How to Communicate Effectively with Anyone, Anywhere

Your Passport to Connecting Globally

Raúl Sánchez and Dan Bullock

Illustrated by **Rod Sánchez**

CAREER PRESS

This edition first published in 2021 by Career Press, an imprint of
Red Wheel/Weiser, LLC

With offices at:
65 Parker Street, Suite 7
Newburyport, MA 01950
www.careerpress.com
www.redwheelweiser.com

ISBN: 978-1-63265-179-2

Library of Congress Cataloging-in-Publication Data available upon request.

Cover design and cover artwork by Rod Sánchez
Interior by Happenstance Type-O-Rama
Typeset in Gilroy and Times New Roman

Printed in Canada
MAR

10 9 8 7 6 5 4 3 2 1

This book is dedicated:

*To God, His global perspective and
His universal Love teach us every day . . .*

*To our dear families, whose hearts full of wisdom
and compassion show us the love that can
connect a human family across the world . . .*

*To all the global communicators who
illuminate our seminars and inspire these
pages, on their way to shaping a better
future for all of us together . . .*

This book is for You.

Contents

4 Connecting with Body and Voice: The Power of Nonverbal Communication **131**

5 Connecting with the World: Negotiation in the Age of Collaboration. **171**

Introduction:
Connecting Globally

The most powerful cognitive shift can happen when an astronaut turns back in spaceflight to view the earth; in that moment, all boundaries fall away and clouds of difference part to reveal a fragile planet that we all share. This is termed the *overview effect,* and in fact, this shift in awareness can be so great that many have said that an astronaut's view of the earth is the key to sustainability and world peace. How do we bring this perspective to our work on Earth in the global marketplace? Astronauts have described this transformative experience as leading to a profound sense of *interconnectedness,* and this interconnectedness is what we need to tap into in our interactions across the global canvas. Cultures are now merging from traditional spheres of communication into one dynamic landscape, and the role of the *global communicator* has taken center stage. But how do we arrive at the skills to communicate and, ultimately, innovate together across the global canvas? We first have to expand our skillset interculturally—we have to develop a global mindset.

How to Communicate Effectively with Anyone, Anywhere: Your Passport to Connecting Globally reveals a new approach to becoming a global communicator—a set of actionable patterns we can use to communicate with culturally-diverse professionals from around the world. How do we connect globally? By recognizing the communication patterns between us. The impact of globalization has resulted in a singular and connected global business landscape with many shared methods of communication. If cultures can be defined as *patterns of thinking and doing,* then in our globalized era, these patterns have begun to intersect and overlap now more than ever—recognizing these patterns is our key to communication success.

Imagine speeding away from the earth into the overview perspective and being able to recognize the general communication patterns of the countries across the world. Feel this instant global consciousness coming into focus, as you tap into these global communication patterns within one single overlapping system of unified perspective and guidance. For example, emailing is all too common for many of us, but effectively emailing counterparts in the US, China,

Brazil, or Germany—or anywhere in the world—requires us to "upgrade" our skills with a singular set of key intercultural strategies that allows us to create an expanded and productive network of global interaction. The same approach is essential when enhancing public speaking skills for the world stage—in our globalized era, we often encounter culturally-mixed audiences all over the planet—therefore, we have to develop an *international presentation style* when delivering ideas in service to others. Globalization has resulted in a communications system of profound interconnectedness, and the patterns in this book are the building blocks for global communication—containing unifying models of messaging and interaction. The result is a set of culturally-powerful "blueprints" that completely change the way we communicate across the global marketplace.

The phrase *How to Communicate Effectively with Anyone, Anywhere* is intended to imply a greater communication practice. Instead of communication strategies that target a homogenized audience from a specific country, we need to find singular communication models that reach diverse and mixed audiences in every country. In our globalized world, we encounter mixed audiences and networks wherever we go. We need to expand to a perspective that views our connections as part of a single, breathing system.

Hence, this book is not a travelogue; it is a practical skill-based tool that can lead us, not just to a future of greater communication, but to greater collaboration and innovation as well. The focus centers on singular models of communication that link our identity across the earth as a whole. Unlike most intercultural texts, which contain chapters organized by country-specific knowledge, this book contains chapters divided by *skills*, such as *effective emailing, public speaking,* and *negotiating.* The unique focus is on *patterns of communication,* singular models that work with diverse audiences and networks from all over the world.

Most cross-cultural training programs focus on culturally-specific values, customs, and facts—but professionals need a more practical and holistic approach. Many of us in the twenty-first century often encounter dozens of cultural contexts every day—often in a single day, at work, socially, or online. New research shows that cultivating skills with a certain **cognitive flexibility** is what unlocks the skills of cultural competence—a *global mindset.* In a truly globally-connected world, professionals could find themselves in any number of locations—therefore, they need to be able to operate in any cultural environment they enter. This would not only require specific linguistic skills for messaging but would also require a new *adaptability* to ever-evolving circumstances and an ability to respond to new contexts—a *cognitive flexibility*—a global mindset leading to global communication skills.

Drawing on our research backgrounds in psycholinguistics and intercultural communication, this book bridges the gap that exists between traditional training in cultural-specific *knowledge* and the practicalities of putting that knowledge *into practice.* Traditional knowledge-based models of cultural competence have yet to show us how to jump from abstract concepts into an actionable set of principles. However, the solution to communicating effectively across cultures resides in integrating "blueprints" we can then actively work from—connecting *perception* to specific *behavioral skills*—ultimately, expanding our ability to operate across cultural settings and enter the future transactions of global business, international relationships, and worldwide innovation.

These contents are based on our years of research and teaching experience as professors, corporate trainers, and intercultural communication specialists at New York University and at entities such as the United Nations (UN) Headquarters. For years, we have educated American and international students and professionals in the "global classroom," a shared space that continues to enrich the multiplex process of *communication competence*—the most valuable skill in the world today, both personally and professionally, and now needed more than ever transnationally. Within this shared space, we've been deeply moved to witness firsthand both US and international professionals working together to bridge gaps in communication and reveal the implicit commonalities we all share as human beings. We researched ways, not just to work more effectively with one another, but to *relate* more deeply with one another. Our research led us to isolate a set of unifying skill-based models that would work both within the US and around the world—models that emerge from our *interdependence* on one another, and models essential to the harmonious intercultural contact of the future.

How to Use This Book

This book is designed to create powerful *shifts,* both within and beyond. After all, key shifts in mindset lead to key shifts in behavior.

There are numerous ways to utilize this book. You may view the chapters in order, or you may select a chapter that pertains to a desired communication skill pertinent to a particular context. However, if you choose to read in order, know that each chapter follows the other in a progressive fashion—and collectively, these chapters form the skillset of a global communicator.

- **Chapter organization:** Each chapter, 1 through 6, in this book contains an easy-to-implement pattern for global communication from such areas as *social styles theory, win-win decision-making,* and *schemata theory.* These patterns are not theoretical, but practical "blueprints" for effective global communication. The first part of each chapter introduces the pattern; the second part connects the strategies to a specific skill, such as *emailing, negotiating,* and *public speaking*—a collection of in-demand performance areas that will inform and enrich interactions across world markets. For professionals looking to take their skillset to the next level, this set of approaches is the key to connecting professional skills to a larger practice of global understanding, ultimately leading to the skillset of a global communicator.

- **Creative exercises:** The exercises outlined in this book are designed for the application of communication concepts, self-discovery, and empowerment. Some exercises are skill-based and are intended to be open-ended—as launch points to ignite further development. Others are knowledge-based, with specific answers included in the chapters' relevant answer keys. All exercises are starting points for the continual evolution of communication work.

- **Key illustrations:** As stated in the book, many research studies suggest that it is more powerful and effective to deliver material through *more than one sense.* The illustrations are a vital communicative aspect of the work: delivering a multidimensional representation of the content, enriching the strategies presented, and enhancing the self-empowering creative exercises throughout the text.

- **World region guide:** A geographic resource is included in Appendix B adapted from the United Nations Children's Fund (UNICEF) Regional Classification and the United Nations Statistics Division.

- **Appendices:** The appendices refer to three larger dimensions of intercultural communication that are used throughout the book: "Global English and Brevity," "Cultural Contexts," and "Cognitive Flexibility," which are referenced alongside strategies that leave room to navigate individual diversity as well as group diversity. Research has shown that, while it is helpful to be aware that cultures share larger values, such as collectivism or individualism because this knowledge may inform communicative decisions, it is also important to keep in mind that cultures do not always conform to a single prototypical behavior. Instead we must discover strategies that not only work across cultures, but also leave room for recognizing the individual within the culture. We must form a developmental viewpoint, a global mindset.

At the most fundamental level, becoming a global communicator is about much more than increasing our earning potential, economic opportunities, and productivity—ultimately being a global communicator is about an *authentic* dedication to human relationships. To truly integrate world cultures, we professionals and global leaders alike must integrate a vigilant commitment to an understanding of those cultures and their many attributes, psychologies, values, and traditions. With understanding comes *connection,* and with the dedication to relationships comes the true connection of trust with which to build influence. Once we begin to develop our intellectual and emotional understanding of world cultures, we open limitless opportunities for connection and expansion into new cultural spheres and global market spaces.

This book is for anyone who is a global professional, who is newly entering the international market, or who is looking for proven ways to enhance their global communication. *How to Communicate Effectively with Anyone, Anywhere: Your Passport to Connecting Globally,* unlike most cross-cultural books with chapters that are arranged by country-specific knowledge, is organized in a practical and easily-digestible way—organized by a distinct set of skills—the *skillset of a global communicator.* Therefore, the skills within this global mindset allow us to master the art of communicating successfully across all cultures, while honoring the larger cultural context and, at the same time, recognizing the individual within the culture.

Traditional views tend to present a study of culture driven from fragmented culturally-specific perspectives; however, this book offers a global look at culture akin to the *overview effect,* a larger perspective on the different continents of the world, and subsequently a wider range of actions for connecting that world. The goal of this book, with exercises designed to impart valuable self-discovery, is to be part instructional text and part empowering workbook. At the same time, the book intends to inform and enrich interactions, as well as bring global awareness to business communities across world markets and international economies.

Finally, as you will discover in these pages, the global communicator is focused on *long-term* thinking as opposed to *short-term* thinking—a perspective that is not always culturally universal but, to the global communicator, is essential to establishing everlasting international professional relationships. Globalization is a long-term process. As the world continues to become more integrated through global business practices, an intercultural perspective will become the driving force for succeeding globally, at the individual, national, and multinational level.

This book is intended to be a profound point of departure, for a better future of effective communication and successful intercultural interaction. It's time to join the next generation of global communicators and facilitate the human connection in our shared thoughts and interactions. Mastering the art of communication is both the journey and the reward of living for all of us in our shared world as we seek to connect even more deeply with those around us. We are shapers of a better future when we work together. Let's begin.

Connecting with the Audience: Public Speaking from the World Stage

> *The only reason to give a speech is to change the world.* **—John F. Kennedy**

Every speaking situation is an opportunity for change. Whether facing a crowd of five or five hundred, we feel an earthquake rising inside. A fire awakening. A spark ready to ignite the hearts and minds of the world. This fire in our minds is an *idea* and it is a tool, coursing through our every word—ready to transform us and our audiences anew.

Whether we are presenting to a small group of stakeholders, a conference room of board members, or a larger audience, the universal goal of any presentation is to create a *connection* between presenter and audience that brings about lasting change. So how do we expand this impact when we're delivering presentations to global audiences?

In the globalized era, presentation skills are more important than ever. Today successful speakers must not only know their subject, but their audiences. As businesses and organizations become more global, the international presentation space has seen a shift in focus from information to *communication*. We now have multicultural teams to motivate, international clients to engage, or global partners to collaborate with, all with diverse needs and communication styles.

On the global stage, we discover that fire breathing within us, igniting our inner self to hold the space and focus on one goal—communicating an idea powerfully. Expression is transformative, and we each have a spark inside that can illuminate the world. So how do we create a bridge with our audience that ignites rippling change?

To ensure that our messages will resonate with diverse audiences with a rich mix of communication styles, we must develop an *international presentation style*. The potential of a presentation style that works for everyone around the world goes vastly beyond career opportunities, managerial interpersonal skills, and organizational productivity. We live in an ever-evolving era of global innovation. Sharing ideas has always been our key to human progress.

Experience has shown us that the communication of ideas has produced such innovations as space flight, the personal computer revolution, the transistor radio, quantum physics, antibiotics, the steam engine, the sundial, and the wheel—we can envision these ideas all lit up, like sparks of light uniting us through the ages, crisscrossing the earth in a glowing latticework of inspiration like part of Earth's electric field.

No matter how giant the leap, looking backward, we can see that every idea in the flow of human progress was advanced by the spreading communication of ideas that came before, like sparklines connecting all around the globe, propelling human history into a fascinating voyage through time to the present moment.

Overall, if you have a big idea, you're already capable of a powerful speech. It doesn't have to be a Nobel Prize–winning invention—it could be a vision of the future or a reminder of what's important. What matters most is the *way* we share that idea. All we have to do is make specific and dynamic combinations of two key presentation components: **delivery** and **content.** When connecting—*how* we say things is just as important as *what* we say.

Indeed, research has revealed that when we share a powerful presentation or story, we actually share the same brain activity as our audiences. That is to say, the importance of a good presentation is not just delivering the information, but connecting with the audience so that they can integrate the information and act upon it in collaborative ways. When presenting on the world stage, we must not be distracted by notions of personal success, but instead focus on what the former United Nations high commissioner for human rights Navi Pillay calls starting "millions of conversations among people around the world." Our goal is *service*—namely, serving as a catalyst for thought, emotion, and action.

We are already a part of this sparkline process of service—of business entrepreneurs creating new innovations, of scientists finding new facts, of artists inspiring new worldviews—and of breakthrough discoveries such as how blood circulates through the human body or how gravity works to propel the International Space Station in orbit around the earth. We are as much a part of the innovative process as we are a part of Earth's magnetic field, the electricity charging the atmosphere, and the electromagnetic impulses firing from one synapse to another inside us, carrying our ideas between our minds to become blazing realities.

All we have to do is shift our focus from *presenting* to our audience to *connecting* with our audience. Then, on the world stage, these ideas of today and tomorrow—ideas inherited from the past and inspired by dreams of the future, a better human future—converge and burn inside of us.

In this chapter, we'll explore how to develop an *international presentation style* that applies cognitive strategies for using visual aids, navigates multiple communication styles, and uses specific transcultural storytelling patterns that tailor our messages to diverse audiences—all while revealing the glow of that universal connection. Ultimately, an international presentation style allows us to fully enter communication patterns across the world, while also influencing global business, cross-border transformation, international workforce development, effectiveness of global teams and organizational missions, and world change.

Globalization is the defining characteristic of our age, and in globalized business markets, we now present to a mix of cultures in one presentation space. Therefore, as global communicators, when we layer our presentation skills with patterns of cognitive strategy and storytelling, we not only create more engagement and impact among multicultural audiences, we also participate in the global innovation process.

1.1 Presentation Fire: Powering the Mind-to-Mind Connection

> *We seek the fire of the spark that is already within us.* —*Kamand Kojouri*

What is the power of a speech? Think of the flames reaching from within us, sparks leaping from nerve cell to nerve cell, carrying our hopes and dreams through our bodies. Leaping across synapses as they travel through us like gathering electrical firestorms. One tiny electrochemical spark is monumentally influential in our lives.

This spark has been the centerpiece of all cultural innovations, from those of our ancestors to the many inventors through the last decade. A fiery force that has become a newfound treasure for us to share, cultivated from our passions, consciousness, and ongoing purposefulness in our careers. The power of a speech resides in more than the courageous act of sharing an idea, but sharing that idea in service to others. And like electrons leaping from atom to atom, we can *transmit* this energy to others. An idea can become supercharged.

Researchers at Princeton University took a closer look at this *energy*, discovering that when we deliver a powerful story, we share nearly identical brain waves with our audience, similar to the way "mirror neurons" work. This research affirms that one of the most powerful presentation vehicles between us as human beings is storytelling. Dr. Uri Hasson, one of the pioneers behind this research, arrived at the findings for this shared human experience when analyzing the brain scans of both storytellers and audiences who were hooked up to MRI machines. His team determined that our brains essentially get in "sync" with one another during storytelling in an amazing event termed *neural coupling*. Sparklines.

In other words, during the live act of storytelling, firing neural patterns in listeners "mirror" those in speakers. No wonder storytelling remains an age-old and fundamental process that we humans instinctively and passionately use to communicate ideas, emotions, and motivations—storytelling transcends culture. The boardroom, virtual room, and conference room environments have become our new metaphorical campfires. However, when we tap into storytelling, we also tap into our ancient roots and a universal process that makes our ideas part of world collaboration, catharsis, and collective memory across cultures.

Forge the mind-to-mind connection from the global stage by telling stories that:

- bond with our audience over a *professional, social,* or *personal cause*
- illustrate a *skill, method,* or *process* important for personal growth or global progress
- highlight how to overcome a *shared challenge* or achieve a *common goal*
- make a *presentation "bigger" in meaning than its data*
- convey our *passion for a topic,* and ignite audience interest in the process

Yet, an idea doesn't simply get its power from storytelling, nor courage in the act of expression—an idea gets its power from *service,* the most important concept of presentations in the global context. The most powerful narratives are those that inspire, nurture, and heal others. As Japanese Buddhist priest Nichiren Daishonin writes, "If one lights a fire for others, one will brighten one's own way." Service is the act of giving back the gift of ideas that have been given to you. As we do this, not only do our own lives change for the better, but also the lives of all those around us.

👥 Global Presentation Tip

Sharing an idea in service to others is our greatest expression as a global presenter.

1.1a The Fire Within and Between: Global Courage and Global Sensitivity

> *When you stop putting yourself on the line, and you don't touch your own heart, how do you expect to touch other people?* **—Tori Amos**

The principle of service as a global presenter is paramount. On the global stage, we do not present for ourselves. The concept of service is founded on the idea that we are all joined at a certain level. Indeed, human rights keynote public speaker and South African social rights activist Archbishop Desmond Tutu stated "Do your little bit of good where you are; it's those little bits of good put together that overwhelm the world."

The key to embodying service as a global presenter is with the right combination of courage and intercultural sensitivity—which, in turn, cultivates our larger skillset as a global communicator. According to notable keynote speaker Stephen R. Covey, all our human interactions are touched by two essences: the amount of courage we have to display our emotions and convictions, coupled with the amount of consideration we have for the emotions and convictions of others. In his landmark work, *The 7 Habits of Highly Effective People,* he presents a matrix with these two variables that delineates the overall paradigms of human interaction.

When we apply these two essences to intercultural presentations, we first develop what we call **global courage,** which inspires us to step out of our presentation comfort zones until the *world* becomes our comfort zone. By honoring the expression of our identity, we merge personal growth with the process of cultural integration and communication. At the same time, we must cultivate a **global sensitivity,** which enables us to present with an awareness beyond our own cultural filters. By integrating the viewpoints of others, we can present through the filter of a global society. When we focus on delivering an idea in service to others, we find the right balance between *global courage* and *global sensitivity*—where a global mindset can emerge.

Combine these two essences when delivering an idea in service to others. Keep in mind that, by definition, culture is an intersection of *shared values, beliefs, and behaviors.* We can deliver powerful stories that merge *global courage* and *global sensitivity* through the following shared cultural dimensions:

- **Shared values:** Connect your stories to *values* that resonate with global audiences. All of us listen to stories with our hearts more than our minds because we look for messages that align with our values. Think of the core value of your presentation, such as integrity, honesty, and empathy, and build your narrative around it. How can you expand stories from personal to human experience?

- **Shared goals:** Forge common goals that motivate *action.* Remember culture is a shared system of beliefs, so bridge goals globally in your speech. What personal stories illustrate us making a *choice* we want our audience to make?

- **Shared solutions:** Finally, fuel the *urgency* for change, while also igniting the *hope* that change is possible. Tap into cultural systems of *behavior.* If our story illustrates a choice, why is it timely for global audiences to make the same choice? What *immediate* steps can the audience take to fulfill a vision of successful action that has a globally-relevant solution?

With the right *elements of motivational narrative,* courageous stories can serve as lightning rods that supercharge a presentation. On the stage, as we revisit the personal and emotional connections of a story from a past situation, global audiences are revisiting their own related experiences at the exact same time. Storytelling is the doorway to our collective "emotional memory" across cultures.

👥 *Global Presentation Tip*

The goal of presentation storytelling is not simply to express ourselves, but to illustrate and to inspire.

Now, a further way to combine *global courage* with *global sensitivity* is to consider the work of social innovator Dr. Mitchell R. Hammer, who developed the widely-adopted *Intercultural Development Inventory (IDI)* as a means to peel back the layers of an intercultural perspective. With a growing need for all of us to *shift perspectives* and *adapt behavior* in the act of global communication, the IDI has created a path toward developing a cultural nuance that addresses the needs of individuals and organizations in today's globalized economy. What's important about this approach for us as global professionals is that when delivering ideas in service to others, we must strengthen awareness and *link understanding to actionable steps.*

1. **Awareness:** First, in terms of a global mindset, a helpful model for expanding our awareness is to experience cultural attributes from a *kaleidoscopic* perspective. Just think of those tube-like cylinders that reveal a palette of colorful patterns when held up to the light. When we look for the intersection of communication patterns, we deepen connections, and then integrate diverse perspectives into the presentation content we offer.

2. **Adaptation:** Second, when entering each presentation space, instead of focusing on our presentation content, we must make the global audience the *centerpiece* of our presentation. By cultivating this adaptive approach, we are able to create an *interactive* presentation space of deeper understanding, respect, and empathy with audiences as we share ideas in service to others.

👥 *Global Presentation Tip*

Evoke a shared state of mind with your audience by communicating with the right balance of global courage and global sensitivity.

So, how does this play out in the three-dimensional space? Life and motivational business coach Tony Robbins is known for engaging his audience fervently in any physical presentation setting—in fact, for the past thirty-five years, he has even invited audience members in his *Unleash the Power Within* seminars to conquer their fears with a "firewalk" over hot coals, which allows them to enter a new era of personal transformation. Robbins dynamically uses the environment and regular crowd interactions to sensitively convey his messages quite literally among his diverse audiences. Here, we realize that increasing *global sensitivity* to other cultures is through increased opportunities for interaction.

Renowned German aviator and public speaker Dieter F. Uchtdorf said in his speech *Happiness, Your Heritage,* "As we lose ourselves in the service of others we discover our own lives and our own happiness." He is known for using his experience as a pilot to draw spiritual metaphors for his audiences, and his analogies have endeared him to international audiences all over the world.

Similarly, when she first burst onto the world stage with her album *Little Earthquakes,* storyteller and songwriter Tori Amos, with her fiery red hair, passionate piano playing, and deeply-personal words, brought a revelation in how to convey a personal story to global audiences through lyrical messages. As she sang about the courage of being true to one's own voice, people marveled how one woman twisting passionately at the piano, armed with nothing but a single bare light, a soprano voice, and penetrating lyrics, was able to spark change across a spectrum of cultures and hearts worldwide. When asked about her performance approach on global tours, Amos said, "When you stop putting yourself on the line, and you don't touch your own heart, how do you expect to touch other people?"

The most seasoned intercultural presenters, entrepreneurs, and storytellers realize this important truth—that for profound connections to occur, every presentation involves the global courage to find strength in our vulnerability and to take *risks.* Only the person who risks is truly free, which brings us to our presentation *message.*

To open the hearts and minds of others, we need to first allow ourselves to be fully affected by our *message.* After all, openness is the foundation for integrating differences and building unity. This is as true of us as presenters as it is of our global audiences—openness through emotion connects us all. **In order to arrive at an effective presentation message, consider: What do we want people to *do, feel,* or *think* after listening to our speech?**

The message and purpose of the most powerful ideas and speeches isn't to build a sales pitch, but to link values from our own real-life experiences to larger issues relevant to our current reality. The potential we illuminate in others is always within ourselves. How can we expand our business or personal topic into greater motivation in terms of individual well-being and larger present-day issues? To establish a blazing neural connection, combine *a call to action, a call to feeling,* and *a call to thought* in every single presentation to release a firestorm nexus of greater impact.

👥 Global Presentation Tip

Every effective presentation message is a call to action, feeling, or thought.

Imagine now the sparks that leap from neuron to neuron *within* your body—then envision these sparks as inspiration and how this motivating force can also be transmitted *between* our bodies. With conductivity as our goal, our ideas and messages can travel around the world as currents across electrical fields and vast distances, even hemisphere to hemisphere. We're interconnected through story in the service of ideas. Every presentation is a collaboration between presenter and audience in the cognitive space—which is why storytelling is a *key transcultural presentation ingredient.* Storytelling in presentations does more than bring us together through the effects of "neural coupling." We not only share meaning with each other, but it's almost as if we share *human experience* itself.

Finally, the "neural coupling" phenomenon from Dr. Hasson's and his team's Princeton research revealed another significant finding that can be applied to our international presentation style: not only did the brain regions of audiences "light up" to mirror the sparks and activity in the storyteller's brain, but other sub-regions of listeners' brains "lit up" *before* the same activity in the speaker's brain—as if the audience were *predicting* the story while the presenter was speaking. This profound finding implies that audiences also have the desire to *understand* the storyteller between parts of a story. Essentially, storytelling is not just a presentation tool for global communication, but also functions as a tool for profound *empathy.*

Overall, an international presentation style fused with *global courage* and *global sensitivity* has larger implications beyond neural coupling for relationships, community, imagination, and beyond. It also has immense potential for the health of societies and the global order. When we infuse our presentations in service to each other with the narrative and cognitive strategies in this chapter, we radiate energy that creates a two-way dynamic between presenters and audiences from around the world. From thousands of years of evolution, storytelling hasn't just been one of the most fundamental forms for exchanging ideas across cultures, but science has also begun to show us that storytelling is one of the most unifying qualities of the global workplace—in other words, one of the most powerful forms of *human* communication today.

The principle of service is not only immensely fulfilling in terms of creating new opportunities and building impactful relationships, but it also advances us along the path to global presentation skills faster than anything else we can do. Once we learn to actively connect these patterns of impact and sensitivity across cultures, we begin to make the connection of true communication.

....

Activity: Building Intercultural Stories

In your next presentation, explore the following steps to build intercultural stories with *global courage* and *global sensitivity* in service to others that evoke the "neural coupling" phenomenon from the global stage. Remember, the change we wish to spark in others, we must first ignite in ourselves:

- As you prepare your presentation, think of how your stories can target important "decision-making moments" in your life, as these meaningful experiences *reveal* the values you hold.

- Then, think about how these "decision-making moments" you share may *connect* with the values of your audience.

- Finally, establish these shared values with statements that ignite support for your message and *motivate* audiences to action.

....

1.2 Passing the Torch: Global Communication Style Patterns

You're lost if you lose your audience. **—Simon Sweeney**

For many years, fire has blazed as the symbolic center of the modern Olympics, with a burning torch honoring the ancient games. This powerful symbol gives us a revitalizing metaphor as presenters—chiefly the way this beacon of light is traditionally passed from person to person, traversing the globe and uniting world communities.

The foundation for an international presentation style is mirroring this same practice in our presentations as one where we exchange the "flame" of an idea between presenter and audience. Our goal is not simply to present for our own self-fulfillment, but to deliver presentations that *share* information and powerful ideas in *service* to others. This pivotal shift in perspective inspires us to deliver presentations for global audiences that *empower* everyone to participate—our audiences enrich our purpose with their goals as much as our own goals do. The audience's perspective always comes first.

As global communicators in our interconnected world, if cultures can be defined as "patterns of thinking and doing," then our goal is to integrate the rich range of style preferences among individuals, groups, professional fields, and world cultures. For example, some audience members may prefer a linear communication style focused on directness, logic, and tasks. In other scenarios, participants may prefer a communication style that is individualistic, colorful, and personality-filled, while still others may favor a style that is indirect, formal, and respectful. Keep in mind that these style preferences can vary by individual, occupation, and culture (see Appendix B on *Cultural Contexts*). So, as global communicators, how do we merge these preferences into *one singular presentation style?*

First, envision yourself rushing outward into the earth's outer orbit to a vantage point akin to the *overview effect* where you can see all of these communication patterns as one single overlapping system. Within this expansive view, we can recognize that these communication patterns interwoven between cultures provide us with a global mindset.

The answer resides, not in focusing on *one* particular communication style for one particular scenario, but in integrating *all* style preferences within a cognitive flexibility that links awareness to action across a range of global scenarios—equipping ourselves with an *international presentation style* that allows us to communicate effectively as global communicators.

Right now, imagine the presentation as a significant moment where you as the presenter are holding the torch—or rather your idea—and are entrusted by your audience with the larger opportunity and colossal responsibility of *sharing* that flame with those gathered before you, so that they, in turn, can pass this torch to others. This goal informs our every decision.

For us as presenters and torchbearers, contrary to popular belief, this consideration calls upon us to reframe the notion of simply "being ourselves" when giving a presentation. Instead, we must focus our energy on tailoring our presentations for communication to *our audience* when sharing an idea in service to others.

👥 Global Presentation Tip

As global presenters, *service* is the most powerful way to create meaning in our lives and the lives of those around us.

As presenters everything changes when we think of ourselves as *torchbearers.* In this way, we completely rethink and refocus the presentation scenario. Presenting becomes a humbling act of *responsibility* to our audiences, to whom we are passing the torch of our ideas.

The first step is to understand the larger communication style patterns of audiences all over the globe, which we have adapted from leading intercultural researchers to reveal a global presentation skills approach that leaves room for cultural, occupational, and individual diversity. We can use these style patterns to arrive at techniques for interacting with teams from countries worldwide. The goal is not just to navigate the styles of a culturally-diverse audience—but to integrate these styles into a holistic approach when presenting to international members in the same presentation space.

The following three general global style preference patterns are adapted from the *Lewis Model* by linguist Richard Lewis, whose work expanded upon such notable intercultural research as *cultural dimensions theory* by social psychologist Geert Hofstede, along with building on foundational intercultural principles from anthropologist and intercultural researcher Edward T. Hall (see Appendix B on *Cultural Contexts*). Additionally, these communication style patterns contain adjusted dimensions adaptable to diverse fields and individual preferences.

Step 1: Internalize the three global communication style preference patterns.

1. **The Linear-Expressive style pattern:** This style tends to be task-oriented, direct, and logical; the goal of communication and presentations

is *information;* therefore, to integrate this style preference in presentations, strongly correlate words and actions, focus on facts, and provide logical solutions.

Style preference: Often preferred by most of the English-speaking parts of the world, including the United States, parts of Northwestern and North-Central Europe, Scandinavia, and Australia/New Zealand.

2. **The Multi-Expressive style pattern:** This style tends to be people-oriented and expressive; the goal of communication and presentations is *personal connection* and *opinion;* therefore, to integrate this style preference in presentations, create a space for empathy, focus on feelings, and provide inspirational and creative solutions. This style is less direct than Linear-Expressive and more direct than Amicable-Expressive.

   Style preference: Often preferred by most countries in Latin America, the Middle East and North Africa, regions of Eastern Europe and the Iberian Peninsula, the Mediterranean region, and sub-Saharan Africa.

3. **The Amicable-Expressive style pattern:** This style tends to be indirect and respect-oriented; the goal of communication and presentations is *harmony;* therefore, to integrate this style preference in presentations, cultivate respect and relationships, provide continual courtesy, and contribute constructive solutions that preserve reputation and social harmony.

   Style preference: Often preferred by most Asian countries, except the subcontinent of India, which is both Multi-Expressive and Amicable-Expressive.

Now, the second step is to interweave these styles into a single practical presentation approach. Remember, as a global communicator, the goal is not simply to focus on separate styles for separate presentation situations, but to integrate *all* these style patterns into our own communication style.

This approach accommodates variations between *individual* and *cultural* preferences, as well as *occupational* preferences (e.g., accountants may be Linear-Expressive, publicists may be Multi-Expressive, and doctors may be Amicable-Expressive). Furthermore, research shows that each style also retains characteristics of the other two styles. Therefore, a presentation style that incorporates all three styles is important for us to win over any spectrum of presentation audiences in mixed presentation spaces.

👥👥 *Global Presentation Tip*

Integrate all three global communication styles as a presenter by including all three rhetorical appeals in every presentation.

Aristotle's canonized book, *Rhetoric,* outlined the first documented and systematic approach to persuasive public speaking. The three rhetorical appeals coined by Aristotle—*logos, pathos,* and *ethos*—are commonly referred to as "modes of persuasion" and can be adapted to align a presentation well with the above intercultural style patterns. When modified, these appeals can accommodate a full global span of audience members in a practical way. This is how it works.

Per the above research, Linear-Expressive cultures are drawn to presentations oriented to logic (logos), Multi-Expressive cultures prefer presentations containing aspects of emotional connection (pathos), and Amicable-Expressive cultures connect with expertise (ethos) as a starting point. The goal in an intercultural presentation is to tailor our ideas across diverse styles in the same room, and we do this by merging *the three rhetorical appeals into a singular international presentation style.*

Step 2: Use all three of the following rhetorical appeals in every global presentation to reach mixed audiences.

1. **Logos (*appeal to logic*):** Include statistics, facts, and relevant research in your presentation that are logical, structured, and linear. This integrates *Linear-Expressive* preferences into your presentation style.

2. **Pathos (*appeal to emotion*):** Interweave emotionally-impactful stories, compelling opinions, and sensory media in your presentation that are personal, authentic, vivid, creative, and entertaining. This integrates *Multi-Expressive* preferences into your presentation style.

3. **Ethos (*appeal to credibility*):** Include relevant information about your character, reputation, credibility, track record, and professional experience in your presentation. This integrates *Amicable-Expressive* preferences into your presentation style.

Consider a presentation scenario where a distinguished speaker from the United Nations is presenting on *The Need to Respond to World Hunger* and shows charts and graphs demonstrating alarming trends in the state of food security and nutrition in the world (logos). Then, the presenter shows haunting photos and relays accounts of children affected (pathos), before finally providing a brief biography as a relief worker abroad for the World Food Programme, with a call for others to join the effort (ethos).

The more we combine rhetorical appeals in our speaking, the more persuasive we will be, and when we include all three appeals in our presentations, we successfully reach across the spectrum of presentation styles.

As torchbearers, we are called to adapt and expand our presentation style to serve a global audience's needs and interests. We learn to do this in intercultural contexts by starting with the inclusion of the three rhetorical appeals in every presentation. Even if a presentation has met our own personal standards of success, if our audience isn't following us during our presentation, we have lost the opportunity to serve and connect in the speaking situation at hand.

Plan your presentation delivery as much as you plan the presentation content, especially for multilingual audiences. Remember, planning a presentation for a global audience requires letting go of self-image and self-standards and instead focusing on adapting our ideas to our audience in *service*, so that we inspire "mental fireworks" within others when delivering a presentation in a shared global space.

Reflection:
From Torchbearer to Global Audience

When planning a presentation, use the following questions in order to analyze your audience so that you can refine your presentation *purpose, content,* and *delivery:*

- Analyze where audience *expectations* meet *motivations;* then, integrate all three rhetorical appeals—logos, pathos, and ethos—into your presentation to connect with the full spectrum of global communication style patterns (Linear-Expressive, Multi-Expressive, and Amicable-Expressive).

- Approach every presentation from a mindset of service. What does your audience *know* and *need to know?* How can you analyze what they bring to the presentation and what they are hoping to receive?

- Increase intercultural sensitivity through increased opportunities for *interaction*. How can you find ways to interact with your audience, not just *during* a presentation, but *before* and *after* a presentation as well?

1.3 The Balance: Optimizing Content and Delivery

> *The sole meaning of life is to serve humanity.*
> **—Leo Tolstoy**

When you enter the stage, in-person or virtually, feel the electricity in your veins and the cognitive fire in your mind—as two towering pillars of public speaking wait to provide a strong platform for success. *Both* content and delivery are important pillars of any international presentation. Try to imagine one without the other. Both pillars are mutually reinforcing and need each other to hold up the structure of your presentation. The most powerful global speakers do not perceive these two elements as separate, but integrate them when erecting the total architecture of an effective presentation that successfully targets the rich spectrum of global communication styles.

👥 *Global Presentation Tip*

Balance content as much as delivery when planning presentations for global audiences—*what* we say is just as important as *how* we say it.

This balance between **content** and **delivery** is also tethered to the concept of *service*. When we embody this principle of service as global presenters, we move beyond self-directed considerations, such as a focus on appearance and other preoccupations in our individual sphere of perception and, instead, project outward all our emotional and intellectual capacity in that presentation moment to fulfill a service to others.

Presenting with the principle of service brings with it newfound freedom. You know those pent up feelings of nervousness people talk about when about to give a speech? Well, the principle of service is the antidote, freeing us from any potential reservations that many experience upon preparing to speak publicly. Instead, the electricity we feel is the *excitement* of sharing with and serving others. The principle of service liberates us—driving us to go above and beyond our own capabilities, as we find fulfillment in the fulfillment of our audiences.

👥 *Global Presentation Tip*

When we embody a principle of service, we unleash the untapped energy within.

For us as global presenters, whether presenting in-person or online, it is important to regularly reflect on the following guidelines for finding an optimal balance between *content* and *delivery* when presenting interculturally:

Optimizing content

- **Research:** Make it customary to include research and content that broadens context for diverse audiences. Create an impact with universal examples recognizable to audiences all over the world.

- **Multimedia:** Use visual aids/media to convey and clarify complex information. While using visual aids/media to punctuate emotional content with pathos, optimize your presentation material with elements of logos and ethos to reach across the spectrum of the three larger global communication style patterns (Linear-Expressive, Multi-Expressive, and Amicable-Expressive).

Optimizing delivery

- **Nonverbals** (see Chapter 4 on *Nonverbal Skills*): Use shifts in body movement to mark shifts in topics and meaning. Alongside purposeful body language, use vocalics (e.g., volume, speed, rhythm) to emphasize key points, while also using thought groups (pausing) to create impactful phrasing in sentences.

- **Chunking:** Deliver key material in smaller, more manageable chunks. Think in microfires. *Content* becomes linked *microcontent,* allowing audiences to better connect information and arrive at understanding. Chunking doesn't mean simplifying, just conveying larger, intricate content in smaller, more manageable portions and complex information in different forms (e.g., graphics, information charts).

- **Global English** (see Appendix A on *Global English*): Use a form of English adopted and standardized by the international business world known as **Global English** that is clear, purposeful, and practical. Avoid idioms ("off the top of my head"), phrasal verbs ("let's get on with it"), jargon ("socio-linguistic and lexical diffusion"), and cultural-specific references ("we're in the big leagues"). If jargon use is necessary, define key expressions/essential specialized concepts immediately and rephrase technical terms promptly.

- **Guideposts:** Use transition signals to indicate the introduction of reasons as well as to *mark* sections of your presentation orally. Just as a driver depends on road signs for direction, so too do your audiences in presentation situations. Make sure your content is easy to follow by providing information in a *logical sequence* ("First of all . . . ," "Before . . . ," and "After . . ."). Also, deliberately *link* ideas with guideposts throughout a presentation ("Let's switch topics. Now, we're going to talk about . . . A case in point . . . Equally as important is . . .") and introduce information in *lists* to guide readers ("There are three key points that . . . Let's look at each of these in more detail. First . . .").

- **Virtual presentations:** In virtual spaces, don't lecture—*present.* As they say, movies are for watching, presentations are for interacting. So, make interaction a *presentation goal* for engaging audiences, gauging cultural comfort zones, enhancing understanding, building community, and sparking feedback loops for intercultural audiences. Also, an interactive approach is pivotal to intercultural communication, as deeper understanding emerges when humans with diverse worldviews construct knowledge together. Don't ask "What will my presentation *cover* today?" ask "What will my audience *do* together today?"

We can use these in-person and virtual public speaking strategies to bend fire and spark our own presentation impact in service to the global community. Once we integrate a balance between *content* and *delivery* into our presentation philosophy, we can consciously set ablaze meaningful professional experiences in any international presentation.

Now, we're going to delve into another layer of presentation skills that provides unique opportunities to connect—the glowing possibilities in the cognitive space.

1.4 Bringing Your Flame into Focus: The Five Presentation Hooks

The mind that opens to a new idea never returns to its original size. —Albert Einstein

How do you grab an audience's attention? Well, have you ever caught yourself staring into the flame of a candle and felt your consciousness clear? You may have been inadvertently tapping into a yogic-Hindu focusing practice called *trataka*. When our attention fixates on a defining flame, our consciousness is absorbed into a meditative state.

In the same way, as global presenters, we must create an allure for our audiences using presentation "hooks," which draw our audiences to the flame of our idea. In this section, we will cover the five presentation hooks that enhance concentration and compel intercultural audiences to participate cognitively in our speech right at the outset.

Neuroscience has mapped out the starting point of a successful presentation to reveal that we are attracted to much more than unique ideas or poetic words. Instead, across cultures, captivating speakers create a universal draw in their presentations—the *curiosity* to learn more.

We need to build *anticipation* in our presentations to create the curiosity that fuels the transformative conditions necessary for deep learning to occur. Let's break down this process. When we become curious, our brains trigger the release of a pleasure chemical called *dopamine* that makes us feel happy. In other words, dopamine is our brain's "chemical reward" for curiosity.

According to researchers at the University of California, Berkeley, stimulating curiosity causes the production of a natural high—not when *receiving* information, but when *anticipating a reward of information*. That's right—the pleasure we feel in a state of curiosity is not derived from the actual reward itself (information), but the audience's *anticipation* of that information. And it doesn't stop there.

Participants in the study who were stimulated and primed for curiosity later were able to more effectively recall *random* information. In other words, an existing *state of curiosity* can lead to improved learning and memory retention, *even about unrelated information we are not actually curious about.* So, to create an engaging and memorable presentation, especially at the outset, think curiously!

We've all experienced this phenomenon—just think of how we vividly remember the *anticipation* of waiting in line for a blockbuster movie more than the movie itself or when we recall the first song of a sold-out concert more than the remainder of the show. Dopamine is the reason we sometimes remember these anticipatory moments where we were burning with curious excitement in more detail than anything else. A good opening hook, in addition to well-placed hooks throughout key sections of a presentation, can urge our audience to stay with us during a speech, regardless of the information itself.

Hooks are essential to an international presentation style, no matter the topic or situation. By learning to pique the curiosity of our audience to build anticipation for our speech, we trigger the kind of deep-seated curiosity that makes the listening and learning process more memorable and effective.

👥👥 *Global Presentation Tip*

Use hooks to build anticipation and invite your audience to participate cognitively in your speech, right from the start.

The following *five presentation hooks* align with the psychology and neuroscience of curiosity and not only enhance our spoken discourse, but our written communication as well. Remember, although we should place hooks at the *beginning* of a presentation, we can also place these purposefully *throughout* our presentation, at the openings of various sections where we want to reinvigorate the flow of our speech.

Effective hooks create *story,* and story is what awakens the fire of curiosity in the human brain. Just keep in mind that a hook doesn't have the same role as a main idea or message. Examine the following two versions of the same hook—which is more enticing?

- **Hook version 1:** "Today, I am going to share with you information about the new net neutrality regulations proposed by the Federal Communications Commission (FCC) and how these regulations may affect electronic communications and the role of internet service providers."

- **Hook version 2:** "Online freedom of speech is in jeopardy."

Notice how the first version functions as a main idea statement, while the second version functions as a *hook* that ignites curiosity about the topic and is, therefore, more effective. As part of an international presentation style, learn to adapt and even combine these hook patterns to strengthen your content and audience engagement.

Use the following **five proven hook patterns** highlighted in Figure 1-1, "The 5 Presentation Hooks," to captivate the attention of world audiences with the cognitive power of curiosity:

1. **Create a question:** Jumpstart your presentation by engaging audiences with a dynamic question that disrupts an expectation or touches upon a concept of shared value. "Can you imagine the world without a single tree?" "What if sleeping near our smartphones had health benefits?"

   Key strategy: Questions can be of two types. The first type, a "yes/ no" question or a "show-of-hands" question, should get your audience to ask "So, what?" Second, an open-ended question should imply that there is a predetermined answer in your presentation; regardless of the question, if your audience is thirsty for more answers, they will be "hooked."

2. **Start with an amazing fact:** Audiences are immediately engaged when they are shocked. So, shock them. Surprise them! Give audiences a key statistic or figure that grabs hold of hearts and minds and derails their expectations. Avoid beginning with "Engaging in environmental sustainability can help us to decrease the greenhouse gases causing global warming . . ." Instead, begin with "New York and Mumbai will be underwater in 2050 if global temperatures continue to rise."

   Key strategy: An amazing fact should fuel anticipation for what comes next in a presentation and provide surprising insights, reveal hidden inspiration, or illuminate an urgent solution.

3. **Share a story or situation:** We are hardwired for story. So, why not lead with a gripping anecdote? The scenario should not focus on an ending, but rather serve as a prelude to the topic. For example, "This afternoon, when the clerk asked me for my driver's license and my credit card, I hesitated. Identity theft may be one of the fastest growing crimes today—however, we can protect ourselves by . . ."

   Key strategy: A story/anecdote hook should start *in medias res,* meaning in the "middle of things" (storytelling techniques are revealed in

Section 1.6), and should be relatable so audiences can cognitively make a "listener-character swap," imagining themselves having the same experience.

The 5 Presentation Hooks

Use these proven hook patterns at the start of a presentation to instantly engage world audiences.

HOOK 1 — Create a Question.

HOOK 2 — Start with an Amazing Fact.

HOOK 3 — Share a Story or Situation.

HOOK 4 — Make a Compelling Observation.

HOOK 5 — Start with an Inspirational Quote. *(and your own words)*

Figure 1-1

4. **Make a compelling observation:** Let's go back to our earlier example, "Online freedom of speech is in jeopardy." A striking observation ignites curiosity in a topic by making listeners' minds beg, "Why?"

   Key strategy: An observation hook should point out an irregularity, a pattern, a discovery, a warning, or a hint at compelling future outcomes.

5. **Start with an inspirational quote (and your own words):** Try to abstain from beginning presentations solely with quotes from others. Chances are when the orator said the quote, they weren't thinking about you or your presentation. Therefore, these "borrowed openings" are related to another context and often require us to accompany the quote with a brief explanation of how it relates to our presentation topic. Sharing favorite quotes may have noble intentions but can waste valuable time and the opportunity to connect with our audience—at the most important juncture of our speech: *the beginning.*

   Key strategy: A quote should support our ideas and be placed after our own words—the beginning of a presentation is an opportunity to lead with originality.

··

Activity: Identify the Hook

Review the following openings and determine which hook combinations are being used. *Two or more hook types are included in each item.*

1. What if there was a way to record all of your dreams and then apply the ideas to your daily life? Would you? A staggering one in every 250 people have reported that they never remember their dreams—but dreams are experiences too and we can invest in our subconscious with this modern-day voice-to-text dreamcatcher . . .

2. Imagine taking a deep dive into the Mariana Trench, known as the deepest place on Earth, thirty-thousand feet below sea level. You are gripped by the sound of metal crunching under pressure. I know it sounds scary—it was for me too. And you'll never guess what I learned about life after what happened next . . .

3. Even if they've never seen a smile themselves, blind people smile when they're happy. Smiling is a basic human instinct.

Answers:
(1) question, start with an amazing fact, interesting observation
(2) share a story or situation, start with an amazing fact
(3) make a compelling observation, start with an amazing fact

....

1.5 The Sensory World: Activating Mental Schemata with Multimedia

> *Tell me, I forget. Show me, I remember. Involve me, I understand.* **—Confucius**

What exactly is a *schema,* and how can we use it to immerse our multilingual audiences in the sensory world of our presentations? Just think about how the light from a hand-held sparkler can outline shapes in the air. These lingering "light paintings" persist as our brains see an "afterimage" of light trails for just a split second longer after they've faded in reality. Known as the *sparkler's trail effect,* this phenomenon is our mind attempting to perceive the quick light movements even after the light has passed. In a similar way, we want our presentation to leave an "afterglow" in our listeners' minds. We want to reach a global audience with a resounding effect beyond the words we use.

The trick to lighting up the cognitive centers of our audience's minds, particularly of intercultural audiences, is by activating what is called **mental schemata** (or **schema**—singular). Essentially, a *schema* is a cognitive framework that helps us understand and interpret information. Commonly referred to in the plural form, *schemata,* these intrinsic, generic mental frameworks were defined by cognitive psychologist Jean Piaget and serve as "mental shortcuts" that have proven vital in intercultural communication situations as a way to help both presenter and audience connect the dots.

Suppose we're delivering a presentation story and we tell audience members that we've recently bought a chair, without providing any additional details about it. The audience would understand that we bought a chair because their *schema,* or *mental representation,* for "chair" (four legs, a seat, and a backrest) is already at work filling in the missing details. But if we were to poll them about the *type* of chair they are picturing in their minds, some audience members may call up the image of a wooden chair; others might picture a metal chair, or perhaps even something akin to an armchair—such is the wonder of communication. The schema for *chair* allowed the communication to be successful, while the particular image that comes to mind for different audience members depends on their own cultural and personal experiences.

How can we use schemata as a tool to connect deeply with diverse audiences? The best way to activate schemata and breathe fire into your presentation is by conveying information through *two or more of the five senses (sight, sound, smell, taste, and touch).*

In the above example, an image, or a piece of fabric from the chair, or a video of the office space designed for the chair, may all have served to heighten communication in that presentation situation and enabled the audience to connect prior knowledge and experience to the new information and language presented.

Successful presenters use schemata to spark active learning centers in our brain and to help audiences more effectively interpret the information in a presentation. Schema helps us not only *organize* new information with background knowledge, but even *predict* elements as we interpret new information. In these ways, schemata give us essential blueprints for integrating new knowledge.

👥 Global Presentation Tip

Activate the schemata of global audiences by presenting information through more than one sense.

Using another example, what if we were planning a presentation for global audiences entitled *Entrepreneurship in the Age of Globalization*? The term *entrepreneurship* may have different levels of familiarity for international audiences, both culturally and linguistically. However, if we include an opening image of Amazon's Jeff Bezos and Zara's Amancio Ortega on our first slide—when audience members walk into the room and see the image paired with the word *entrepreneurship* in the presentation title, the audience will immediately begin to engage in the cognitive connections that activate their bank of preexisting information, cultural knowledge, and language skills, while priming them cognitively for new information.

Visual aids are the prime place to start when tapping into schemata. As Jacqueline Dunckel and Elizabeth Parnham write in *The Business Guide to Effective Speaking,* effective visual aids not only "show information which is not easily expressed in words," they also "cause the audience to employ another sense to receive information."

Ways we can "activate the schemata" of any audience and present information through more than one sense when introducing a topic are to:

- Introduce topics and supporting details with photos, sound files, or videos.

- Use engaging and interactive props—including hands-on activities and 3D model demonstrations—that present information through more than one sense.

- Deliver dynamic stories, with powerful gestures, vocal variations, and other ways of building context.

- Highlight compelling background information, quotes, bio excerpts, and sensory language.

- Harness real-time technology via interactive polls, digital brainstorms, screen rankings, and data visualizations of multiple-choice surveys.

The goal of a presenter is to be a living fire that touches all. Activating schemata is the key to guiding audiences toward understanding. Helping others to connect knowledge from past experiences to new information is acutely important in an intercultural situation, which often contains a rich blend of new and preexisting knowledge frameworks.

In our international presentation style, always explore additional ways to build schemata, such as using visual aids. However, be sure to remember that these elements only *accompany* our delivery of the content. As presenters, we are the axis of the presentation. We narrate, create relationships between ideas, and ignite messages in every speaking opportunity. As Dunckel and Parnham elaborate, "The great danger in using visual aids is that presenters place the major emphasis on visual aids and relegate themselves to [a] minor role . . . You are central to the presentation. The visual aid needs you, your interpretation, your explanation, your conviction, and your justification."

Always look for ways that you can brighten the fire of international presentations by activating the schemata of multilingual and multicultural audiences, and you will enhance the linguistic meaning and cultural significance of your message. You are the architect of meaning in your presentation.

1.6 Releasing "Lightning in a Bottle": The Six Universal Storytelling Patterns

> *If history were taught in the form of stories, it would never be forgotten.* **—Rudyard Kipling**

The "bottled lightning" in your presentation is your stories. Release it. However, remember that the electricity of a presentation is its *theme,* which is the guiding topic your presentation is about—your theme connects your audience to human experience.

Your presentation theme must be universal enough that *your* story becomes *your audience's* story. Once you've formed this connection, your audience goes out into the world armed with your knowledge, concept, and message like a handheld thunderbolt ready to release an energy of change into the workplace or into the world at large.

The theme in every presentation can be summed up in this single word: *change.* The theme is the *change* connected to your message—*a call to action, feeling,* or *thought.* In the principle of service, the audience is the true "hero" of our presentation. *They*—not us—are going to bring our change to the world. If the presentation were a quest, once our presentation ends, the fading flame of our words ignites the beginning of the audience's heroic quest. As part of an international presentation style, one of the most powerful ways to channel the electrical charge of your theme and message to global audiences is through the power of storytelling. Remember, narrative transcends culture.

👥 *Global Presentation Tip*

Use stories as a way to not just build meaning in your presentation, but ultimately, support the role of human decision-making for your audience.

So, what storytelling patterns work best for presentations across cultures? The most notable example comes from mythologist and writer Joseph Campbell, who references the transcultural power of myth in his opus, aptly titled

The Hero with a Thousand Faces. Campbell compares mythologies from around the world to reveal a powerful truth: all cultural narratives are a variation of a single great and common story—*the monomyth.*

At the root of most world myths exists a universal pattern: a hero leaves home, ventures into the unknown, and returns with newfound knowledge or wisdom. Along the way, the hero meets a guide or teacher for their quest. This monomyth pattern is true regardless of origin or time of creation. And, this pattern has now become prevalent in Hollywood movies in the last several decades (just think of Star Wars!).

Our presentations function the same way—as a quest—and once we acknowledge that the audience is the hero, not us, we begin to embrace our true role as the *guide*—in this way, we are like Yoda, Mr. Miyagi, Merlin, or the Fairy Godmother, imparting advice to heroes on their journey. This role informs our approach to storytelling—*or rather story-sharing*—which has always been a human way of meaning-making and sense-making.

For one thing, storytelling, across global societies, is how we learn to make choices. Just reflect on this for a moment. When we feel a story deeply and emotionally, we learn from that story as if we were learning from firsthand experience. Stories guide us to what we "ought to do" in the future—we connect our values to action through stories. And in terms of upcoming decisions, how often have we stored the courageous stories of others to access later as fuel when we are called to act with bravery in the future?

Ultimately, linking stories to our presentation message ensures that the audience not only remembers the information but also knows where to channel their passion—they know what the next steps are.

👥 *Global Presentation Tip*

The ultimate goal of a presentation story is to motivate your audience to join you in a quest with a shared purpose.

Storytelling enhances every presentation, whether we are presenting data, delivering a business report, or pitching an innovative concept. As an integral component of an international presentation style, storytelling is a vital way to connect with global audiences. For example, some of the most resonant and universal story themes are overcoming adversity, making surprising revelations, challenging the status quo, taking risks, being true to our dreams, coming of age, and sharing hopeful messages.

Remember, presentations are meant to be *shared,* not *told,* and this slight shift in thinking can make a significant difference in how we adapt our content for our audiences in service to others. Through story-sharing, we gain not only a deeper understanding of our own experiences, but also a better understanding of each other and the rich perspectives through which we view our shared world.

Global Presentation Tip

Remember, your audience is the "hero" of your narrative. Prepare and inspire the "hero" to take your journey.

When we deliver a narrative, our goal is to inspire audiences to participate *introspectively* and *cognitively* in our presentations. As research has shown, when we listen to a presentation with vibrant story elements, our minds become electrically charged with excitement—across cultures, our language-processing areas are activated with the same wildfire of thought lighting up other areas of the brain that become energized during events *occurring in reality.* Research has even indicated that the same neural networks burn with excitement whether we're experiencing an event in a story or in real life! These findings mean our audiences are much more likely to remember and be impacted by a presentation that contains stories.

Story-sharing also creates *narrative empathy* that forges new connections and increases the quality of our messages. As Lisa Cron, author of *Wired for Story,* describes, "Stories allow us to simulate intense experience without having to actually live through them . . . to experience the world before we actually have to experience it." This effect is called "mentalizing," which brings about shared feelings to create an "empathetic experience," allowing us to share in the storyteller's moments as if they were our own, in a revealed universal connection.

Global Presentation Tip

Use the six storytelling patterns to take audiences on a cognitive journey and powerfully communicate your content.

Whether you call it storytelling or story-sharing, taking audiences on this cognitive journey is an indispensable part of an international presentation style and speaker-audience relationship. Dynamic connections stir embers into flame when we use the storytelling methods outlined in Figure 1-2, "The 6 Universal Storytelling Patterns." These narrative patterns clarify concepts and channel the thematic electricity charging our message.

The 6 Universal Storytelling Patterns

Use storytelling patterns to build connections and take global audiences on the journey of your ideas.

1

Monomyth
Focus on the hero's journey into the unknown, who then returns with a discovery helpful to their community.

2

Petal Structure
Short different stories orbit a central concept.

3

Global Sparklines
Continually contrast "how things are" with "how things should be," as you reveal the global impact of your idea.

4

In Medias Res
Begin in the middle of a story, then return to the beginning.

5

Unifying Ideas
Different ideas converge to form one larger idea.

6

False Start
Begin predictably, then shift to an unexpected new beginning.

Figure 1-2

In the body of your presentation, use the following **six universal storytelling patterns** to engage global audiences in the sense-making process—you'll be motivated by the response!

1. **Monomyth:** As mentioned previously, this storytelling pattern is focused on the central figure of a hero who embarks on a journey into unknown territory, then returns with a discovery, treasure, or new-found wisdom that will help their community. Think of the "hero's journey" in worldwide sensational stories such as *The Lion King* and *Star Wars* (as well as many world myths, religious stories, and folklore).

   Key strategy: Use this narrative pattern to show your audience the benefit of taking risks and how you acquired newfound wisdom or results in a project or personal triumph.

2. **Petal structure:** This story scheme organizes multiple anecdotes around a central message. The stories can be disconnected or part of a larger narrative—as long as the "petal" stories are all related to a single message. For example, the Netflix series *Black Mirror* consists of multiple episodic stories that weave together to portray humanity's evolving relationship with technology.

   Key strategy: Use this method to show how pieces of a larger story or process are interconnected, while weaving a rich tapestry of evidence or emotional significance around a central theory or idea.

3. **Global sparklines:** This powerful discourse pattern is the blueprint for the most resonant speeches in the world; it contrasts an ordinary world with an ideal or improved world. Think of Martin Luther King Jr.'s "I Have a Dream" speech, which continually intertwines and contrasts two worlds: "how things are" and "how things should be." By drawing attention to challenges in personal lives, society, and business, this pattern, credited to Duarte Design CEO and presentation guru Nancy Duarte, fuels the desire for change. Turn Duarte's sparklines model into *global* sparklines by revealing the global impact of your idea as you lead your audience from reality to vision.

   Key strategy: Use this pattern to create hope and excitement for an improved world, while engaging an audience to join you in your vision.

4. **In medias res:** This storytelling method drops you in the middle of the action prior to setting the story scene. In the *James Bond* franchise,

many stories begin with a "chase scene" that immediately pulls the audience into the action before the film goes back to fill in the details. Just like a 007 movie, this recognizable story motif framework works well if there is a lot of background information to your presentation story or leading to your narrative's turning point.

Key strategy: Use this pattern to begin at a pivotal moment in your tale before going into the backstory and then finally giving the audience the resolution they are thirsting for.

5. **Unifying ideas:** In this pattern, different strands of thought converge to form a single idea. The merging of storylines differs from the "petal structure" in that several parallel stories of equal importance come together to achieve a single goal. Consider the story of how one of the most influential music bands in the world, the English rock band the Beatles, first began with the creative collaboration between John Lennon and Paul McCartney.

Key strategy: Use this pattern when acknowledging how great minds or ideas came together for a common purpose.

6. **False start:** This storytelling pattern produces the "dopamine effect," the rush of curiosity and sense of excitement that begins with a seemingly predictable plot and then abruptly shifts to a new beginning. Think of J. K. Rowling's inspiring Harvard commencement speech, where she surprisingly begins her speech with the benefits of failure rather than dwelling on the graduates' achievements or the story of her success.

Key strategy: Use this method to disrupt audience expectations with surprise, immediately engaging them to focus on a newly revealed primary message.

We live and create through the sparklines of stories. Just as music has the potential to transcend cultural boundaries, a great story has the power to move us and unite us across cultural and generational dimensions. The deeper the "real-life" theme comes from our personal experience, the more it will connect with the human experience of our audiences.

As international presenters, we grow with our audiences by utilizing a combination of storytelling patterns in our presentations, so that we arrive more deeply at the importance, weight, and fire of a message—together.

1.7 The Hourglass Speech Canvas: An Intercultural Presentation Model

> *If something comes from your heart, it will reach the heart of your audience.* **—Fawzia Koofi**

There may not be a "one-size-fits-all" template for a perfect speech; however, there is an **hourglass speech canvas** presentation model that provides a single effective framework for global presentations. This singular presentation model is a presentation "map" that catches fire with audiences interculturally across the world.

A canvas itself is symbolic of endless possibility. Artists create art in service to others, and the idea of a *presentation canvas* awaiting our expressive gestures and the color of our ideas is an important metaphor as we weave hooks, stories, and presentation schemata into our public speaking fabric. We term this model a "canvas" because, while it contains key intercultural presentation components, it gives us room for flexibility and creativity.

In today's globally-connected and technologically-linked world, this is truly the potential era of vast and collective service. We can reach vast amounts of people, whether via online or in-person presentations. The principle of service guides us as presenters to raising the consciousness of the planet. So how do we do this? As *audience* members, all of us have diverse ways of learning and intaking information. As *presenters,* we must optimize how we organize our ideas when sharing them in service to others.

👥 *Global Presentation Tip*

Organizing your ideas for a spectrum of diverse audiences is the key to an effective presentation process.

Essentially, the *hourglass speech canvas* is effective because it targets two means of organizing information—represented by an inverted cone and an upright cone. First, these two cones target two larger cultural dimensions: high-context and low-context communication styles. Anthropologist and intercultural researcher Edward T. Hall outlined these two frameworks for approaching intercultural communication (see Appendix B on *Cultural Contexts*).

The Hourglass Speech Canvas

Combine cultural styles, effective techniques, and inductive/deductive reasoning in this one unifying presentation pattern for all audiences.

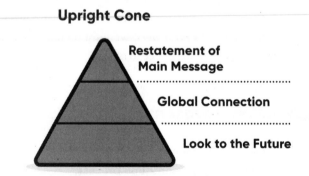

Inverted Cone

Hook

Key Details

Main Message

PATTERN 1: Distilling Information

- Reflects high-context communication styles; information builds from a hook toward the main message

- Reflects deductive thinking and learning styles; elements are sequenced from general to specific, focus is on synthesis

Upright Cone

Restatement of Main Message

Global Connection

Look to the Future

PATTERN 2: Expanding Information

- Reflects low-context communication styles; information builds from the main message to a larger conclusion

- Reflects inductive thinking and learning styles; elements are sequenced from specific to general, focus is on development

Figure 1-3a

According to Hall, culture with **high-context communication** styles, which tend to be a pattern of Eastern cultures, generally prefer information presented in an inverted cone format, with a gradual "funneling" of information

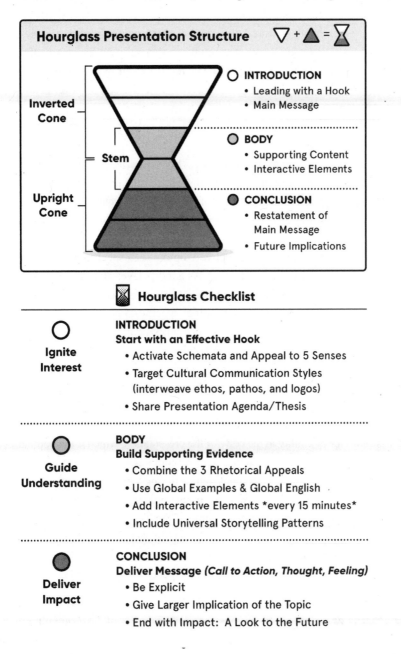

Figure 1-3b

that builds toward the main message or point of the presentation. The focus is on synthesis and on developing knowledge from multiple sources of information. This general-to-specific sequence is represented by the inverted cone at the top of the hourglass model.

On the other hand, cultures with **low-context communication** styles, which tend to be a pattern of Western cultures, generally prefer information presented in an upright cone format, with the main message or point introduced at the outset that builds toward a larger conclusion. The focus is on details and on developing knowledge from one statement, principle, or source. This specific-to-general sequence is represented by the upright cone at the bottom of the hourglass model.

When merged together as an "hourglass," both patterns of communication build toward a unified presentation model that clearly and impactfully communicates information across the spectrum of global professionals.

Furthermore, just as artists paint possibility into existence for the world, the hourglass canvas actualizes powerful communication possibilities. To start, this method of organization effectively optimizes a spectrum of learning styles with its inverted and upright cones. As another layer of an *international presentation style,* this model contains a combination of deductive reasoning (general-to-specific) and inductive reasoning (specific-to-general) approaches that meld cultural and learning styles into one unifying presentation pattern.

Additionally, in terms of content, while this model targets *both* low-context and high-context communication styles, it also preserves the most important *parts* of a presentation—an effective introduction (inverted cone) and an effective conclusion (upright cone), as these essential components leave the most lasting impression and impact. At the same time, the body (or stem of the hourglass) provides room for flexibility in the body of the presentation, which is the optimal place to "feed the fire" and make adjustments by compressing or expanding body sections depending on audience responsiveness during a presentation.

Overall, the hourglass canvas appeals to the intercultural style preferences that span the global communication patterns of the world. See Figure 1-3 and reflect on how the elements of this chapter fit into this *hourglass speech canvas.* How can you use this canvas to ignite your next intercultural presentation?

Creative strategies for using the *hourglass speech canvas* include:

- **Inverted cone:** Start with an introduction or opening to a presentation that is organized in an inverted cone reminiscent of *Eastern* cultural style patterns, leading with an impactful hook and connecting information—followed by a main idea or thesis.

- **Stem:** Highlight supporting content in the body, or middle of the presentation, that responds to time needs and audience interest. This is also the place to plan "extra sections" or dynamic presentation components that can be rotated as necessary, such as interactive elements that can be flexible as time permits. Include content that is adaptable to contract or expand as needed.

- **Upright cone:** Finally, deliver a memorable closing, or final portion of a presentation, that focuses attention just like the structure of any newspaper article in *Western* culture, where the main message or thesis is stated at the outset (in this case, it would be a gripping restatement of the main idea), alongside specific recommendations and contexts, eventually broadening to a larger conclusion that touches on the greater significance of the presentation and future implications.

We first deliver our message with a hook and overview, leading to our main idea, then give supporting details, and finally circle back to a restatement of our main idea while broadening our message toward larger implications. Artists create art in service to others to bring color and vitality to people's lives. Similarly, we can use the *hourglass speech canvas* presentation model to ignite interest and inspiration across audiences with a series of sparkline connections that electrify our overall message all the way through to the end of the presentation.

1.8 Effective Conclusions Are New Beginnings: Evolving along Global Sparklines

> *A single question can be more influential than a thousand statements.* **—Bo Bennett**

If you get the chance, take time to marvel at the outstretched arcs of trailing green light that ripple across the night sky in high-latitude regions of the earth. Encountering the mystical phenomenon of an aurora may give you rivaling feelings of reality and fantasy, as your mind is set ablaze by astonishment and inspiration.

In a similar way, the most powerful presentations have the potential to impart the same reaction when fueled with oscillating patterns that link us between dream and reality. As mentioned earlier in this chapter, one of the most powerful storytelling patterns for achieving an emotional connection and bridging these sparks from one person to another is what communications expert Nancy Duarte calls *sparklines*. Her examination of the most impactful speeches revealed this singular and fundamental model.

According to Duarte, *sparklines* are a fundamental blueprint of every powerful speech in human history—revealing flashes of insight by contrasting "what is" with "what could be." Essentially, when we look at this blueprint through our lens as global presenters, we see that these speeches feature key oscillating points between *reality* and *vision*. By adapting this model to our purpose as global presenters, we discover expanded storytelling and presentation patterns that can be broadened transculturally.

Presentations that fluctuate between reality and hope with an expanded global relevance contain the key to rippling this illumination across the world. When we seek to expand this blueprint to global audiences, we must rhythmically contrast reality with an imagined future, while also including an additional element—revealing the global impact of our ideas through the creation of **global sparklines,** indicated in Figure 1-4. This added dimension optimizes our speeches for a more global reach—by contrasting planetary *reality* with a shared *vision,* we show our audiences how to actualize **globally-connected possibilities.**

As analyzed by Duarte, Martin Luther King Jr.'s "I Have a Dream" speech is a powerful example that embodied the sparkline technique when he contrasted the *reality* of historical social injustice ("sweltering with the heat of injustice . . . of oppression"), with his *vision* of a harmonious and equal society ("I have a dream that one day . . ."). Through our lens of *global* sparklines, we see that the pulsating dynamic between *reality* and *vision* reverberated to future world audiences called to further actualize the concept of human rights in a global impact still being felt today.

A modern example related to the sweeping global impact of a technological wonder stems from Steve Jobs's 2007 speech introducing the first iPhone to the world. Duarte analyzed how Jobs highlighted the contrasting *reality* of previous phones that limited us, with his *vision* of the new iPhone as a revolutionary communications device capable of internet, music, phoning, and creativity. Through our lens of *global* impact, this announcement also rippled across worldwide audiences whose imaginations lit up with the larger potential of this device for accelerating the connectivity and empowerment that drives innovation across the world.

Global Sparklines

Tap into the blueprint of the most powerful speeches in human history, a storytelling pattern where you rhythmically contrast reality with an imagined future. ***Reveal the global impact of your idea as you show your audience how to actualize possibilities.***

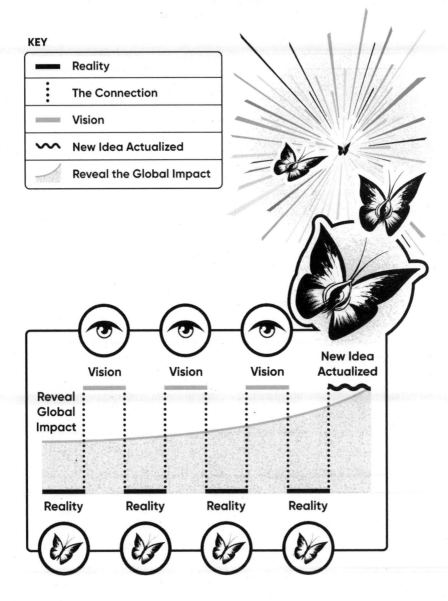

Figure 1-4

👥 *Global Presentation Tip*

Reveal meaningful connections between vision and reality as you deliver a presentation in service to others. Service opens the path to enlightenment for all of us.

To infuse your next business speech with the heightened awareness and impact of global sparklines, hone your central idea with the following two key parameters:

1. Help audiences improve themselves and their own lives.
2. Contribute to a better world.

The greatest presentations are in service to others. No matter whether the speech is a routine boardroom presentation or a keynote address, these elements will turn any idea into meaningful waves of influence. While our words, ideas, and passions ignite part of the communications process, the true magic manifests in the collection of sparklines that fuel our global presentations within the principle of service. To expand consciousness, our spoken stories must fluctuate between *vision* and *reality*, connecting us to our audiences and synchronizing the electrical impulses within our minds and bodies. When presentation *global sparklines* fluctuate between dream and reality, electrical charges ignite within and between our bodies, creating powerful communication situations. These sparks leap from synapse to synapse among our network of neurons, triggering impulses that fire across our minds, sparking ideas from one person to another on this planet. We catch fire with renewed perspectives that are set ablaze with new shared meanings.

This awareness ignited by global sparklines is especially relevant when crafting a presentation *conclusion.* Every presentation conclusion should evolve along global sparklines, and is an opportunity for us to change, together. Not just the change conveyed in the presentation itself, but the change the audience will carry forward—*doing* something differently, *thinking* differently, or *feeling* differently upon leaving the room, even after the speech has ended.

For us as global presenters, our conclusion is an opportunity to motivate and inspire audiences by sharing the larger implications of our presentation. What are the lingering possibilities? What larger solution, prediction, or vision can we share? Avoid just giving a restatement or summary of your presentation; don't fizzle out—go out with a bang!

The most effective way to deliver a lasting resonance and create an impactful conclusion is to deliver a *look to the future*. The most powerful conclusions allow the audience to linger in the presenter's world and wander between hope and reality—after the presentation has concluded. The dream should still be in reach, at their fingertips.

Yes, when we come to a close, remember that every presentation is an opportunity for change. And we each possess a fire that breathes within us and can be passed onward to others, conveying our knowledge and thoughts as if cast from the same flame. As French general Ferdinand Foch once said, "The most powerful weapon on earth is the human soul on fire." And this is true. The passion of a single soul can set the hearts of the world aflame, for when you discover the deeper reason for being in a speaking situation, you become unstoppable.

Yet, above all, always keep in mind that the presentation situation is a gift—a most profound opportunity—a unique chance to share the full force of our passion, ideas, and message with a gathered audience in person. As presenters, we serve as catalysts of change. The human voice is a catalyst for thought, emotion, and action. We can place a spark in someone's mind, a flame in their heart, and a fire behind their decisions.

However, as catalysts for change, we are not the source of change alone—the change that happens is a collaboration between audience and speaker in the cognitive space, an interplay between listeners, narratives, cultures, and our words. This is incredibly humbling and liberating. When we view ourselves as catalysts for change and not the source, we begin to enter that vast network of human ideas that has propelled us from the past to now and, from now, collectively into the future.

Activity: Evolving Global Sparklines

Review your next presentation and expand your topic or data analysis using the two sparkline parameters from this section: (1) *help audiences improve themselves and their own lives* or (2) *contribute to a better world.*

- Even if you are presenting on a business product or service, reflect on how you can tie it to a larger message.

- Then, how can you link your message to the greater good and expand your idea to societal issues and global audiences?

....

1.9 Torchbearers in an Interconnected World

> *Change will not come if we wait for some other person or if we wait for some other time. We are the ones we've been waiting for—we are the change that we seek.*
> *—President Barack Obama*

As torchbearers, we can illuminate aspects of shared humanity. Spreading ideas in service to one another is one of the greatest achievements of the human spirit. When we see presentations in this way, we can fully honor the uniqueness of diverse societies by creating a collective space where similarities drive our stories forward. Once the principle of service is in place, we are able to successfully navigate every presentation decision.

The concept of service must be a way of global presentation life. What this means is asking yourself in every presentation, How is this presentation helping my service to humanity? To be effective, global presentations must go beyond career goals or other short-term professional goals. Instead, they must be part of one tapestry of life based on service. When we think of presentations in terms of service, we think of the entire system of humanity.

Furthermore, in the act of service, storytelling does more than bring us together, as in the researched experience called "neural coupling." We not only share understanding, but we also share human experience itself.

Presenters who are storytellers can resolve unnecessary distinctions between values, feelings, ideas, and ways of seeing the world. By creating openness, storytelling in presentations is the foundation for integrating our diversity of ideas and building unity in the world. As French literary theorist Roland Barthes stated in his signature essay, "Introduction to the Structural

Analysis of Narratives," "Narrative is present in every age, in every place, in every society; it begins with the very history of mankind and there nowhere is nor has been a people without narrative. All classes, all human groups, have their narratives. . . . Narrative is international, transhistorical, transcultural: it is simply there, like life itself."

When we begin to develop an international presentation style that integrates these cognitive and storytelling patterns into our presentation skills—constructing the story of our ideas—we begin to give shape to a new view and shared perspective, a collective human memory of ideas organized by stories in time and arriving closer to what Yale professor and author Peter Brooks described as "our very definition as human beings." As torchbearers sharing the story of our ideas in service to others, we begin to unite perspectives and build on cultural truths in a global way.

Global presentations infused with story-sharing rekindle passion and awaken the mind beyond the rim of consciousness, to what can be known inside, yet not entirely told—merely implied in the act of telling. Only then do we begin to understand together the difference between longing and wonder. By tapping into these global sparklines of storytelling when presenting to multicultural global audiences, we are no longer separate in longing, but united to participate in wonder alongside connected societies at our own renewal as a shared human race.

We all share this three-pound universe inside, this network of a hundred billion nerve cells composing the human brain, from where the sparks of all ideas come and the eternal flames of story continue to link us in global sparklines throughout our careers and across generations. As we begin to recognize these patterns that connect us, we begin to see a new map of communication that, in the light of our fire, illuminates a new reality—one where we not just create unity in our professional lives, but sustain it in our messages and service as well.

How do we build meaningful networking relationships that create a greater purpose of generosity, discovery, and collaboration?

Connecting with People: The Power of Meaningful Networking and Relationship-Building

> *Networking is the art of building and maintaining connections for shared positive outcomes.*
> —**Devora Zack**

We have arrived at this point in our lives because of the people we know. Everything in the world is connected—both business and Nature exist in relationships. Even Nature operates the same way, with its own network of constantly-flowing daily communication.

If we were to divert our attention to the earth under our feet, we would discover an abundance of chatter unfolding beneath the soil, between an elaborate system of roots, and across a vast network of trees and plants. Just as Nature has configured a hidden complex communication system—where different plant and fungal networks busily communicate to support fellow plant species with information, water, and nutrients in exchange for resources—we also participate in this type of information exchange in our own professional and personal networks.

The purpose of networking has evolved in the globally-connected era, becoming more than a self-serving process. Instead, networking is connecting—a commitment to *genuine relationships*. We must form a culture of professional networking that creates a greater purpose of generosity, discovery, and collaboration.

When we think of the parallel lines of communication among trees, it's clear to see how having a supportive network and relying on others develops our professional selves. In the past, prized networkers were those who "made it hard for the other person to say no." The goal was to create buy-in from the other person. But when you're "selling yourself," how can you open up a meaningful dialogue? No one has ever gotten anywhere meaningful without *meaningful relationships,* and it is the same with networking.

Although previous strategies drove us to be "mega-connectors" in the office, boardroom, industry event, or global space, these approaches just created a culture of hungry job seekers who targeted corporate elites. However, we unintentionally remained siloed in our own niche industries by focusing on specific, yet limited, networks.

Today, the successful approach involves a culture of generosity, of helping others. We must figure out the other person's needs and wants and then provide a *solution* or *opportunity.* This successful approach also involves networking outside of our industries and connecting with others besides the obvious corporate elite contacts. When we do, we increase our opportunities, not just for professional growth, but for innovation as well.

The US Bureau of Labor Statistics and Yale University reported that 70 percent of all jobs are found through networking and this number is likely to continue increasing year after year. Further research shows that companies prefer to hire via internal networks, such as CareerXroads's report that cites only 15 percent of positions were filled through job boards; the others were internal hires or referrals. These figures are eye opening! The era of primarily sending cover letters to advertised positions is vanishing. Networking is not an optional skill, but *essential,* particularly in a workforce connected across the world. Networking allows us to:

- tap into *existing* opportunities
- create *new* opportunities

In addition to paving the way for a posted position, professional networking creates opportunities for us *outside* of job postings, leading to either an "invented" position tailored to our talents or new projects altogether. And across cultures, networking now also has a grander purpose of *connecting* over joint goals for mutual success and global influence.

With the accelerating rate that globalization and technology further intertwine our cultural dimensions and cultivate our interconnectivity, modern-day networking has become a vital skill of global professionals. The global approach is two-pronged: create new relationships and revitalize existing relationships.

In this chapter, we will focus on how we can tap into *patterns of interaction* to cultivate influential and powerful relationships in the global age. Across physical and virtual spaces, we will examine how to form more genuine connections and cultural partnerships that result in meaningful opportunities for career, perspective, and innovation. In addition to learning how to build an effective *networking pitch* by using an adapted model common in behavioral or competency-based situations, we will also explore how to integrate our networking pitch naturally into any conversation, using effective speaking techniques from the field of linguistics.

In a globalized world, the true networker focuses on relationships, not only to discover new industry opportunities and ideas, but also to gain meaningful ways to truly connect culturally with those around us. It's time to network with a greater purpose.

2.1 The Global Rainmaker: Networking for Discovery

> *Man cannot discover new oceans unless he has the courage to lose sight of the shore.* **–André Gide**

We have to rethink the concept of networking as a form of rainmaking. Rainmaking is a Native American practice of prayer and ritual dancing that has been around for hundreds of years, as a tradition to summon life-giving rain in a drought. Similarly, in the world of professional networking, rainmakers are those who are able to generate floods of new business opportunities. The source of this magic? Connecting with others outside of our own traditional market space.

As networkers, we have to reframe networking from being a results-driven practice to being a *discovery-driven* practice. Networking, as a form of communication, has as much to do with input as with output. In other words, networking is about much more than finding a career opportunity—networking is also a way to test new ideas with different people, gain new perspectives, and learn new things. To be rainmakers in the modern business world, we have to venture out of our core networks to meet those from different cultures, industries, and even generations.

🗣 *Global Networking Tip*

Be a modern rainmaker and reframe networking from being results-driven to *discovery-driven*.

The modern rainmaker builds influential relationships not just by *revitalizing* regular in-person or online interactions, but also by creating *unforeseen* interactions in new market spaces. Indeed, research has shown that networking can provide a cognitive benefit associated with innovation.

According to Jeff Dyer, Hal Gregersen, and Clayton M. Christensen, who authored *The Innovator's DNA,* networking is one of the behavioral skills that entrepreneurs use to create innovative business ideas (alongside questions, observations, and experiments). How? Creativity is important, but without a network, we cannot fully spark our imaginations, reinvent ourselves, test our inventions, nor share our ideas with the world. The entrepreneurs behind Airbnb, eBay, and PayPal succeeded not only by asking questions of their markets, but also by testing their budding ideas on the public and building fruitful enterprises from those interactions.

Networking is a communication practice, but it is also an *idea-generating* practice—and this idea generation spans cultures. Just think—there you are at an event or a webinar, poised to network with an intercultural audience, who are from countries spanning the globe. Imagine the network of ideas and minds just waiting to inspire you and join with you in the process of global innovation.

🗣 *Global Networking Tip*

When you network for discovery, you not only gain ideas, but build the trust essential to long-term partnerships and global innovation.

Is there a standard global networking formula? According to a study by Yu Tim God and Hongzhi Zhang in *The Journal of Higher Education,* social scenarios remain one of the most difficult challenges for intercultural counterparts due to not having the shared prior knowledge that is required for establishing shared meanings in conversation. This challenge can present a disconnect when professionals navigate diverse groups in networking scenarios, regarding such aspects as customary greetings and cultural norms relative to respect, honor, and seniority.

However, the deeper challenge is trust (see Chapter 5 on *Negotiation Skills*), which cannot be built when networkers are selling themselves, are promoting their company, or are simply hungry to access resources. Instead, as rainmakers, we should network to share opportunities, while gaining new perspectives and ideas in the process. We have to network to "partner," especially when networking interculturally.

According to Dyer, Gregersen, and Christensen, when we are **delivery-driven,** we only meet people like us, in our fields, with similar resources as our own, which can limit the potential of our careers. However, they state that when we are **discovery-driven,** we become open to those who are different from us, outside of our fields, with ideas or perspectives that lead to opportunities previously unimagined.

There is no one formula for navigating the networking journey, but there is a successful approach: *networking for discovery.* All of us have different comfort levels of social interactions, so with the diversity of cultures, beliefs, and attitudes in the world, seeking an exact standardized *formula* may actually make us fall short of arriving at our true *potential* as well as that of our ideas. Instead, all we need to do is cultivate a commitment to fostering meaningful relationships, just as we would in other areas of our lives.

When we are in a room full of people, we have to refine a networking purpose that distinguishes between two types of professionals: *discovery-driven* or *results-driven.* In the following approach, adapted from the work of Dyer, Gregersen, and Christensen, we can see that networking for "knowledge and ideas" versus "assets and status" sends us down different networking paths and, consequently, toward different networking opportunities:

GLOBAL PROFESSIONALS	
Who are results-driven	Who are *discovery*-driven
NETWORK FOR ASSETS:	**NETWORK FOR *IDEAS*:**
Want to expand status in global networks	Enrich **awareness** via global relationships
Seek assets from cultural partners	Pilot **ideas** with cultural partners
See own culture as initial frame of reference	Expand **cognitive skills** and global mindset
Land short-term opportunities for self-interest	Cultivate **long-term** global partnerships
Promote own goals and company's goals	Explore **shared goals** and intercultural possibilities to innovate

RESULTS-DRIVEN PROFESSIONALS SEEK:	DISCOVERY-DRIVEN PROFESSIONALS SEEK:
Exclusive and domestic groups	**Diverse** groups
Partners with similar views and from similar fields	Cultural partners with **different** views and from **different** fields
Industry leaders and superiors offering assets, power, status, or leverage	Specialists and non-specialists offering **creativity, global outlooks,** and **new perspectives**

When we are driven by obtaining *knowledge and ideas,* we exhibit a verbal and nonverbal curiosity to learn, while affirming the ideas of others. Alternatively, those who seek *assets and status* with the intention of personal gain always struggle with hiding an agenda-driven interest in building their careers or enhancing their business.

Globalized business culture is moving toward a networking culture that is collaborative, with the partnerships that lead to multinational innovation as the goal. These opportunities are manifested when our *networking purpose* changes and guides us toward intended audiences and future partners. Professional networking is just as much about the counterpart in the conversation as it is about the motive for networking. When we know our purpose, we naturally shift our mindset to meet greater goals—in professional networking, these goals are joint opportunities that we create with others as modern-day rainmakers.

2.2 Building Global Ties Interculturally: Patterns of Interaction

If the bee disappeared off the face of the Earth, man would only have four years left to live. **—Albert Einstein**

When it comes to vastly expanding our professional networks, we need to look only as far as Nature's greatest networker—the bee. These insects have a hefty responsibility that supports the interconnected network of plant life, which in reality supports the ecosystem of all living things.

Bees are ardent pollinators of over 80 percent of all flowering plants in the world, which includes a third of what we eat! At the center of their entire delicate balance of duties is communication, which is orchestrated by the queen bees in "hives" all around the globe. With more than twenty thousand to fifty thousand bees to communicate with on average, queen bees have a sophisticated way of interfacing to ensure that their hives function to spread the pollen that is integral for our crops, fruit, and vegetables to flower and grow globally. Just like in this bee analogy, we need to expand our perspective from our immediate networking "hives" to the many near and far relationships that we can forge in our real and virtual spaces, including across cultural spheres.

When we network, patterns of communication tend to occur. All of our connections online and offline consist of two types of interaction patterns: **strong ties** or **weak ties**—both of which serve different functional purposes, according to sociologist Mark Granovetter in his popularized research involving social networks in *The Strength of Weak Ties*. *Strong ties* are connections with those closest to us and within the same group (e.g., family members, close friends, and mentors). *Weak ties* are connections with those further from us in "different groups" (e.g., acquaintances and colleagues).

Although at first it may seem counterintuitive, Granovetter recommends that we focus on the power of *weak ties*. Now, this focus may run contrary to our instincts. Aren't those closest to us and who know us well the ones most likely and willing to help us? The reality is that *weak ties* are, in fact, the ones who can offer us new information and greater resources. In other words, *weak ties* offer important relationships because they lead to varied ideas and perspectives, especially transculturally.

Expanding this model to the global context, we find that establishing connections with people beyond our general expertise as well as our cultural sphere can help strengthen our network and opportunities over the long-term. Just think about it for a moment—when we stay within our network of strong ties, we can end up with "groupthink" or a lack of cultural diversity in imagination, representation, and values. In the short term, we are even less likely to find a job this way. If our close friends are our core network, they will likely know the same people and already have the same information we have.

Now, adapting this concept to the global perspective, in our interdependent world, global "ties" will continue to grow increasingly interconnected and substantial—therefore, we use the term **soft ties** for weak ties and **solid ties** for strong ties. Globally, *soft ties* will eventually become *solid ties*. *Soft ties* are just as important as *solid ties* because they bridge the connection between closely-knit groups or cultures with other groups or cultures. In this way, *soft ties* prevent static patterns of social interaction from forming—which increases interpersonal connections and skills.

We are not only more likely to get a professional opportunity through serendipitous acquaintances from far-flung social and cultural circles—we are also likely to expand our skill sets and gain information relevant to the global order. *Soft ties* help us to not miss out on important trends and information that did not originate from our particular groups or communities. When we tap into the power of *soft ties,* we increase the flow of ideas, resources, and opportunities between cultural and global communities.

🐝 *Global Networking Tip*

Cultivate soft ties as much as solid ties to tap into the power of your global network.

Sociologist and University of Chicago professor Ronald Burt demonstrated via his research that "brokers"—those who span connections across clusters or "hives" of solid ties—often receive greater promotions, salaries, and innovative ideas. Brokers are important intermediaries. Furthermore, according to business school professor David Burkus, author of *Friend of a Friend,* we need to be "brokers" because those who have "both access to diverse information and the ability to combine that information to create new ideas provide value not just to the company, but to themselves."

In networking, just as in culture, our diversity, whether in opinion, customs, or background, is what makes any interaction worthwhile. Networking involves leaving our comfort zone in order to create new opportunities and reach larger goals. When we think of our networking goals as seeking out new information, gaining fresh ideas, and building a global network, this mentality will help us attract others, accelerate connections, and expand our diverse social circle in both online and in-person environments.

Now, what if we apply this *soft ties* principle across the varying cultural demographics of people in the business world network? See Figure 2-1, "Solid Ties and Soft Ties: Building a Global Network." Notice how both *solid ties* and *soft ties* can be combined to create an expansive *global network.* To take this a step further, we should consider how to build **global ties** through the creation of *intercultural ties* among business communities to enhance the diversifying "hives" of global professionals and encourage more cultured perspectives.

Much like the bee, if soft ties were removed from the global order, all communication would break down. The global order would cease to operate properly. Diversity matters, and establishing intercultural connections can be advantageous for professional networks and the development of empathy.

Let's examine just how effective and powerful *risk* can be as we continue to structure our global network. Each time we step out of our comfort zone, we find a bigger world—until there is no difference between the world and our comfort zone. The world becomes our comfort zone.

Solid Ties and Soft Ties: Building a Global Network

Use a combination of solid and soft ties to broaden your global perspective, network, and opportunities.

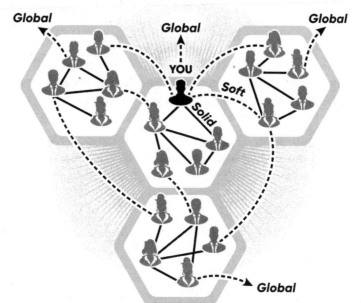

TIES	ROLE	DESCRIPTION
Solid ———	Interconnectors	People that are family members, faithful friends, or close peers.
	Mentors	People you trust, respect, and admire.
Soft - - - -	Influencers	People with influence you aspire to know.
	Grounders	People you admire anchored by similar beliefs positioned to become leaders.
	Connectors	People who can introduce you to a bountiful network.
Global - - -▶	Diversifiers	People with diverse and far-reaching contacts, offering cultured perspectives.

Figure 2-1

2.3 Smart Networking with a Conscience: Diagnosing Your Network

> *Giving connects two people, the giver and the receiver, and this connection gives birth to a new sense of belonging.* **—Deepak Chopra**

Think of a nearby garden—or maybe the public park. Do these green spaces exist as part of the backdrop of your day-to-day flurry of to-dos and schedules? Or, are these landscapes seen as sanctuaries to enter and reflect upon well-springs of possibilities? More importantly, are you a part of a garden?

Gardens are fascinating cultural landscapes all over the globe, from the growing of flowers and vegetables in Western cultures, to the arrangement of stones in Eastern cultures. According to University of Leicester professor Gordon Campbell, author of *A Short History of Gardens,* gardens stand as a metaphor for "the interdependence of humans and . . . the natural world." Campbell states that gardens are "partly constructed and partly natural," products of our desire to create order and patterns in partnership with Nature. The metaphor of a diverse community all living and working together in the "garden" we know as the earth is important. How we see ourselves in Nature's multicultural microcosm is a reflection of how we conduct ourselves in the networks of the multicultural world.

Just as the garden represents our global consciousness, as we cultivate our garden, we must also forge more influential connections, by analyzing which shared activities have the power to build greater networks. On the surface, shared activities seem to be the foundation for professional networking, but they aren't enough. We need to measure whether we are creating the *right* activities, according to two criteria that Brian Uzzi and Shannon Dunlap of Northwestern University's Kellogg School of Management call the *self-similarity principle* and the *proximity principle.*

Activity: Diagnose Your Network

Refer to the following chart based on the accompanying guide to diagnose your virtual and in-person network and reveal your "networking garden."

1. **The Contact:** Assess your core network and plan to pay it forward. Start with a self-imposed audit and write down the names of individuals that you consider to be the most important people in your network in one column—*start with at least five people.*

2. **The Connector:** Think of who introduced you to each person (e.g., a friend or yourself), and list the contact's name in the second column. If you reached out to the person yourself, list "myself."

3. **The Global Nurturer:** In the third column think of how you may repay the favor to those contacts, either by introducing them to an individual in your core network or another way. Focus on listing three key needs and wants of that person and how you can contribute to their progress.

4. **The Diagnosis:** Now, self-reflect and take notes in the fourth column. Which Connector appears the most and is your Superconnector? Do you have a Cultural Superconnector? If you, yourself, are your own Superconnector, how can you branch out? Finally, which contacts took you outside of your usual market and cultural spaces?

SAMPLE NETWORK DIAGNOSIS			
The Contacts	**The Connector**	**The Global Nurturer**	**The Diagnosis**
Jen-Hsun Huang	Bill Fernandez		
Steve Jobs	Bill Fernandez		
Tim Cook	Myself		

Note: The person who appears the most in the Connector column is your Superconnector; if you are listed many times in this column, work to diversify your networking practices.

If you find you've introduced yourself to your key contacts more than 50 percent of the time, your network is too "inbred" and you are building your network according to the *self-similarity principle*. This concept describes our tendency to seek out and network with those who are most like us, in terms of jobs, training, and perspectives.

Research by Columbia University professors of management Paul Ingram and Michael W. Morris demonstrated that many executives who make new contacts tend to fall victim to the *self-similarity principle*. In their study of a mixer attended by approximately one hundred business people, the majority of executives only spoke to people they already knew and with whom they had a "pre-mixer relationship"—apparently the most successful networker was the bartender! In fact, according to Keith Ferrazzi, author of *Never Eat Alone,* the best Superconnectors are frequently said to be restaurateurs, recruiters, journalists, lobbyists, fundraisers, publicists, and politicians because they are in constant conversation with people in different industries and markets.

We've all had this experience—we walk into a business function and immediately find ourselves drawn to those who give us a sense of familiarity, especially if the conversation seems more like a reunion rather than an introduction. After all, who isn't excited about the uncanny experience of meeting a stranger who relates to your ideas, industry, and yes, even Netflix shows!

Additionally, some favor the approach in Ken Coleman's book, *The Proximity Principle,* where strategically positioning yourself in the right place at the right time will grant you access to the right opportunities (or people). Regardless of preference, we should not fall victim to another aspect of the *proximity principle,* where people tend to build their networks based on the people they physically or virtually spend the most time with, such as coworkers and close contacts, as this dynamic creates a buffer against a diversity of ideas and opportunities.

Instead, we should use what Uzzi and Dunlap call the *shared activities principle* and build our networks with activities that bring together "a cross-section" of "disparate individuals around a common point of interest," rather than "connecting similar individuals with shared backgrounds."

Let's be open to networking around activities such as sports, cross-departmental projects, community service activities, and vocational conferences—even in artistic or creative areas outside of business. The goal is to connect with diverse professionals over a shared passion or goal. In this way, our interactions are genuine, are grouped around a shared passion, and generate bonds of loyalty.

🖧 *Global Networking Tip*

Forge connections with diverse individuals through new shared activities and patterns of interaction.

Our own social appraisal of our interactions gives us the power of choice. We can choose how we build the relationships in our online and offline professional networks to reflect our needs and interests. The better option is to reach out through larger cultural networks to become more informed of world topics and more mindful of diverse thinking across the spectrum of business.

On the global scale, self-reflect on these principles in order to leave behind safe networking habits. Make a conscious effort to expand your practice and invest in opportunities to participate in powerful shared activities with those of other cultures—you will be surprised by the positive results that await you.

2.4 Awakening the "Cultural Ambivert": Global Networking Styles

> *The way of the world is meeting people through other people. —Robert Kerrigan*

Across a wide range of cultures, the lotus flower blooms with significance. Collectively, from ancient texts up to the present day, many cultures interpret the lotus flower as representing spiritual enlightenment or rebirth. For some, we arrive at this awakening in our own habits and patterns, but as introverts or extroverts, we look for a new approach to revitalizing ourselves in professional networking encounters.

Like a lotus flower emerging from murky waters, what we have termed the **cultural ambivert** is leading the charge to bridge the networking gaps across East and West networking practices. First of all, what is an ambivert networker? We seem to be on the verge of becoming a culture of *ambivert* networkers without realizing it—at least that's what the research is saying. Many are starting to embrace the ambivert networking style, a balance between preferring interactions with many people and preferring minimal contact—a combination of extrovert and introvert networking styles.

Culturally, there are competing views as to which personality is preferred in networking situations. Many Western ideals may often appear to prize personalities that are sociable and expressive as projecting success in today's competitive workforce—a belief that may be carried over to professional networking contexts. Conversely, some traditional Eastern ideals are more attuned to personalities of reservation and respect (see Appendix B on *Cultural Contexts*). However, while it may seem that only extroverts win over people and ideas, the reality is some extroverts are too assertive and self-absorbed to successfully navigate networking situations that require sensitivity to others. Sociological research has demonstrated that introverts can be just as skilled in professional networking situations, with their natural abilities to reflect upon and internalize information, as indicated by author Susan Cain.

According to research in her book *Quiet: The Power of Introverts in a World That Can't Stop Talking,* introverts make up 33–50 percent of the US population. This means that at a networking event, at least one in four people in attendance are likely to be an introvert in terms of personality type or in terms of experiencing situational introversion. Introverts will approach conversations with different degrees of directness and body language indicators (see Chapter 4 on *Nonverbal Skills*).

However, neither is better than the other. Ambiverts are successful because they *combine* both extrovert and introvert approaches in a networking scenario. Findings by management and psychology professor Adam Grant at the Wharton School of the University of Pennsylvania have indicated that two-thirds (60 percent) of people are true ambiverts, or what he describes as being good salespeople.

Ambiverts approach each exchange by adapting between introvert and extrovert styles in the process of gathering information, exposing opportunities, or closing a deal. Being highly receptive to another person as introverts are, while being sociable with strangers as extroverts are, can help ambiverts to carefully consider responses based on deductive reasoning, while being outgoing and building strong human connections.

Try being an ambivert networker the next time you enter an in-person networking conversation. You may just take a liking to this persona, especially when networking with multicultural audiences.

The cultural ambivert *is a rainmaker who is:*

- adaptable to the directness of Western personalities and the indirectness of Eastern personalities
- able to adjust their communication style between low-context and high-context cultures (see Appendix B on *Cultural Contexts*)

The virtual space also offers new opportunities for ambiverts. You don't have to be an extrovert to take the first step to making an online connection or to becoming a digital video content creator; all you need is an active user profile or a web camera as well as a willingness to take the kind of risk that leads to opportunity. Research shows that many introverts become extroverts online because the age of social media frees introverts to choose platforms that enable full control over their own communication.

We must all reach beyond the comfort of our close network of go-to individuals and make a strategic investment in becoming a cultural ambivert, extending ourselves through virtual networking across different time zones and international borders. In this way, we will broaden global prospects, expand worldviews, and collaborate on unique solutions to shared challenges.

In Buddhist tradition, the three wise monkeys covered their eyes, ears, and mouth to negative thoughts in order to perceive a more profound positive reality. To use this mindset to transform our global reality, see Figure 2-2, "The New Cultural Ambivert." A further and outward-facing interpretation of this proverb aligns with our framework for best practices in becoming a cultural ambivert that *sees, hears,* and *speaks* intently with others for more effective and meaningful intercultural networking.

The New Cultural Ambivert

Cultural ambiverts adapt their communication style *online* and *in person* between *high-context* and *low-context* cultures to be "rainmakers" in the global networking context.

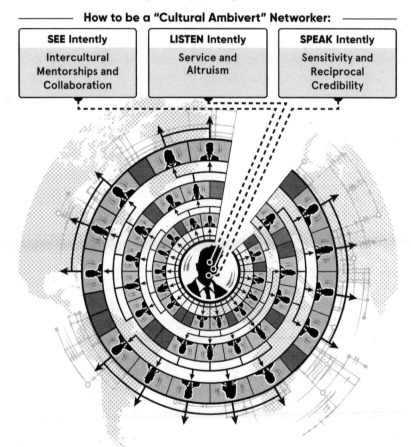

———— How to be a "Cultural Ambivert" Networker: ————

SEE Intently	LISTEN Intently	SPEAK Intently
Intercultural Mentorships and Collaboration	Service and Altruism	Sensitivity and Reciprocal Credibility

Figure 2-2

Here's how to be a cultural ambivert who networks in this neutral space effectively:

- **See intently—intercultural mentorships and collaboration:** Fostering existing online networks is a starting point, but also try forming collaborative networks internationally by seeking multiple virtual mentors for valuable intercultural exchanges, while also being a mentee for others from diverse cultural backgrounds. Have conversations with culturally-diverse professionals from all around the world at varying levels of seniority. Additionally, consider expat communities, which can serve as intermediaries in guiding you toward building networks on the ground in specific countries. Be passionate about learning, be a resource for others, and ask thoughtful questions to underscore your value and loyalty.

- **Listen intently—service and altruism:** In the virtual space, be more *interested* than *interesting*. Build community interculturally by practicing active listening in the virtual space. Prioritize others' experiences, perspectives, and culture before your own. Look for areas of potential collaboration that recognize the person and their value in the interaction. Collaborate without asking for anything in return and give tailored solutions and knowledge abundantly. You may be surprised at the unforeseen opportunities that come from those who serve others.

- **Speak intently—sensitivity and reciprocal credibility:** Step outside of your virtual comfort zone and sign up for industry newsletters, attend virtual webinars, or register for international conferences, both online and in-person, where diverse professionals are gathering. Actively participate in online discussion boards and in knowledge-sharing virtual networks to build *reciprocal credibility,* the social act of mutually constructing positive reputations, as part of the larger intercultural conversation. When we feel reciprocal credibility and trust, we tend to balance the relationship as well, so ask personalized questions, provide knowledge freely, build trust, and be reliable. Solidify your digital networking platform and develop a valued intercultural standing as a global networker.

Whether in-person or online, we have to nurture meaningful diversity within our own networks and avoid networkers who try fast-tracking their understanding of a person's culture only when the networking opportunity calls for it. Instead, adopt a more globalized outlook in the growing international market, by applying the actionable concept of ambiverts embracing new traits.

From an intercultural perspective, *cultural ambiverts* may create the biggest advantage through their nimble methods of recognizing cultural cues in networking dialogues. As cultural dimensions cross boundaries into the mainstream, we must become sensitive to others and manifest key behavioral traits to solidify and expand our network into new virtual and international environments.

Activity: Conversation Culture

If you tend to be introverted, remember those conversations that seem to occur naturally while you are in transit or in places where people are literally waiting—such as at the airport, on a train or bus, or in line at the supermarket. These places are prime areas to practice networking because people aren't waiting with a networking agenda, such as when at the doctor's office, a sporting event, or the gym.

Instead of grabbing your smartphone and scrolling through your news or social media feeds, take a moment to interact in these situations with a real live human, especially in intercultural situations. While some people may think these impromptu conversations are just a means to pass the time, the creative networker harnesses these opportunities to learn more about others around them.

2.5 The Need for Speed: Crafting the Elevator Pitch

> *Have something to say, and say it with passion. Make sure you have something to offer when you speak, and offer it with sincerity.* **—Keith Ferrazzi**

Who knew that the elevator, which is even faster in energy-efficient skyscrapers, would create time limits for our ideas? Nowadays, if meeting an executive in an elevator, we're sometimes even tasked to articulately express a pitch in less than thirty seconds! The networking pitch doesn't always occur in an elevator, but it is called the elevator pitch for two reasons:

1. The elevator is often the space we commonly encounter a target executive and have their undivided attention.

2. More importantly, linguistics tells us that we often have about thirty to sixty seconds to speak before someone interrupts us.

So, how can we be more effective with our words and ideas at this speed in prime networking territory? We've just entered the battle for quick-fire professional sound bites and impact. It's time to build an effective elevator pitch.

🗣 *Global Networking Tip*

Your elevator pitch should communicate how you or your idea will solve a problem, meet a need, or provide an opportunity.

We can build the pitch by applying a behavioral interviewing technique called the **Situation, Task, Action, and Result (STAR) method.** This modified STAR "Pitch Builder," shown in Figure 2-3, can help us to better organize and adapt our professional elevator pitch across any intercultural networking situation.

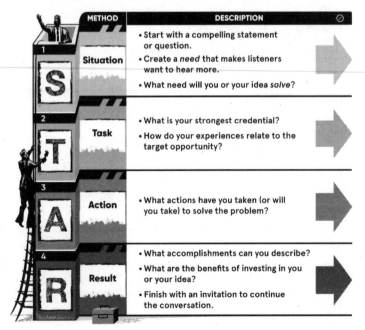

The Networking Pitch Builder

Use the **STAR** Method to tell stories rather than list facts in an effective networking pitch. Create a *need*, then share your idea as the *solution*.

METHOD	DESCRIPTION	⊘
Situation	• Start with a compelling statement or question. • Create a *need* that makes listeners want to hear more. • What need will you or your idea *solve*?	
Task	• What is your strongest credential? • How do your experiences relate to the target opportunity?	
Action	• What actions have you taken (or will you take) to solve the problem?	
Result	• What accomplishments can you describe? • What are the benefits of investing in you or your idea? • Finish with an invitation to continue the conversation.	

Figure 2-3a

Overall, the pitch structure deliberately creates a "need," which then positions you or your idea as the "solution." This sequence creates a problem-answer sequence that is psychologically satisfying to the other person. Use the following steps of this adapted communication technique to build an effective pitch that showcases your skills or your idea:

- **Situation:** Start with a hook that is an attention-grabbing statement or question (see Chapter 1 on *Presentation Skills*). Create a need that makes listeners want to hear more. What need will you or your idea solve? What value can you offer connected to a need in your target industry?

  Sample stem phrases: "Have you ever . . . ," "What if . . . ," "Over X percent of . . . ," "Did you know that . . ."

- **Task:** What are your strongest credentials? How do these relate to the task and target opportunity?

How will you or your idea meet a NEED or provide an OPPORTUNITY?

SAMPLE PITCH

Did you know that we spend one-third of our lives sleeping? We should cherish our sleep to live a wonderful life.

Hello, I'm a Sleep Specialist at the *Forty Winks* corporation. Our policy is "Good sleep for everyone," and today I'll show you our most popular product — a pillow. We've recently received funding from celebrity investors, such as *Van Winkle Capital*, and we are also partnering with *Sheep Airlines* to design pillows for their passengers.

All our pillows are made-to-order: you choose the solidity, height, color, and contents. We'll make the perfect pillow just for you. Also, we're committed to environmentally-friendly manufacturing, with 80% of our pillows made from recycled materials. According to a recent survey, 95% of our customers are satisfied with our products.

Sleep is one of the best things we can do for our health. To partner in developing these superior sleep products, why not invest in us? Our goal is to provide the best sleep for all people. Here's my card if you're interested in learning more.

Figure 2-3b

- **Action:** What actions have you taken (or will you take) to solve the need?
- **Result:** What accomplishments can you describe in relation to the need? What are the benefits of investing in you or your idea? Finish with an invitation to continue the conversation.

🗣 *Global Networking Tip*

Use the STAR method to tell stories rather than facts in a networking pitch.

This pitch format in Figure 2-3, "The Networking Pitch Builder," works for a variety of pitch scenarios, such as networking, job interviews, a book pitch, a business idea, a film pitch, or even speed dating! The key is creating a relatable "need" with the *situation/task* steps and a "solution" with the *action/result* steps. However, remember to see this pitch format as a blueprint and keep it flexible according to what has been called the *accordion model*. Depending on the situation, there will be times where we must condense or expand our elevator pitch.

In other words, sometimes we must narrow our elevator pitch to ten to fifteen seconds and offer key talking points, while at other times we have the opportunity to elaborate on those key points for one to two minutes. Prepare for both scenarios. Also, be aware of intercultural considerations regarding listening and speaking, such as adjusting the pace of our speech for ease of the exchange.

Now, is the pitch our entire strategy? No, the pitch is a blueprint that has to be interwoven into the conversation. Every pitch situation is not a speed-dating event. We can easily envision that rehearsed professional walking up and delivering their entire pitch, memorized, without the art of small talk, such as "My name is Mei. Did you know that 85 percent of positions are filled outside of job boards? I'm an HR manager with a new approach that . . ."

Instead, we have to use "topic-initiating strategies" to open the pitch, such as in the following four-part format shown in Figure 2-4, "Flow of the Networking Pitch": *conversation opener, networking pitch, conversation pre-closer,* and *closer.* The goal is to combine conversation strategies around an effective pitch.

Let's look at how you can initiate, shift, and exit a topic smoothly in a networking situation.

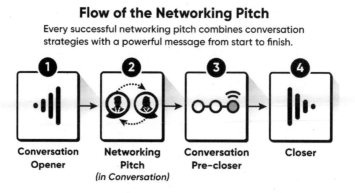

Flow of the Networking Pitch

Every successful networking pitch combines conversation strategies with a powerful message from start to finish.

Conversation Opener | Networking Pitch *(in Conversation)* | Conversation Pre-closer | Closer

Figure 2-4

2.6 Engaging a Cultural State of Mind: Leading with Conversation Openers

> *One good conversation can shift the direction of change forever.* **—Linda Lambert**

Creating conversations is how we create relationships. Then why is it so hard when networking? Judy Robinett in her book *How to Be a Power Connector* writes that most of us initiate conversations with strangers only 2–3 percent of the time in all of our conversations.

Well, instead of viewing ourselves as "pitching" a person, we should reframe our approach as presenting an *opportunity* to the other person. Research studies indicate that over 50 percent of our perceived notions underestimate the genuine willingness of others to help us when making a request or favor—and this spans culturally as well.

In Nature, everything starts with a seed. Every seed must have the right conditions and be nurtured to grow. Similarly, conversations in professional networking scenarios are a seed that can be nurtured to grow—with the conscious and linguistic effort of engaging others *naturally* with a conversation opener and then building interest toward a given topic.

So, how do we initiate a topic naturally? We've all been in situations where a job-hungry executive quickly introduces themselves and immediately jumps into their pitch. Instead, we have to build rapport with small talk. While there are some exceptions (such as parts of Scandinavia and parts of Central Europe—see Appendix B on *Cultural Contexts*), many cultures view small talk as an important "social lubricator" that builds trust and interest from the other party.

When we view conversation as a *system,* as in the field of linguistics, we see new interrelationships. In other words, we shift awareness from our immediate words, to building the larger pattern of the exchange itself. We can then predict responses and engage in something called "topic management" in order to create a path to our pitch.

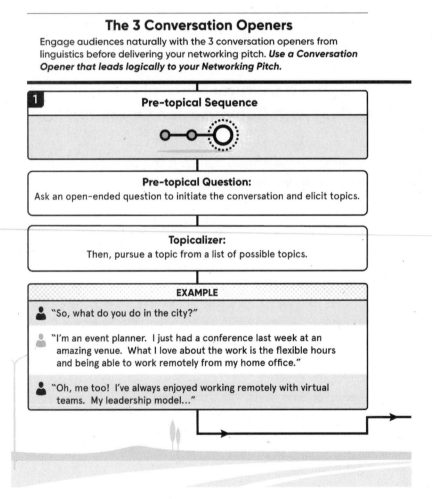

The 3 Conversation Openers

Engage audiences naturally with the 3 conversation openers from linguistics before delivering your networking pitch. *Use a Conversation Opener that leads logically to your Networking Pitch.*

1 **Pre-topical Sequence**

Pre-topical Question:
Ask an open-ended question to initiate the conversation and elicit topics.

Topicalizer:
Then, pursue a topic from a list of possible topics.

EXAMPLE

👤 "So, what do you do in the city?"

👤 "I'm an event planner. I just had a conference last week at an amazing venue. What I love about the work is the flexible hours and being able to work remotely from my home office."

👤 "Oh, me too! I've always enjoyed working remotely with virtual teams. My leadership model..."

Figure 2-5a

So how does a **conversation opener** lead us to our goals? The opener is the "small talk" that leads to the "big talk," or purpose of our conversations. The opener is the "icebreaker" that initiates the pitch. In network courting practices, starting with an "icebreaker" and then leading the other party to your pitch takes a bit of planning, but is essential to forging meaningful business interactions.

Consider the following conversation openers derived from research studies in the field of discourse analysis and linguistics. See Figure 2-5, "The 3 Conversation Openers." These openers are part of "structuring practices" in topic management that can help you initiate and establish the topic of your choice.

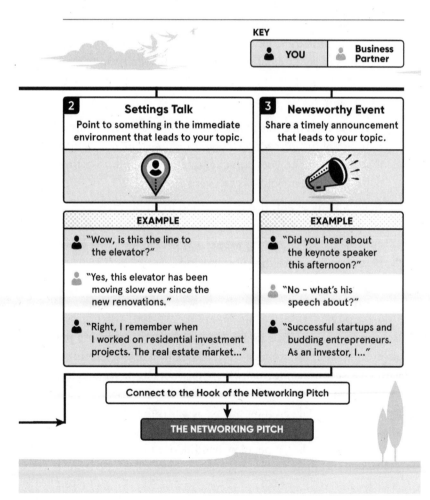

KEY

| 👤 YOU | 👤 Business Partner |

2 Settings Talk
Point to something in the immediate environment that leads to your topic.

3 Newsworthy Event
Share a timely announcement that leads to your topic.

EXAMPLE

👤 "Wow, is this the line to the elevator?"

👤 "Yes, this elevator has been moving slow ever since the new renovations."

👤 "Right, I remember when I worked on residential investment projects. The real estate market..."

EXAMPLE

👤 "Did you hear about the keynote speaker this afternoon?"

👤 "No – what's his speech about?"

👤 "Successful startups and budding entrepreneurs. As an investor, I..."

Connect to the Hook of the Networking Pitch

THE NETWORKING PITCH

Figure 2-5b

The Three Conversation Openers

Use the three conversation openers to initiate a dialogue that naturally leads to your pitch:

1. **Pre-topical sequence:** Use this topic initiation method to explore possible topics and get to know one another.

   - **Pre-topical question:** Begin with an open-ended question about identity or activities (e.g., "Tell me about the most exciting projects you're working on at the moment.").

   - **Topicalizer:** Then, after the response, transform a possible topic into an actual topic (this initiation sequence is the third turn in the topic initial elicitor sequence) (e.g., "That second one's really fascinating! I worked on a similar initiative last year, facilitating digital storytelling trainings as part of an employee exchange program with our Swiss colleagues . . .").

2. **Settings talk:** Use this method to point to the immediate environment of the interaction (could be a question or a statement) that then leads to your topic (e.g., "Every year, this venue gets better and better, right? As an event planner, I . . .").

3. **Newsworthy event:** Use this method to report on newsworthy activities that lead to your topic (e.g., "Did you hear about the earthquake in China this week? I was talking to my business partner in Shanghai this morning and . . .").

How do we set ourselves up for success? Start by targeting a few select people in the room. Then, begin a conversation with one of the openers highlighted above, such as *settings talk:* "Wow, this morning mixer is really packed, isn't it? I'm glad no one slept in." Then, after the response, lead naturally to your pitch, such as "Did you know that we actually spend one-third of our lives sleeping? We have to cherish our sleep to live a wonderful life. I'm the president of the Forty Winks Corporation, and I'd love to tell you about our most popular product, a pillow . . ."

> ### 👥 *Global Networking Tip*
>
> **Use a conversation opener that works as both an icebreaker and a logical lead-in to your pitch.**

While some networkers plan key points when conversing in professional networking situations, the key is to plan which *conversation opener* to use—and then use it to lead logically to the topic of your pitch. Above all, our goal in any networking situation should be to make the other person feel valued and appreciated.

Small talk establishes relationships. Eastern cultures value this polite conversation protocol, while some Western cultures may tend to place value on qualifications, achievements, and successes. Instead, always enter an intercultural networking situation with humility, appreciation, and respect—establishing a foundation of character. Then, you have a solid place to discuss your own successes and can readily shift the conversation toward your pitch, while also finding common ground and acknowledging the other person's successes.

Activity: Pitch Perfect

- First, review the hook or first line of your networking pitch and apply the three conversation openers (*pre-topical question/topicalizer, settings talk,* and *newsworthy event*) as a way to initiate the conversation and guide the dialogue toward your pitch. Remember, the conversation opener is not the same as the "hook" of your pitch (the situation step) and does not replace the hook, but rather leads to it.

- Then, think about how you can link anticipated responses to the hook of your pitch (see Chapter 1 on *Presentation Skills*).

2.7 The Grand Finale: Concluding Memorably with Conversation Closers

> *Networking is about making meaningful, lasting connections that lead to one-to-one relationships.*
> **—Les Garnas**

Closing a conversation is vitally important to any relationship just as much as opening it. Why? When we close a dialogue in person or online, we must make sure that both we and the other party disengage from the conversation in a natural way that doesn't leave the relationship vulnerable. Instead, a good closing deepens the relationship by solidifying the next interaction. And if networking in person, remember to ask for a business card!

To close a conversation naturally, we have to look at what the field of linguistics and conversation analysis calls "pre-closings." These linguistic expressions are called **pre-closings** because in most cultures, we rarely end a conversation with an abrupt "Goodbye" (unless we are dramatically ending a bad first date!). Instead, linguistics tells us that we must give a *pre-closing signal,* such as "Alright then" or "Well, it was really good seeing you," before naturally delivering the final and "terminal" exchange of "Goodbye," such as in the following example.

Pre-closing Example

- **Pre-closing:** "Well, Rodrigo, I look forward to stopping by your office to meet in person next Wednesday."
- **Terminal exchange A:** "Sounds good, Salva. Have a great night."
- **Terminal exchange B:** "You too. Goodbye."

In networking situations, once we receive what we want or achieve what we set out to do—be it getting a business card, follow-up appointment, or information—it is important not to overstay our welcome. We can use a pre-closing sequence to initiate closure before ending the exchange with a final goodbye.

When gradually closing a dialogue, use the following conversation pre-closings from the field of discourse analysis and linguistics to help you naturally signal that the discussion is finished. See Figure 2-6, "The 5 Conversation Closers," for the pre-closers that will help you close the conversation after getting the business card or opportunity, while paving the way for the next interaction. **First, use a pre-closing sequence,** which signals the end of the conversation, **before definitively ending the exchange** with a final farewell.

The Five Conversation Pre-closers

Use the five conversation pre-closers to end a conversation naturally at the close of your pitch:

- **Pre-closing signal:** Indicate the closing of a dialogue by giving a pre-closing signal that neither adds anything new to a current topic nor raises a new one (e.g., "Well, anyway" or "Alright then").

- **Reason-for-the-exchange sequence:** Restate or summarize the purpose of the conversation (e.g., "I'm really glad we talked about the project proposal.").

- **Solicitude sequence:** Express concerns, well-wishes, regards to third parties, and holiday greetings (e.g., "Give my best to the team—have a great weekend!").

- **Arrangement sequence:** Make or restate plans to contact one another or to get together; this sequence further emphasizes the relationship (e.g., "I look forward to seeing you at the gala on Friday.").

- **Moral/lesson sequence:** Use a moral or lesson to summarize the topic so far; this sequence is a highly-impactful means of deepening the relationship by demonstrating attentive listening and empathy (e.g., "Remember, when one door closes, another one opens.").

Is the goal of the networking pitch to land a job on the spot? No. Just envision that executive with a résumé in hand, expecting to be hired right then and there. Or the startup CEO sending a digital pitch to a potential product design partner, while also attaching a draft contract to his email. Or a writer with their manuscript at the ready, expecting the editor at the conference to read it

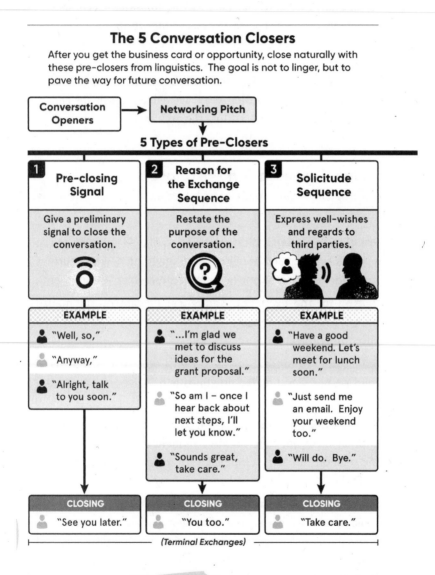

Figure 2-6a

immediately and give them the publishing contract. This is why conversation closers that pave the way for future interaction are so important. Once you get the business card or set up the appointment, wrap up the conversation. The purpose of the pitch is not to close the deal, but to get the other party interested in continuing the conversation.

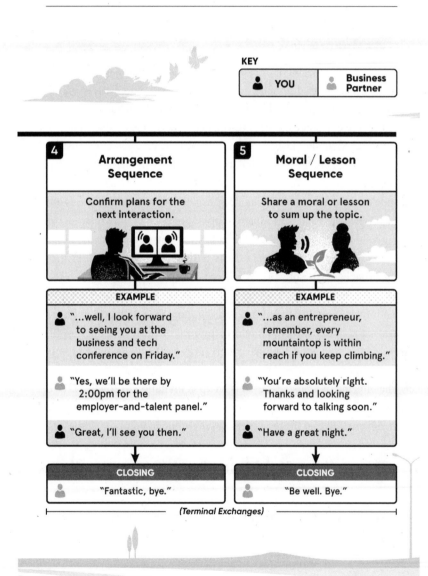

KEY

YOU — Business Partner

4 — Arrangement Sequence

Confirm plans for the next interaction.

EXAMPLE

"...well, I look forward to seeing you at the business and tech conference on Friday."

"Yes, we'll be there by 2:00pm for the employer-and-talent panel."

"Great, I'll see you then."

CLOSING

"Fantastic, bye."

5 — Moral / Lesson Sequence

Share a moral or lesson to sum up the topic.

EXAMPLE

"...as an entrepreneur, remember, every mountaintop is within reach if you keep climbing."

"You're absolutely right. Thanks and looking forward to talking soon."

"Have a great night."

CLOSING

"Be well. Bye."

(Terminal Exchanges)

Figure 2-6b

> ### 🔊 *Global Networking Tip*
>
> **The purpose of the pitch is not to close the deal, but to begin the relationship.**

Also, when networking with global professionals in person, keep in mind cultural customs that align business card exchanges with respect and seniority. Many Eastern cultures tend to regard the business card as a direct reflection of identity. Therefore, traditionally, it's common practice in Eastern cultures for the senior person to present their business card with both hands.

During the exchange, make sure you also receive the card with both hands. The business card should be treated with utmost care as it is considered an extension of self. On the other hand, many people in Western cultures typically trade business cards informally with a quick glance before shoving the card in their pocket; however, this act can be considered disrespectful in Eastern societies, as if the card (and person) are of no importance to you. Instead, examine it attentively and place it on the table in front of you or carefully in a card case. While casual receipt of business cards is culturally acceptable in the West, these approaches will not work in Eastern culture.

As you wind down the conversation, always make sure to obtain follow-up contact information. Instead of making your goal the job opportunity, view the *business card* or digital contact information as the most tangible objectives of a networking event. Once you have a business card, you have the promise of a follow-up interaction where you can send materials for a job or creative project. The offering of a business card is an open invitation to connect on a deeper level—a building block of initial trust (see Chapter 5 on *Negotiation Skills*) and an affirmation that the other person sees value in your initial conversation.

2.8 The Follow-Up: Mind-Anchoring Practices

> *Respect for people is the cornerstone of communication and networking.* **—Susan RoAne**

Following up is the key to creating a lasting impression after a networking scenario and navigating to the next opportunity. We like to call this approach **mind-anchoring.** Now, just think of how palm trees stay rooted even in one-hundred-mile-per-hour winds from a hurricane. Despite being flexible, these remarkable wonders are masters of persistent engineering. As a metaphor for the post-networking scenario—*do just as palm trees do*—**foster ways to positively anchor yourself in the minds of the people that you meet.**

In any culture, try the following "mind-anchoring" practices to plant the seed for a future meeting with that person or even a later introduction to other professionals in their network:

- **Build a pattern of rapport:** *Always send a message of gratitude,* via LinkedIn or email (see Chapter 3 on *Effective Emailing*) or even an old-fashioned handwritten message. Beyond a simple "thanks," the goal of the message is to convey the value of the relationship, while redirecting the recipient's attention back to ways *you* can contribute to joint interests. Regardless of culture or professional status, everyone wants to feel valued and validated. Restate key points that differentiate you from the crowd based on your conversation, so that the person can easily recall you and your unique attributes. Use this opportunity to include any information that you may have left out in the initial conversation to further entice interest.

- **Be a resource:** Forward relevant resources related to your conversation, such as industry updates, news articles, events, and other opportunities—although do so sparingly and appropriately. For example, if a new initiative that the company is working on mirrors what was mentioned in the conversation, share it! The key is using this method as a springboard to extend yourself, demonstrate your investment in the relationship, and showcase your value so that the other person will reciprocate in kind.

- **Be consistently in touch:** Don't just engage your network when you need a favor—this word of caution extends interculturally as well. Professional relationships are personal too. We are hardwired to interpret patterned behavior that reveals a person's intentions and ambitions. Professionals are apt to look for patterns to ensure our networking intentions are noble. Thus, consistency in all networking situations translates to a measure of authenticity of character, so avoid falling into the trap of making last-minute pleas for help. Instead, pick up the phone or keep the relationship moving forward by sending a message of gratitude or a gift to demonstrate that you really value the relationship—no special occasion required. Contacting people in your network unexpectedly during off-peak times of the year to express your gratitude or sincerity goes a long way in any culture.

Ideally, a networking exchange doesn't stop with the first conversation, but extends over a series of conversations that build rapport, relationships, and opportunities.

> ### 🤝 Global Networking Tip
>
> Use *mind-anchoring* practices to communicate the value that you bring to another professional's network.

This stage of the networking process should essentially communicate your value to the other party, and the best way to do that is to position yourself as a go-to resource, not just to that professional, but to their network as well. Once seen as a resource, you enter the talent pool for consideration for the next relevant opportunity, not to mention solidify a genuine relationship. Rapport-building can be time-consuming, particularly with an extended global network, but it is also well worth the effort to inform other people of your interests and passion for shared topics so that they recognize the value in you.

2.9 A Global Mentality: The Crossroads of Strategy and Etiquette

> *You will achieve the greatest results in business and career if you drop the word "achievement" from your vocabulary. Replace it with "contribution."*
> **—Peter F. Drucker**

A good day begins with a good mindset, as the saying goes. A mindset can change everything—not only how we perceive reality, but how we are perceived as well. Consider the many networkers that take on the *quid pro quo* mindset, which essentially means doing a favor in exchange for another favor. However, this not only leads to ineffective practices, but also eventually leads to a negative perception and reputation.

Instead, focus on the power of goodwill and do a small favor for someone—a courtesy that holds little inconvenience to us, but is of high value to the other party—and don't expect anything in return (see Chapter 5 on

Negotiation Skills). This overlooked approach will demonstrate integrity by earning respect, fostering trust, and acquiring more loyalty in the relationship.

Think of your networking approach as a crossroads between *strategy* and *etiquette*. An intersection of these crossroads of interaction helps us build a solid foundation in our professional networking practice.

BASIC NETWORKING STRATEGY	
Know your wants	Know what you want and position yourself creatively to get it.
Know their needs/wants	Determine the other party's needs and wants—favors come at the expense of what you can provide to others.
Reverse-engineer questions	Create questions in reverse with the answers you want in mind; doing so enables you to showcase skills while also learning from others.

However, the process doesn't end there. The real work happens when we begin to integrate strategy with what is more important in the interaction—*generosity*. Giving is valued in all cultures and can make all the difference in how the other person perceives you and your intentions. When someone shows their kindness by being considerate about how you feel, think, or act—it feels good, doesn't it? The same is true when you are on the side of *giving* in a networking situation—it creates a genuine depth and feeling in the conversation.

BASIC ETIQUETTE STRATEGY	
Be prepared to give	Networking as relationship-building requires offering a benefit to the other party.
Be prepared to adapt	Networking globally requires cultural and style flexibility.
Genuineness	Networking that focuses on mutual interests creates the most meaning and impact.

Lastly, using Global English is also part of intercultural networking etiquette (see Appendix A on *Global English*). In any networking scenario, we must judiciously select meaningful phrases that convey literal intentions minus cultural and region-specific idioms or fixed expressions (e.g., "top of the morning," "the daily grind") to avoid confusion or misinterpretation with a global audience. These catchphrases, although considered to be the flavor of local conversations, don't always translate exactly in another language and could do more harm than good in your next networking opportunity.

Major multinational companies, such as Volkswagen, as well as leading banks and pharmaceutical companies, require their employees to learn the international language of Global English. Particular focus on Global English has grown due to lax language and business jargon used by people who speak English as their first language. Many make no attempt to adjust their speech to accommodate Global English, and their networking potential suffers.

As a result, communication breaks down and becomes less clear for intercultural audiences, according to British linguist and expert in English as a lingua franca Jennifer Jenkins. When using English in the workplace or in general networking conversations, we're tempted to use idioms, or culturally-specific catchphrases, as *shortcuts* for communicating meaning instead of saying things literally. However, these expressions leave intercultural audiences to wrestle with the intent and meaning behind these expressions in a conversation.

Have you heard the American business phrase "It is what it is" and tried to interpret the literal meaning of this phrase in the context of a conversation? Ultimately, this expression is defined as accepting an outcome or situation that is unchangeable; however, cultural counterparts may wonder whether the comment is positive or negative (besides sounding completely nonsensical in translation!). Global English has been the fastest-growing dialect to bridge the world and unify communication across the rich diversity of countries and the global workforce.

2.10 Culture of Change: Global Greeting Patterns

> *Your value will be not what you know; it will be what you share.* —**Ginni Rometty**

Ever wonder why we are more relaxed around people when we are in Nature or at the beach? Numerous studies point to a harmonizing pulse from the earth that connects us, particularly syncing with our minds and hearts. Some believe that this synchronization to natural environments—namely between our brainwaves and heartbeats—impacts how we interact with others on the planet.

At any given moment, the earth resonates with various low frequency patterns (7.83 hertz on average) that produce a natural vibration for reconnecting ourselves with Nature. First predicted by Dr. Winfried Otto Schumann, Earth's natural resonances, referred to as Schumann resonances, are a springboard for exploring how our alpha brainwaves coincidentally vibrate at the same frequency as the electromagnetic waves of Earth. Harmonizing with this pulse is believed to be restorative, making us feel relaxed and seemingly more ready to connect with those around us. Our connection to the earth is deep and between us at the same time.

Now you may be asking, how might this information improve the way that we network with one another? Beyond the science, there have been hypotheses that these Schumann resonances can contribute to making us more present and open toward *interconnectivity.*

Global Networking Tip

Being present when meeting others is just as important as knowing the right words to say.

Professional networking is one of those skills that we "learn by doing" when we cultivate intercultural awareness. That awareness is important when forging relationships with international professionals across a room full of new connections and symbolic handshakes. The famous handshake in Western cultures is more than a symbol of goodwill. The bow in East Asian cultures forges respect. How about the subtleties involved in an exchange of kisses in France? Nowadays, even the "fist bump" has become more mainstream in professional circles. In the interchange between virtual and in-person formats, cultural nuances still remain, yet intersect and combine as well. In our globally-connected world, we now also share common and overlapping ways of greeting each other and establishing connections—see Figure 2-7, "Global Greeting Patterns." The key is tapping into larger interaction patterns while being aware of subtle cultural norms.

A global awareness of common "greeting" gestures can sometimes be a defining factor in creating and maintaining global business relationships. Overall, being *present* in an intercultural networking situation is the key to interacting respectfully and connecting meaningfully. In the intersection of "greeting" patterns around the world, we find a significant opportunity, not just to make a good first impression with global professionals, but also to navigate everyday business interactions with respect and appreciation for the cultures of the world. And that awareness is spreading. As our world becomes more globalized, intercultural guides regarding business etiquette have begun to indicate that "greetings vary," as Eastern cultures become more westernized and Western cultures become more aware of Eastern practices.

GLOBAL GREETING PATTERNS

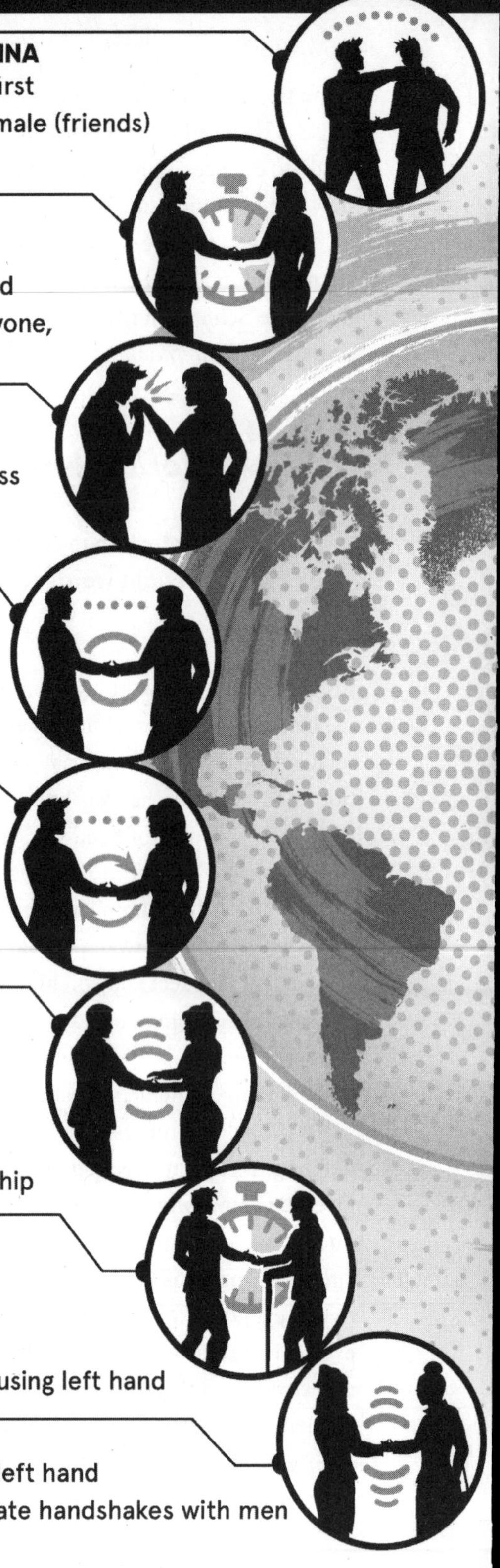

COLOMBIA / SPAIN / MEXICO / ARGENTINA
- Firm handshake with everyone, eldest first
- Cheek-kissing: male-female & female-male (friends)
- Hug & back-patting for men (friends)

TURKEY / ISRAEL
- Men take cues when greeting women
- Direct eye contact, forgo using left hand
- Earnest/lingering handshake with everyone, elders first

RUSSIA
- Men usually kiss a woman's hand
- Men-women handshakes only in business
- Very firm/short handshake
- Hug & back-patting for men (friends)

UNITED STATES / CANADA
- Firm handshake
- Direct eye contact, good posture
- Smile, quick first-name basis
- Kiss both cheeks (French Canadian)

BRAZIL
- Firm/lingering handshake
- Strong eye contact
- Handshake before & after meetings
- Cheek-kissing: male & female

SOUTH AFRICA / KENYA
- Women initiate handshakes with men or nod head in greeting
- Smile, direct eye contact, lingering handshake
- Hand clasping signals respect & friendship

UNITED ARAB EMIRATES / IRAN / IRAQ
- Greet eldest/senior person first
- Light/lingering handshake (friendship)
- Right hand over heart (respect)
- Handshakes initiated by women, forgo using left hand

EGYPT / ALGERIA / MOROCCO
- Light/lingering handshake, forgo using left hand
- Same-gender handshakes, women initiate handshakes with men

Figure 2-7

AUSTRALIA / PHILIPPINES / NEW ZEALAND
- Firm handshake with everyone, direct eye contact
- Women initiate handshakes with men

CHINA / JAPAN
- Greet eldest/senior person first, age matters
- Bow slightly, follow with a handshake (China)
- Degree of bow demonstrates level of respect, handshakes also welcome (Japan)
- Most senior person initiates the handshake

GERMANY / ITALY / GREECE
- Firm/short handshake, direct eye contact
- Include titles/honorifics
- Women initiate handshakes with men

UNITED KINGDOM
- Light/short handshake
- Appropriate distance when talking
- Include titles/honorifics

SWITZERLAND / NORWAY / SWEDEN
- Firm/short handshake with everyone
- Direct eye contact, smile
- First-name basis (Norway/Sweden)
- Include titles/honorifics (Switzerland)

FRANCE
- Brisk/light handshake
- Kiss both cheeks (friends)
- Handshakes with women are common
- Include titles/honorifics

SOUTH KOREA
- Senior person initiates handshake, slight bow, or both
- Use a soft grip, include titles/honorifics
- Bow common, followed by handshake (men)

THAILAND / INDIA / INDONESIA
- Perform the *namaste* (palms together at chest level, fingertips upward; slight bow), reciprocal bowing
- Same-gender handshakes, women initiate handshakes with men, forgo using left hand

Above all, **respect** is a universal value throughout the international community and is communicated in various ways, through the use of personal space (see Chapter 4 on *Nonverbal Skills*), titles, or first names. Depending on levels of formality and with whom we are networking, we need to make judgement calls when conversing across cultures. For example, many Eastern cultures focus on titles, while other cultures may prefer a more informal approach and focus on *first names* depending on the context of the conversation.

We must integrate cultural perspectives from Eastern and Western thinking when forming networking relationships. These "give-and-take" differences that influence networking structures are due to individualistic and collectivistic values embedded in each culture, as indicated by Hofstede's cultural dimensions (see Appendix B on *Cultural Contexts*).

Being *present*, with an intercultural awareness, is not only an essential mechanism for connecting people to success, whether for career growth or dealings in their respective industries, but the key to a broader perspective. Networking with global professionals is much more than a game of collecting business cards and boosting one's own reputation—both online and offline.

To really captivate the people that we seek out to become part of our active networks, we need to think in broader terms, with a globalized perspective, of how joint opportunities and new connections fit within our global-ready network. The world is growing into a more interconnected place—where understanding is our most valuable asset. Ultimately, in our interconnected world, everyone wants to be a person of value in our global system.

2.11 Meaningful Networking: Creating Change and Opportunity

> *Networking is not about just connecting people. It's about connecting people with people, people with ideas, and people with opportunities.* **—Michele Jennae**

As the delicate ecosystem of Nature flourishes when all of the parts work together, we must also communicate globally to build a better future. There is tremendous value in networking with others across the world, and creating this system of bridges has become an enterprise larger than ourselves in globalized business.

In all its patterns, communication has grown out of intercultural understanding and our inherent longing to establish relationships outside of our individual perspectives. Networking prospects abound if we can see and create new patterns of interaction.

With an estimated 7.7 billion people inhabiting the earth today, the new reality is that human-to-human interactions are at our every turn. When we network by identifying and creating an opportunity that did not previously exist, we partner with others over joint opportunities in a natural, yet indispensable, way. We call this *meaningful networking*. Then, we enter a global community where we can contribute to the success of many, and if done correctly, the same favors will ripple across the global sphere and return to us.

Networking helps us achieve our full potential, just as relationships allow the world to reach its full potential. Real networking is connecting. Only then will we realize that humanizing the experience is all that is needed. The way to create change and opportunity is achieved when we connect networking to a greater purpose. It is then that we discover mutual interests, mutual understanding, mutual goals, and mutual successes—all of which build meaningful global influence.

In the digital sea of communication, what principles guide our messages to the right digital shores?
MESSAGES
MESSAGES
MESSAGES
MESSAGES
MESSAGES

Connecting in the Digital Sea: Effective Emailing and Behavioral Psychology

> *There are two ways of spreading light; to be the candle or the mirror that reflects it.* **—Edith Wharton**

Can you imagine life without email? Globally, we send more than 293 billion emails *every day.* It's difficult to imagine a world where messages aren't flowing around us in an endless invisible sea of communication. The reason is that in this digitized world as in the real one—expression is the pivot of existence.

Upon diving into the virtual frontiers of electronic communication, we realize that we've left our physical selves behind—what remains is the glow between mind and network. These frontiers are liberating and exciting because we can communicate across the far-reaching corners of the globe in less time than it takes to blink, even keeping pace with half the speed of light (93,000 miles per second). So, what new principles guide our interactions?

When entering these digital currents, many people often unnecessarily place the same pressures on themselves to communicate as they do when writing a letter in the physical world. However, research shows that mastering email writing is different from writing a "perfect letter" or memo. We may write what amounts to a perfect virtual letter and still not get a response; why? This is because studies show a strong relationship between emailing and behavioral psychology—namely, the science behind *face-to-face communication.* Emailing is *dialogic,* part of a collaborative chain, and this insight greatly impacts our strategies for constructing effective messages.

Let's imagine that each of us is a lighthouse among others across the vast waters of the digital sea of communication. A lighthouse doesn't use its own light to guide messages across the dark waters to unseen shores. The secret to guiding our messages to the "right" shores is to pay attention to what the lights from those lighthouses across the distance are telling us. We must still humanize the digital experience. We must remember that all of us are lighthouses of communication. We all have the power to be beacons for each other.

All we have to do is consciously shift our focus away from targeting and analyzing ourselves as writers (which adds a lot of unnecessary pressure) and instead *observe* and analyze certain traits about our *readers.* In other words, we have to focus on specific patterns of *observable behavior.* New research shows us that we just have to understand email as another aspect of *interpersonal communication,* even though its interactions take place in the digital realm.

In this chapter, we're going to walk you through key insights from the field of behavioral psychology, so that we can evaporate email anxiety and target a set of four distinct preferences called *reader styles* to arrive at more effective communication. This clear model is about to change the way you communicate in any online environment, whether emailing those within your own culture, or those from any culture in the world. Overall, this approach allows us to not only humanize the email experience, but also become true global communicators in the digital world.

Part I. The "Reader" Styles Model for Effective Emailing

3.1 A Singular Approach for Emailing Globally

> We are; therefore, we evolve. **—Geert Hofstede**

E-communication has the potential to build powerful bridges between international business audiences and global partners. However, past studies, including several from researchers at Stanford, Cornell, and Yahoo!, utilizing Dutch social psychologist Geert Hofstede's *cultural dimensions theory,* reveal that countries prefer to email more frequently those countries with whom they share cultural and economic similarities.

These research findings partly reveal that cultural differences need to be bridged in email just as much as they do in person—but, they illuminate something else much more important. These findings also reveal that *if we can change our style to be closer to the styles of others, we can better communicate with and, ultimately, understand others.*

Global Emailing Tip

Mirror the style of your reader to email effectively.

The secret to effective emailing is based on this principle of *reflection* and rooted in the field of behavioral psychology—an approach that we've been researching and teaching for years to professionals from universities, corporations, and organizations around the world. This approach works both within and across cultures. Therefore, we can use the *reader styles* model in this chapter in order to interact effectively—electronically with *anyone,* regardless of their cultural background.

The most significant aspect of this research, coupled with data from behavioral psychology, is that each of us has a communication style that can be described by one of *four reader style behaviors*—regardless of gender, age, ethnicity, or nationality. This four-quadrant model is based on levels of *assertiveness* and *responsiveness* and is informed by differences in "high-context" and "low-context" cultural preferences (see Appendix B on *Cultural Contexts*). In other words, this means that when we email individuals *across* cultures or *within* a particular culture—even our own—the most effective way to work toward e-communication success is to understand a person's preferred *reader style.*

In essence, this approach is the gateway to working successfully with others in the virtual space and to building a satisfying relationship with them as well. In the following pages, we'll show you that once you tap into this set of interactional styles and think of emailing as part of interpersonal communication, then you truly tap into the power and impact of your digital correspondence.

3.1a Testing the Waters: A Mental Exercise

> *I learn by going where I have to go. —Theodore Roethke*

First, let's engage in a simple and empowering mental exercise. Visualize yourself in front of that glowing screen, about to type a message, as in Figure 3-1.

Now, what is going through your mind? What are your key challenges and considerations when producing effective emails?

Figure 3-1

Now, let's really think about this for a moment. We're sitting there, with frantic topics of concern running through our minds—*openings, closings, organization, subject lines, cultural nuances, levels of formality,* and *grammar.* Overwhelming our minds results in only one thing—"pressure" on ourselves as the writers.

Yet, again, emails aren't one-way, self-contained messages. Writing an email is not the same as writing a perfect letter. We may write an email worthy of the Nobel Prize in Literature and still not obtain a response. The reason is that emails are *intertextual,* part of a collaborative chain. Emails are a *dialogic* process and must, therefore, draw upon aspects of interpersonal communication. So, why do we put so much unnecessary pressure on ourselves as writers, when the solution simply involves a *specific way of analyzing our readers?*

Instead, we need to completely reframe our approach to emailing and achieve personal and interpersonal growth in the process. See Figure 3-2. Think of the following phrase as the key to producing effective messages:

⛵ *Global Emailing Tip*

Creative ways to demand response.

And how exactly do we engage in these creative ways to demand responses from individuals all around the world? The answer resides in targeting something called the *reader's communication style.*

CREATIVE WAYS TO DEMAND A RESPONSE

Figure 3-2

3.2 Connecting in the Digital Sea: Reader Communication Styles

> *Don't build links, build relationships.* **—Rand Fishkin**

Creative ways to demand response means that by modifying our own emailing behavior to mirror the reader's communication style, we can create a bridge for successful communication across any culture. This framework is the best-kept secret to effective emailing. And not only does this approach help us get the response that we desire, but it also results in a greater sense of communication and understanding between professionals in the intercultural workplace.

As a core principle, adapting our style to our reader's style is not Machiavellian nor manipulative. In contrast, the aim of this approach is for our messages to motivate and achieve responses in ways that are natural and rewarding for our recipients. When we modify our style to reflect that of others, especially in other cultures, we demonstrate that we sincerely value the right of others to be unique, and that we respect their uniqueness.

⛵ Global Emailing Tip

Adapting your communication style to others is a key principle of interpersonal effectiveness.

This is the larger benefit of this approach—establishing a key framework for *interpersonal effectiveness*. The first step is tossing away a consideration that is all too common among many of us when we sit down to write that all-important business email—*email anxiety*. If you're like most people when drafting a high-stakes email, you freeze up in front of the glowing screen like a deer in headlights.

However, research shows that the immediate way to alleviate these concerns is simply to adjust your framework for emailing—instead of targeting yourself, the writer, all you have to do is concentrate your emailing focus on the reader in very specific and targeted ways.

We have all been in a situation where we wrote what we thought was "the perfect" email, a message worthy of Shakespeare, deserving eager attention from any high-ranking CEO or other influential figure. But for some reason, our recipient didn't respond. Were they just too busy? Did our email get lost in a void of "to-dos" that just never quite made it to the final list?

Instead of spending a bulk of time and energy cycling through mental checklists in frantic self-analysis, the answer we seek may have less to do with our own writing abilities and more to do with how we analyzed our reader.

This principle of *adaptation* is important in communication both interpersonally *and* interculturally. Interpersonal relationships are the key to well-being. Developing these skills requires commitment and a values-driven perspective. So, the first step to effective emailing is to ground ourselves in the key values of interpersonal effectiveness tied to this framework for intercultural communication in the digital space.

....

Activity: Values Clarification

"True or false" values clarification: Look at the following values of *interpersonal effectiveness,* which are applicable to emailing in intercultural contexts. Determine and affirm the *four* items that are indicative of this skill. Respond with TRUE or FALSE. **See if you can find the** *one value* that *doesn't* result in *interpersonal effectiveness.*

WHAT ARE THE VALUES OF *INTERPERSONAL EFFECTIVENESS?*	TRUE OR FALSE
1. Every positive and reciprocal relationship is an asset—so, we should continually cultivate these relationships.	
2. Adjusting our behavior to improve a relationship isn't insincere, but demonstrates *goodwill* and a genuine, deep respect for differences.	
3. One of the most essential values in an interpersonal situation is *every person is as important as you are.*	
4. Developing these communication skills requires effort—and this effort represents personal growth and cultural understanding.	
5. Other people must adapt to us—controlling or modifying our own actions isn't the solution to an unsatisfactory relationship.	

Answer:
Item 5 is not a value of interpersonal effectiveness.

Final reflection:
Now, reflect on the values above. How can you incorporate these principles into your own value system and email practice? Which values are more difficult to embrace than others? What about the value that you crossed out? Is it challenging to let go of the idea that others have to adapt to us? In what ways is it liberating to know that controlling your actions, not the actions of others, is the most effective way to create a productive emailing relationship?

....

3.3 Mirroring Dialogues with Changing Currents: The Four Online "Reader" Styles

> *There are as many solutions as there are human beings.* **—George Tooker**

Now, let's delve into the crux of this approach—the four reader communication styles. We can use these styles to build rapport and communicate effectively in any email situation. Research has shown that each of us has a preferred interactional style when communicating. These four distinct *reader communication styles* (e.g., **Expressive, Driver, Amiable,** and **Analytical**) are deeply rooted in the field of behavioral psychology and are adapted from the statistical and clinical work of industrial psychologists David Merrill and Roger Reid in "Social Styles Theory."

 **Global Emailing Tip**

Each of us communicates predominantly using one of the four reader communication styles, regardless of cultural background—however, our goal is to learn how to become any of the four styles when the situation requires it.

For years, our work in the teaching of intercultural communication and business communication has been to apply the four reader styles in modern and relevant ways to effective emailing. The work of Merrill and Reid was completed in the 1980s, in a pre-internet era when "Social Styles Theory" was intended to aid face-to-face office interactions—in short, this communication model helped people develop better interpersonal skills.

In fact, the general approach has been so effective and corroborated by research that companies to this day still use "Social Styles Theory" to train managers to work better with others in face-to-face office situations. However, since these are fundamentally "interaction" styles, with our modifications, applying them has proven just as effective within *online* environments as within in-person settings.

When adapting this approach to effective emailing, as in the **Reader Communication Style Model** in Figure 3-3, "The 4 Reader Communication Styles," we found that the online reader is motivated by a preferred "reader style," regardless of their cultural background or whether they were emailing in a work or nonwork environment. In other words, *regardless of a person's age, gender, ethnicity, or nationality, each individual person has specific behavioral preferences in text* and this knowledge can help you engage with your email recipient in their preferred *reader communication style.*

Let's establish that no single style is better nor worse than another style (nor is synonymous with personality). Each style is simply different, and any style can be successful, as long as it makes your recipient feel comfortable. Effectiveness isn't achieved by mastering one style, but by being able to adopt *all four* styles. How do you know which of the four unique reader styles applies to your intended recipient?

Each style is based on *observable* patterns of behavior, each with their own characteristics. The benefit of this approach is that we are not trying to get into our recipient's head, but instead are focusing on observable actions and behaviors.

The good news is that, as email remains a textual medium, once we integrate these reader styles into our awareness, we can readily analyze and identify the characteristics of these styles in the digital messages we read. Ultimately, we can then take the time to craft our messages, using the following "interaction" styles model to create more impactful and motivational digital responses, requests, and exchanges across cultures.

Each of us wears multiple *hats* throughout the day, and it is no different in the virtual space. However, we all tend to exhibit one of the four online reader styles predominantly in every online interaction. At the end of Section 3.3d, we will give you a self-assessment quiz so that you can determine which style you primarily use and how to adjust it for successful communication with the other reader styles, both interpersonally and interculturally. But first, let's start by defining the four reader types and the individual characteristics that set them apart from one another.

3.3a Style 1: Expressive

Let's begin with the *Expressive* style, which is often the easiest to grasp in terms of form and characteristics. Research shows that the communication style of an *Expressive* personality is often characterized by creativity, passion, enthusiasm, action language, and phrasing messages in terms of the "big picture."

The 4 Reader Communication Styles

Identify the reader's communication style. Then, **mirror the style of your reader** to email effectively.

EXPRESSIVE

- Uses an energetic & enthusiastic tone
- Presents ideas creatively
- Paints the big picture/vision before going into detail
- Uses "action" language
- Is excited about new ideas
- Looks for opportunities to recognize achievements
- Seeks to inspire
- Uses exclamation points
- Provides lots of visual stimulus
- Uses vivid descriptions

Spontaneous / People-Oriented

Dominant "TELL"

DRIVER

- Uses bullet points
- Values directness; bottom line on top
- Focuses on results and outcomes
- Conflict is ok
- Looks only for necessary details
- Looks for options that make the decision easy
- Looks for specific action required
- Values time, brevity, and efficiency
- Makes definitive statements
- Avoids using excessive emotion

Controlled / Task-Oriented

Figure 3-3

Learn to become all four reader styles when the situation requires it.

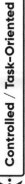

AMIABLE

- Uses conversational language (more than formal)
- Highlights positive benefits to people
- Writes in terms of "one team"
- Harmony; no conflict
- Focuses on relationships (team impact)
- Offers personal commitments
- Provides solutions to minimize the effects of change on people
- Uses small talk to establish rapport
- Is friendly, cooperative, and patient
- Shows empathy to those affected by recommendations

Spontaneous / People-Oriented

Easygoing "ASK"

Controlled / Task-Oriented

ANALYTICAL

- Uses appropriate jargon and technical terms
- Values structure and logic
- Is methodical, focused on process
- Provides all necessary details
- Is skeptical, thorough
- Looks for all the facts in order
- Looks for evidence to prove any claim.
- Values processes explained step-by-step
- Talks specifically – not in generalizations

Now, let's say Einstein is present in our current email era. Let's also say that going by many of his observable characteristics, including his signature hairdo, Einstein's preferred communication style is *Expressive.* One day, Einstein receives two emails from two different lab employees in two different styles. Both are grammatically correct and accurate in terms of language usage and composition. But, as an *Expressive,* which email do you think he will respond to first?

Student A writes:

Dear Dr. Einstein,

Attached, please find my report for the upcoming research presentation.

Thanks,

Lukas

Student B writes:

Hi Dr. Einstein,

I really enjoyed compiling this data report for your upcoming presentation on the theory of relativity! I was inspired by your prepared presentation points and included more data sets to support them. I'm really intrigued by your notion of how objects cause space-time distortion— fascinating! I would love to hear more sometime. Please just let me know if anything else is needed. Have an excellent weekend!

Kindest regards,

Abri

Now, both emails are well-written in terms of grammatical accuracy and fluency. But which email would demand a response from the *Expressive* style? In terms of behavioral psychology, if Einstein's style were *Expressive,* he would very likely respond to Abri first (student B). In fact, he would feel *compelled* to do so—excited at the opportunity to interact in this way since the *Expressive* style is largely more *people-oriented* than *task-oriented.* He may put off responding to Lukas (student A) until much later or, as sad as the case may be, never respond at all. Einstein may not know how to respond or may believe that Lukas's message was a mere announcement that did not require further action.

This introductory example illustrates that mastering effective emailing involves more than linguistic ability. Instead of trying to hone our maestro skills with language, all we have to do is focus on *mirroring* the reader's communication style: we simply adapt our email style to be closer to that of our recipient when delivering a message, and we will motivate the responses we seek. To target the *Expressive* style, follow the tips below.

How to Target the Expressive *Style* via Email

- Describe the "big picture" before going into detail.
- Present ideas creatively using "action" language.
- Use an energetic/enthusiastic tone that is people-oriented.
- Describe ideas in the five senses, weaving in sensory language.

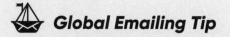 *Global Emailing Tip*

The *Expressive* "reader" style is people-oriented in a way that is dominant (telling others) rather than easygoing (asking others), as this style exudes confidence, inspiration, and charisma when bringing new ideas to the table.

Cultural context: The *Expressive* style can tend to be the style preference pattern of most of Latin America, parts of Southeast Asia, the Middle East, parts of Eastern Europe, the Mediterranean, the Iberian Peninsula, and the majority of sub-Saharan Africa. Always recognize the individual within the culture, as all styles exist across all cultures. Remember that individual preferences as well as occupational preferences may vary. Focus on observable patterns.

As you can see, the *Expressive* style—the enthusiastically-charged style of the quintessential "ideas" person—is often the most immediately-identifiable style to observe and target in email. Now, let's explore how to recognize and target the differing characteristics of the other three social styles.

3.3b **Style 2: Driver**

In contrast to the *Expressive* style, the *Driver* style is direct, avoids excessive emotion, prefers only necessary details, and focuses on results. Picture a boss with glowering eyes and a "no-nonsense" manner. We have all encountered *Drivers* in the workplace that are very task-oriented. We once had a supervisor who was on the extreme *Driver* end of the spectrum and communicated with team members as if with enlisted men and women in the military. She even had laser beam eyes (when she looked at you, you always felt that you had done something wrong, even just by breathing!). Let's refer to her as Ursula. Consider if we wrote an email to Ursula such as the one below:

> *Hi Ursula,*
>
> *I hope you had a great weekend in the Hamptons with your daughter! I would love to hear all about it as I want to take my cousins there this summer. What restaurants did you go to? You must've had an amazing time. Per our discussion this morning, attached is the contract you requested. I look forward to hearing all about your trip!*
>
> *All my best,*
>
> *Nadia*

Now, years later, we compassionately realize that Ursula was probably blowing a circuit in her office upon receiving these types of emails—shuddering at and dreading the thought of responding to these types of questions. Such emails would take her hours to respond to and she often wouldn't respond at all—even if the contracts mentioned in the email were time-sensitive. Why? Because her interaction style was *Driver,* not *Expressive.*

Over email, Ursula usually did not want to discuss her weekend or her day, or *anything personal.* Such an email may have seemed like a chore for her to write. In contrast, for example, if you approached Ursula with an email such as the following, you were likely to receive an immediate response:

> *Hi Ursula,*
>
> *Good morning. Attached, please find the contract for your review. I'm happy to assist if anything else is needed.*
>
> *Best regards,*
>
> *Nadia*

Upon receiving this *Driver*-style message, Ursula would immediately respond with a message such as "Approved. Please send forward. Thanks, Ursula." In fact, she may have even been prompted to immediately respond to such messages even from her smartphone while on her lunch hour.

What is important to realize in the virtual space is that those who tend toward the *Driver* style prefer not to engage in excessive emotion or linger on intimate details. A *Driver* tends to be focused on the *task,* not the person. And so, when we adjusted our communication style to mirror Ursula's, we were better able to obtain the response we sought. In fact, it also led to us appearing more competent and efficient in her eyes.

How to Target the Driver *Style via Email*

- Be direct, providing only necessary details.
- State specific actions required.
- Use bullet points and lists.
- Make definitive statements.
- Avoid excessive emotion.
- Focus on results, outcomes, and the bottom line.

⛵ *Global Emailing Tip*

Keep in mind that the *Driver* "reader" style does not mind conflict and, ultimately, values time and efficiency.

Cultural context: The *Driver* style can tend to be the style preference pattern of most of the English-speaking parts of the world, including the United States, parts of Canada, parts of Northwestern and North-Central Europe, Scandinavia, and Australia/New Zealand. Always recognize the individual within the culture, as all styles exist across all cultures. Remember that individual preferences as well as occupational preferences may vary. Focus on observable patterns.

It is important to note that the *Driver* style is not necessarily characterized by an impersonal tone; in reality, *Drivers* are simply task-oriented. This style can be very effective in using directness and efficiency in the successful completion of tasks.

Now, which style should we use when emailing *a total stranger?* Which style do we use when we're not sure of the preferred communication style of our recipient? Which style is more appropriate to use in a cover letter, for instance? Read on and we'll show you.

3.3c Style 3: Amiable

The *Amiable* reader style is friendly, personal, warm, and cooperative, and prefers "chitchat" language rather than professional jargon. This style often refers to relationships in terms of "one team" and highlights positive benefits to people. Furthermore, the *Amiable* style is also patient, is empathetic to those affected by decisions, and avoids conflict at all costs.

How to Target the Amiable *Style via Email*

- Use "chitchat" language and idioms when appropriate (and if initiated by the recipient).
- Always write in terms of "the team."
- Display empathy toward those affected by change.
- Highlight the positive benefits to others.
- Focus on relationships and team harmony.
- Avoid conflict language; minimize conflict by providing solutions.

Global Emailing Tip

The *Amiable* "reader" style is also the default style in initial correspondence, whether in a cover letter for a job or in an email sent to a complete stranger.

Cultural context: The *Amiable* style can tend to be the style preference pattern of countries in East Asia and most parts of Central Asia, except the subcontinent of India, which is a hybrid of *Expressive* and *Driver* styles. Always recognize the individual within the culture, as all styles exist across all cultures. Remember that individual preferences as well as occupational preferences may vary. Focus on observable patterns.

Given the friendly and empathetic nature of an *Amiable* reader, it should be clear that colloquial language and rapport-building dialogues are paramount to winning over this person via email, especially when establishing initial contact.

When writing a cover letter to a stranger, we should use language characteristic of the *Amiable* style, employing phrases such as "I *offer* X years of experience in . . . ," "I would welcome the opportunity to *contribute* to . . . ," and "I would be very interested in joining your *team* . . ."

Now, let's consider another case study with an *Amiable* boss named Brad. Boss Brad is amiable and easygoing, with a ready smile and carefree attitude. The following scenario illustrates important considerations regarding the "dos and don'ts" of emailing an *Amiable* boss.

We were overseeing a company training program when one day an unexpected issue arose. The lead instructor sent a last-minute email resigning that morning due to another job offer, and several angry attendees from a visiting group of international professionals were in the conference room, demanding to speak to a "higher-up" about withdrawing from the overseas partnership program. In fact, so many people were in the conference room that if all of them withdrew, the partnership program between three multinational companies was in danger of completely collapsing. We decided to send an email to Boss Brad, such as the following:

Dear Boss Brad,

We have a problem. We have several participants from today's training in the conference room, threatening to withdraw from the program. The lead instructor resigned this morning and we still don't have a replacement instructor. With so many people poised to withdraw, the partnership program is in danger of collapsing or operating at a huge loss. Please just let us know what you recommend or if you'd like to go to the conference room to speak to them.

Best,

Raúl and Dan

The first line—"We have a problem"—was our first mistake. This email is a nightmare to an *Amiable* personality, which is why Boss Brad did not immediately respond. What was surprising is that after sending the above email to Boss Brad, we could see him through the window to his office, sitting there, reading the email on his computer. He was *in* the office and knew *we* were in the office. He may have even seen that the attendees were in the conference room, and still did not respond.

Rather than wait for a reply that may have never come, we decided to step up and support the team as best we could by entering the conference room and, thankfully, saved the training after some customer service gymnastics.

After everyone left, we went to Boss Brad's office and knocked on his door. Upon opening the door and saying "Come in," he sighed worriedly, saying, "I know . . . we have a problem." And in that moment, we learned a very valuable lesson when emailing *any* boss.

When emailing your supervisor about a problem, always include a list of *solutions*. And you will always get a more desirable response. This is particularly true for an *Amiable* reader, who sometimes avoids conflict at all costs.

From that point forward, whenever emailing "Boss Brads" about an issue, we were sure to state, "In terms of solutions, we could do X, Y, or Z. Which would you prefer?" When we did this, Boss Brad was much more likely to immediately respond with "Let's do Y." Or sometimes "Great—which solution do you prefer?"

An *Amiable* personality is concerned with relationships and harmony—above all else they prefer solutions to problems. When presenting an issue, always take extra care to provide solutions. We will not only get the response we want, but respect and goodwill as well.

3.3d Style 4: Analytical

In contrast to the other three styles, the *Analytical* "reader" style prefers to use specialized/technical terms and thrives in "jargonland." The *Analytical* personality is skeptical by nature and welcomes a web of evidence, logic, and facts to support any claim.

How to Target the Analytical Style via Email

- Use appropriate specialized/technical terms.
- Provide evidence and data to prove any claim.
- Be methodical in explaining step-by-step processes.

- Show logic by having all the facts in order.
- Contextualize requests with specifics, not generalizations.

⛵ Global Emailing Tip

The *Analytical* "reader" style is often skeptical by nature, so remember to use jargon to establish credibility and ensure your email is thorough, with facts and data that support claims.

Cultural context: The *Analytical* style can also tend to be the style preference pattern of most of the English-speaking parts of the world, including the United States and parts of Canada, parts of Northwestern and Central Europe, Scandinavia, and Australia/New Zealand. Always recognize the individual within the culture, as all styles exist across all cultures. Remember that individual preferences as well as occupational preferences may vary. Focus on observable patterns.

Let's take another case in point. We had a professional in one of our workshops named Tiffany, an event planner, who was tasked to email the marketing director about increasing funds for hosting resident on-site events at a popular real estate building complex in Paris. Being an *Expressive* emailer, Tiffany's initial message, which went completely ignored, sounded something like this:

Hi Brigitte,

Hope you're doing well! I just wanted to connect with you about increasing the budget for our new building amenities. The response and interest have been great! I've attached photos of the most recent gathering that really show residents enjoying the event in the lobby. The event was so much fun—and they're really looking forward to the lineup of events in the fall just as much as we are. Enjoy! And I look forward to hearing back!

Warmest,

Tiff

Now, why did Brigitte ignore Tiffany's message? Tiffany said that she watched Brigitte respond to other people in her department on other email threads *that same day,* but she didn't respond to her own message. Tiffany was flabbergasted, as she needed an answer before the end of the budget cycle.

After observing Brigitte's interaction style by reviewing previous emails, we noticed that Brigitte was clearly an *Analytical* writer and reader. So, Tiffany tried again and rewrote the exact same request in the *Analytical* style:

Dear Brigitte,

It was great speaking with you last week following our annual investment meeting. Attached, please find a full budget proposal to align with our upcoming strategic initiatives in regard to promoting our new real estate portfolio. As you can see from the attached spreadsheet, we are happy to report that interest has increased 26% in terms of new inquiries for potential retail tenants since the introduction of the new residential amenities. We believe that expanding the budget for these residential amenities will have a tremendously beneficial impact in our demographic in the Parisian market. If we could please set up a time to review the attached budget proposal and chart projections, I would greatly appreciate it. Thank you kindly in advance for your consideration.

Warmest regards,

Tiffany

Brigitte immediately responded with "Yes, let's set up a time to meet. I have reviewed the figures and would like to cross-reference them with data from our leasing office so that we can also include language referencing the new building amenities in our promotion collateral. I look forward to meeting with you."

And, although Tiffany's message to her was the same request simply rewritten in a different communication style—it was written in an *Analytical* format that resonated with Brigitte, who likely appreciated the thoughtful analysis from Tiffany's email. Remember, the *Analytical* style is skeptical by nature and prefers proof to back up every claim, along with logic and specialized terminology indicating expertise. Once Tiffany modified her request to the *Analytical* style, she was able to swiftly obtain the response that she sought.

Remember, effective emailing is not about you, the writer, but about becoming more attuned to understanding the recipient's preferred reader communication style. We just have to become a mirror that reflects back understanding when interacting with various types of readers, either from within our country or from all around the globe. Every email is essentially *a request,* and the ultimate goal is to be able to write our request in all four "reader" styles when the situation requires it.

The beauty of the emailing process is that we're able to take the time needed to craft our responses in the best way possible. Keep in mind these ways of adjusting your style to deliver your message to someone who doesn't share the same communication preferences or cultural context and you will be well on your way to arriving at a newly-created bridge of communication.

Activity: "Double Write-Up"

Now, try rewriting a *request* in *two different styles.* This exercise works best using two *contrasting* styles (either *Expressive/Driver* or *Amiable/Analytical*). What differences do you notice? Consider which style would be preferable based on the situation. Why?

Self-Assessment: Which "Reader" Style Are You?

Complete the self-assessment in Figure 3-4. Then use the "Self-Assessment Scoring Guide" in Figure 3-5 to determine your social style. This self-evaluation will yield results that can be applied to pinpoint your preferred email social style.

After taking the test and charting your results on the accompanying grid, reflect on the results in terms of the style you tend to gravitate toward. Which style is your *preferred* social style? Which styles were second, third, and fourth? Now, how can you adapt your style as needed to tailor your message to the styles of global audiences?

Remember, while this assessment is incredibly useful to show you what your preferred style of communication is—ultimately, your goal is to be flexible and become all four styles when necessary in order to gain that edge in *interpersonal effectiveness* when engaging in global email communication.

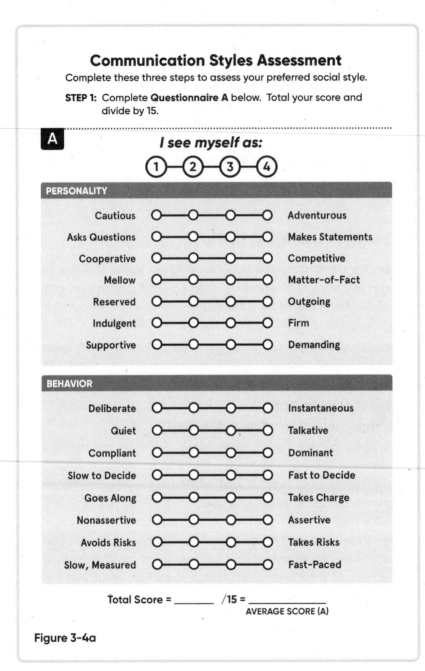

Communication Styles Assessment

Complete these three steps to assess your preferred social style.

STEP 1: Complete **Questionnaire A** below. Total your score and divide by 15.

A

I see myself as:

①—②—③—④

PERSONALITY

Cautious	O—O—O—O	Adventurous
Asks Questions	O—O—O—O	Makes Statements
Cooperative	O—O—O—O	Competitive
Mellow	O—O—O—O	Matter-of-Fact
Reserved	O—O—O—O	Outgoing
Indulgent	O—O—O—O	Firm
Supportive	O—O—O—O	Demanding

BEHAVIOR

Deliberate	O—O—O—O	Instantaneous
Quiet	O—O—O—O	Talkative
Compliant	O—O—O—O	Dominant
Slow to Decide	O—O—O—O	Fast to Decide
Goes Along	O—O—O—O	Takes Charge
Nonassertive	O—O—O—O	Assertive
Avoids Risks	O—O—O—O	Takes Risks
Slow, Measured	O—O—O—O	Fast-Paced

Total Score = _____ /15 = _____
AVERAGE SCORE (A)

Figure 3-4a

STEP 2: Complete **Questionnaire B** below. Total your score and divide by 15.

STEP 3: Use the chart on the next page to score the self-assessment. Plot your *Average Score (A)* and *Average Score (B)* on the next page.

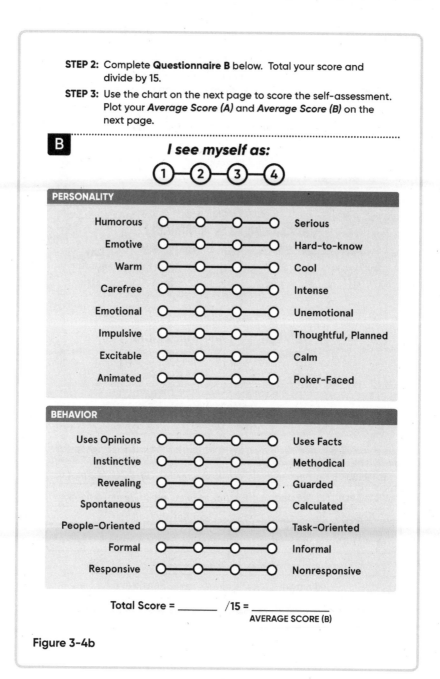

Figure 3-4b

Scoring Guide

- **AVERAGE SCORE (A)** is your **influence** rating on the horizontal axis.
- **AVERAGE SCORE (B)** is your **sensitivity** rating on the vertical axis.

Plot both scores below to assess your preferred social style!

Effective Emailing & Behavioral Psychology

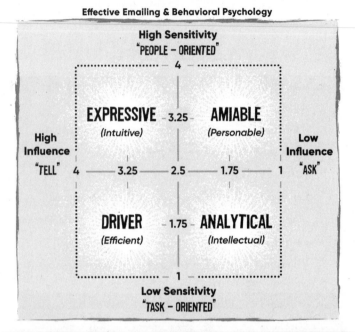

STYLE	APPROACH	DESCRIPTION
EXPRESSIVE	*Intuitive*	Focuses on creativity, ideas, visuals, passion
AMIABLE	*Personable*	Focuses on relationships, teams, & harmony
DRIVER	*Efficient*	Focuses on tasks & results
ANALYTICAL	*Intellectual*	Focuses on logic, data, & analysis

SOCIAL STYLE ESSENCES

Influence:
The tendency to seek control
or let others control scenarios.

Sensitivity:
The tendency to express or
be reserved with emotions.

Figure 3-5

Part II: The Mechanics for an Effective Global Email Culture

> *Compassion is the keen awareness of the interdependence of all things.* **—Thomas Merton**

Having discussed a larger framework for developing an effective practice when emailing *individuals* across all cultures, we now turn our attention to the simple mechanics of emailing, such as subject line and tone, which are just as important when communicating interculturally. As global communicators, how can we contribute to an overall effective email culture and lay the groundwork for more successful and satisfying relationships all around the world?

Every sixty seconds, more than 203,470,000 business and consumer emails are sent around the world. That's about 3,391,203 messages per second! Just think about how that number will grow with the anticipated forecast exceeding 347 billion emails sent daily by 2023. As one of our primary forms of e-communication, effective emailing is no longer optional, but essential to the success of businesses and individuals.

Every email projects an image of you and your company and can, likewise, cost you or your firm in the areas of reputation and future success. Therefore, it is vitally important to engage in an effective emailing practice from an individual to an organizational level—which also means we have the power to impact email culture from the organizational to the *global* level.

Now that we've touched on a larger-order framework and approach to effective emailing with the four reader styles, we will cover some of the most practical yet overlooked email mechanics critical for corresponding with a *broader audience* and shaping global email netiquette:

- the global subject line
- the power of punctuality around the world
- presenting content using *Global English*
- writing with tone and differing levels of formality
- active and passive voice strategies
- the ever-important presence of cultural context

3.4 A Few Words: The Global Subject Line

Do not say a little in many words but a great deal in a few. —Pythagoras

What if we said the Fountain of Youth, known for its restorative waters, does exist? Did we get your attention? A stream of questions likely flooded your mind, such as: "Where is this place?" "How is this possible?" and "How can I get access to it?" Imagine if we placed this information in an email subject line such as "The Fountain of Youth Discovered—Details Inside." We can all relate to the subject of this message, which entices our curiosity since we all know that aging is an inevitable part of life. Who wouldn't want to know this information?

In this way, effective subject lines motivate email recipients to open a message by *promising needed information* to carry out a task or to make a decision. Furthermore, tactful subject lines *create a sense of desirability* that connects to the interests of email recipients (see Chapter 5 on *Negotiation Skills*).

On the global stage, the subject line must say (or imply) it all. Just as a news headline or a tweet grabs a reader's attention, so must the subject line—the trick is to keep the subject line short while also being impactful (no more than five to seven words). In the international context, the subject line is one of the most important elements of an email since our message header must compete with other message headers for attention in global inboxes throughout the day. **In the sea of requests, an effective subject line captivates the attention of our recipient, ensures that our message gets read, and contributes to productive global communication.**

We tend to judge the content of a message based on the first few words—and instead of those words being the first line of our message, those words actually appear in our subject line. So lead with the purpose of your message in the subject line. Think of the email "headline" as the introduction to the first part of your message that recipients will read. An *effective* subject line gets our email read and acted upon. Let us remind ourselves that an ineffective subject line will result in our email going unanswered or, at worst, ignored indefinitely in the purgatory of abandoned or deleted email messages.

So, what is the key strategy for writing an effective subject line across cultures? In the age of smartphones and high-speed communication, we are inundated now more than ever in a constant stream of information. Follow this essential approach to attract recipients with an effective subject line:

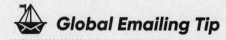

Global Emailing Tip

An effective subject line gets the recipient thinking about the message before they open it.

This key subject line approach for a global audience benefits your request in two ways:

- **A good subject line ensures that your message is already prioritized before it has been read.** Perhaps your reader viewed your email on their smartphone or another device while on the go. A good subject line will ensure that your recipient is able to prioritize your message within their list of to-dos that day.

- **A good subject line gets your recipient already working on your request *mentally* and *immediately*—without even opening it.** With a clear subject line, your recipient can begin processing your request without even needing to read the entire message. This also makes the request more efficient in the sense that the recipient can plan to make needed arrangements, gather important resources, and collect the necessary information required to respond to your request (either physically or digitally) even before finally sitting down to read the remainder of your correspondence.

Regardless of cultural context, a clear, concise subject line has the power to elevate the success of any communication when emailing an international audience. Keep the following two communication norms in mind during any intercultural email exchange:

- **Specificity:** Always be specific and clear in a subject line when emailing a global audience. Avoid vague subject lines like "A small favor" or "A quick question" and, instead, briefly include some context to specify the question or favor in the subject line. Subject lines also help your reader organize and file incoming messages, so keep this in mind when filling a subject line with a concise phrase that describes the topic of your message.

- **Tone:** In terms of tone, avoid subject lines like "Urgent! Please read!" and instead write a focused subject line that acts as an announcement clearly indicating the importance of your message, such as "Marketing Strategy Presentation Tomorrow." A powerful subject line may also help you to later edit your email for impact and decide whether you need two emails instead of one—*remember to keep to one topic per email and per subject line.*

Keep in mind that a good subject line functions like the headline in a newspaper article or the opener to a compelling conversation—grabbing the reader's attention with a preview of the content so that the reader can not only decide if they want to read more, but also predict the content of the message. An email subject line works the same way in terms of creating value for the recipient and must be a "welcome invitation" to your message, inclusive of all language backgrounds and cultural preferences.

Activities: The Winning Subject Line

1. **Open sesame:** Take a moment and look at your inbox, but look at only the subject lines. With a quick glance, select three or four that immediately grab your attention and get you to click "open." Note the two relevant cultural dimensions defined by anthropologist Edward T. Hall—*high-context cultures,* which tend to be relationship-oriented, favor personable and informative details, whereas *low-context cultures,* which tend to be task-oriented, prefer direct and concise communication (see Appendix B on *Cultural Contexts*). Now, consider how you would write these subject lines for both *high-context* and *low-context* cultures. What would you change?

2. **"Subject line" challenge:** For this exercise, take a moment to reflect on the following situations and create subject lines for an intercultural audience that consists of a few words (five to seven words maximum) but conveys the topic in an interesting and impactful way. Some key points to remember as you complete the exercise:

   • Include only one main topic directed toward the recipients' needs.

   • Sequence the ideas based on the anticipated reader's reaction.

   • Distinguish the topic.

   • Use jargon carefully since it can often lead to frustration and confusion.

Exercise:

a. As a public relations manager, create the announcement of a new product.

b. Explain that customary employee bonuses will not be paid because of declining sales.

c. Send a follow-up message with an attached résumé to a career fair recruiter.

d. Alert subscribers of your online newsletter to an upcoming networking event.

Answers:

Sample responses may include **(a)** *Try Our New Pan Pizza—Let Us Handle Dinner,* **(b)** *Employee Bonus Distribution,* **(c)** *Follow-Up Conversation—Career Fair,* **(d)** *Free Global Networking Seminar—Register Now.*

··

3.5 Timing Your Emails: An Ecosystem of Punctuality around the World

> *Punctuality is the soul of business.*
> *—Thomas Chandler Haliburton*

Our emails do not buzz through the air, but underwater via 750,000 miles of fiber-optic submarine cables, which are responsible for the flow of global internet data owned by such tech and telecom giants as Google, Singtel, Telxius, and Verizon. That's right—the cloud is under the sea, encoded in light that crisscrosses the world. We often don't realize that our data traffic depends on these submerged cables connecting the continents across the ocean floor, as we time our email to funnel in hyperspeed to our recipient's overseas inbox right before their 9:00 a.m. meeting. Luckily for us, despite any overseas distance, the electronic transmission of email is nearly instantaneous. The power of punctuality itself resides exclusively in our hands.

Email punctuality has the power to make or break deals, especially when running up against deadlines, and email timing can make all the difference in the global workplace, as it communicates professionalism and commitment. Since business emails often cross time zones or long hallways, it's our job to give the other party reassurance that their request is being fulfilled, so *always acknowledge important emails,* whether from a supervisor, a stakeholder, or an international business partner. Acknowledging an important email makes an impact in terms of courtesy and goodwill, especially when a request will take time to fulfill overseas.

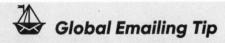 **Global Emailing Tip**

Respond to important messages promptly, especially across time zones. If you receive a request by email that will take a few days or longer to complete, send a response saying so.

When emailing overseas, work and sleep hours often become blurred and can occur simultaneously. Just think about it—an email exchange from a sender in Japan to a colleague in Canada can stretch over drastic time differences, especially when the recipient in Canada waits until the next day in their own time zone to respond to an email. Most likely, if we wait one day to respond to a message, the reality for your recipient across the globe is that not one but two days will have passed.

We often send a reply email only when we are ready with "the answer." However, instead of only responding when you have fulfilled a request, get in the habit of sending a short acknowledgment message upon receipt of the request. Messages such as "I will submit the document to you by this Friday" or "I will share my thoughts with you by next Monday" make all the difference when emailing a supervisor or a stakeholder overseas. Developing this simple routine behavior of giving details in terms of date and time zone as to when you expect (or will provide) a reply goes a long way toward getting things done globally and establishing a relationship of professionalism and respect.

3.6 An International Language: Mastering the Global English Mentality

Life isn't about finding yourself. Life is about creating yourself. —George Bernard Shaw

Similar to how water can take the form of free-flowing rapids in canyons in one part of the world or become a shower of crystalized snowflakes sweeping over the sky in another, the languages we speak can have many different forms and functions under specific conditions, while still remaining recognizable in their basic form. One of those languages that has many forms in the globalized era is English.

Currently, in the globally-connected world, many varieties of *English* comprise the way we communicate transculturally, but with the rise in intercultural business correspondence has come the need for one shared vernacular that is practical for all cultures. *Global English* is a purposeful type of English usage adopted by the global business world that does not assume a certain cultural or native proficiency of others and is thus focused on clarity (with limited idioms and cultural references).

In email and other digital contexts, while it may seem natural for us to use idioms, phrasal verbs, slang, and culturally-specific references to events or attitudes, instead, in international correspondence, we must work to develop a *Global English* standard. One easy way to adopt this standard is by focusing on "plain English." The world is moving toward a new use of international business English that is practical, purposeful, and useful to most corporations globally (see Appendix A on *Global English*), so we need to update our language use accordingly to craft our messages for optimal intercultural correspondence in today's global marketplace.

⛵ *Global Emailing Tip*

When using Global English:

- **Focus on general business or commercial terms, rather than specialized vocabulary.**
- **Double-check that jargon, acronyms, or technical terminology are written in plain language contexts.**
- **Take care when using humor and irony, to avoid misunderstanding.**

....

Activity: "Professional Talk"

Practice converting the sentences below into *Global English.* What idioms, cultural references, acronyms, business-isms, phrasal verbs, and sarcasm would characterize the sentences as non–Global English? Overall, how will the awareness of Global English help you write clearer messages when communicating with an international audience?

1. The budget proposal needs to be firmed up one more time, but not at the eleventh hour. Let's tackle it in the morning ASAP. We need to complete this proposal by the book, so we don't end up back at square one and have to go back to the drawing board. Otherwise, we'll have to pull a Jerry Maguire on Monday.

2. There's some gray area here in the branding piece of the marketing plan that we'll need to clarify to make sure that the team sees eye to eye. We have to stay ahead of the curve, so make sure we don't drop the ball on this one before the presentation.

Answers:

Sample responses may include the following: **(1)** *The budget proposal needs to be updated in advance of the cycle deadline. Let's complete it this morning and include all the sponsor policies.* **(2)** *The branding section in the marketing plan is unclear—we just need to include more information about our pricing strategy before our presentation next week. The more details that we include the stronger our proposal will be.*

....

3.7 Email Decoding: Tone and Register

> *Life's most persistent and urgent question is: What are you doing for others?* **—Martin Luther King Jr.**

When drafting an email, it is also important for us to reflect on the *register* of our messages. Register refers to the formal and informal tone of the language that we use in email.

The four reader styles mentioned earlier, in combination with the section covering *tone* in Chapter 6 on *Writing Skills,* allows us to navigate between formal and informal registers to convey tone in a way that will get us that desired response. What's also important is being mindful of how we close an email, which can make all the difference in how our international counterparts will react to our message.

Consider how the different openings and closings to the same email below affect the tone of the message and, in doing so, the reader's potential reaction to the request:

Dear Sammy,

If you could please complete and submit the 75-page market report by tomorrow that would be great.

Thanks -

Super Supervisor Matek

Now, compare the above email with the same request written in a slightly different tone:

Dear Sammy,

I hope all is well with you. You have been an incredible help with the strategic plan. If you could please complete the 75-page market report by tomorrow that would be great. Thank you so much for all your help finalizing this project—I know it is a tight turnaround, and we are very grateful for your support on this initiative.

Kindest regards,

Super Supervisor Matek

In order to create a more receptive tone with our email messages, particularly if they contain challenging requests, open and close such messages with a positive tone. Phrases of well wishes in your opening sentence and phrases of authentic appreciation in your closing paragraph, such as "I appreciate your help," or "I look forward to hearing from you," or "Please just let me know if you need any additional information," go a long way toward establishing rapport and goodwill—while also motivating the recipient to cooperate with a desired response.

In email, with lack of voice and body language, we are heavily reliant on the word choice, and so it is important to maintain a polite and courteous undertone in the exchange to foster reciprocation, especially in long-distance and intercultural exchanges.

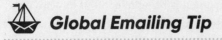

Global Emailing Tip

Take extra time to include a closing statement of gratitude in global emails that establishes a larger tone of appreciation and respect.

3.8 The Whispering Waves: Navigating between Active and Passive Voice

> *Each person's life is lived as a series of conversations.*
> *—Deborah Tannen*

In the flow of both written and spoken speech, *active voice* is generally preferred because it is more direct, more concise, and easier to follow. However, culturally and professionally, there are some situations where *passive voice* would be more effective. Before describing these situations, let's first review the difference between these two styles in relation to tone.

Active voice emphasizes the "agent" or "subject" of the sentence. In other words, the "doer" of the action is emphasized, such as the subject "Elvis" in the sentence "*Elvis* opened the door." However, *passive voice* emphasizes the "action" or "object" of the sentence, such as the object "door" in the revised sentence: "The *door* was opened by Elvis."

Now, watch for a moment what we do with the sentence using the passive voice:

> *The door was opened by Elvis.*
>
> *The door was opened ~~by Elvis~~.*

What did we just do? Elvis has left the building! Are we grammatically allowed to remove Elvis from the sentence and still have a complete thought? Yes. And what we did in this case was *hide* the subject of the sentence so as to avoid disclosing the person responsible. In other words, we concealed the "doer," and used the passive voice as a *strategy* to avoid blame or to avoid indicating who is responsible. This method of discretion is very useful and constructive in terms of not putting someone "on the offensive" no matter the culture.

Global Emailing Tip

Use *passive voice* to avoid blame or to avoid indicating who is responsible.

For example, consider our previous *Driver* boss character, Ursula. On a grueling Friday afternoon, we had to ask Ursula for multiple signatures on a ten-page contract that had to be executed that day due to an impending production schedule that was slated to start the following Monday. After Ursula reviewed and signed the contract, we sent the document to the partnering company across town. However, at the end of the day, we received a call from their legal team stating that there was a page still requiring Ursula's signature. To make matters worse, due to the production scheduled for the following week, the entire contract would have to be redrafted alongside the production schedule. So, we had to email Ursula to notify her of the situation and that she would have to work with us to re-execute the whole agreement with new dates that coming Monday.

After many attempts at drafting, we found ourselves sitting in the office, frantically deleting and rewriting emails to Ursula that began with "You forgot to . . ." or "You didn't sign . . ." or "You missed . . . ," until we realized that using passive voice would be the perfect solution. We could avoid a tone of blame focused on a person and establish a focus on the *task* at hand when using the passive voice, such as the following:

> *Hi Ursula,*
>
> *The contracts weren't fully executed. Due to additional signatures, the contracts will have to be reprinted and re-executed on Monday.*
>
> *All our best,*
>
> *Raúl and Dan*

Then, Ursula immediately responded with:

> *Yes—I can come to the office early—I apologize if any missing signatures were on my account. I'll see you in the morning and I appreciate your work on this.*
>
> *All best,*
>
> *Ursula*

Passive voice is a strategy many professionals use, especially when communicating announcements and notices in email (or even posting signage around the workplace). Just imagine if you noticed a sign on the door at the dentist's office written in active voice: "We are closed today because Drs. Keita, Lincoln, and Olmos went on vacation." The sign is more likely to be written in passive voice, such as "The office is closed"—eliminating the doer of the action. Phrases such as "The period of payment has closed" or "The office is closing early today" are clear indicators that the agent (the subject) has been hidden.

No matter the case, whenever we want to avoid identifying who is responsible, particularly when emailing a supervisor or global partner, passive voice works well to avoid a tone of blame and, instead, creates a more principled tone of respect.

Activity: Active and Passive Voice "Switch Up"

Part 1: See if you can revise the following sentences to reflect *active* voice:

1. It is recommended by the Internal Audit Department that the company obtain all records.

2. The market is being impacted by social media and other emerging technologies.

Part 2: Now, rewrite the following sentences in *passive* voice, using the noun form of the bold verb and using the verb in the parentheses:

3. They will **appoint** a new marketing director within two days. *(make)*

4. People have **accused** the local council of filing false claims. *(make)*

5. Sports fans will certainly **resist** the proposed new multiplex arena. *(show)*

Answers:

(1) *The Internal Audit Department recommends that the company obtain all records.*

(2) *Social media and other emerging technologies are impacting the market.*

(3) *The appointment of a new marketing director will be made within two days.*

(4) *Accusations of filing false claims were made against the local council.*

(5) *Resistance to the proposed new multiplex arena will certainly be shown.*

Final reflection:
Now, reflect on when active voice should be used in the above cases and when passive voice should be used—which sentence in each pair was more effective in terms of rhetoric and etiquette? What about interculturally?

3.9 Taking a Deep Dive: Context Is Still Everything Internationally

> *Coming together is a beginning; keeping together is progress; working together is success.* **—Henry Ford**

As global communicators, we must sidestep conventional approaches to the emailing process and, instead, take a larger approach to understanding and connecting with intercultural audiences in the digital realm. Remember, a useful starting concept for understanding cultural dimensions in online business communication is the distinction between *low-context* and *high-context* cultures, a distinction made famous by anthropologist and cultural researcher Edward T. Hall. This distinction can make all the difference when communicating on the world's digital stage.

In general, it is helpful to consider whether you are emailing *low-context cultures,* such as in the United States, parts of Canada, parts of Northwestern and North-Central Europe, Scandinavia, and Australia/New Zealand, or *high-context cultures,* which include countries in East Asia, Southeast Asia, the Middle East, parts of Eastern Europe, most of Latin America, the Iberian Peninsula, the Mediterranean, and the majority of sub-Saharan Africa. A *low-context* culture tends to value time, directness, and efficiency and usually prefers to get right down to business on email rather than exchange a lot of personal information. However, a *high-context* culture, instead of seeing email as a quick form of communication, tends to value detail and the importance of relationships when conducting business.

The expectations of readers from different cultural and linguistic backgrounds vary greatly, as ideas about appropriate business writing styles differ from culture to culture.

In some cultures, writing that is direct and concise may be seen as efficient and considerate of the recipient's time, whereas in other cultures, such writing could come across as curt or impersonal. Of course, there are also individuals within the same culture that share different individual preferences in terms of interaction and understanding—therefore, mindfulness is a central component to an effective intercultural communication practice.

Keeping low-context and high-context cultures in mind, it becomes clear that in addition to viewing emailing as a way to build relationships, high-context cultures also regard emailing as a form of courting a client or business partner. Therefore, when emailing high-context cultures, take care to personalize your emails and add a few sentences up-front to build a personal connection with the reader by asking about family and appropriate topics in addition to discussing business. In this way, we will build better business relationships abroad that lead to greater opportunities and long-lasting partnerships.

However, again, individuals vary greatly within a culture—which is why focusing on understanding an individual's reader communication style preference is a more precise, effective, and powerful way to make our readers more comfortable in their interactions with us and garner more positive responses to our messages. No matter a person's ethnicity, gender, or nationality, they will prefer to communicate in one of the four social styles covered in this chapter (e.g., *Expressive, Amiable, Driver,* and *Analytical*) and will respond when we approach them through a human lens, by mirroring back their preferred style of communication.

If we keep reader communication styles in mind when we correspond online with intercultural readers, the process of reflecting on inherent habits and behaviors not only gives us a deeper understanding of other cultures, but also gives us an expanded self-awareness. We learn why we express ourselves a certain way and then enhance our powers of expression with additional communication styles, increased sensitivity, and ultimately, greater communicative ability.

3.10 Lighthouses in the Digital Sea: Toward a More Collaborative World

> *Paradise has never been about places. It exists in moments. In connection. In flashes across time.*
> **—Victoria Erickson**

Our world has grown more interconnected through technology, bringing us closer to the concept of a "global village" coined by media and communication theorist Marshall McLuhan. While our digital connectedness has made the world seem paradoxically smaller and yet expanded at the same time—it remains up to us to put global understanding into action in this age of on-demand global connectivity.

Culture is a combination of visible manifestations and unseen influences, and nowhere do these ripples flow more richly than the vast waters of virtual space. Ultimately, as global communicators, we are called to reflect on the myriad of ways readers and writers of diverse cultures present and interpret information. We must develop an openness and adaptability that looks beyond surface ambiguity and inconsistency. More than messages, we are sharing *responses* to one another. We can create *human connection* in a digitally-connected world.

The primary approach to effective emailing is *mirroring our reader's business communication style.* However, in addition to adjusting our style to mirror that of others, we've done more than connect successfully—we've allowed for a greater understanding to be reflected between human beings. Remember, we are all lighthouses of communication. By adjusting our communication style to suit the recipient of our communication, whether in email or in-person, we will not only better position ourselves to obtain a desired response, but also contribute to an expanded reciprocal sharing and mutual understanding between people.

In this chapter, the broad application of adapting to the interaction styles of others is effective both when emailing individuals from another culture and when emailing individuals within a particular culture. By adjusting our style of communication and our expectations of readers from diverse cultural and linguistic backgrounds, we will not only obtain our desired responses, but also build our network and long-lasting fruitful business relationships to come. We find common ground through dialogue, as well as human well-being.

The nature of business is collaboration. Becoming aware of and sensitive to the social styles and business email etiquette of individuals in different countries is the key to establishing long-lasting business relationships around the world and ultimately discovering new horizons of success as partners in the evolution of the global marketplace.

How can we breathe power into our bodies and voices for a greater future of global communication?

Connecting with Body and Voice: The Power of Nonverbal Communication

> *Nonverbal communication forms a social language that is in many ways richer and more fundamental than our words.* **–Leonard Mlodinow**

Breathe in—as if you're breathing in the world. Our breaths unite us among geographic distances, powering the energy of our body movements, uniting us across this shared air in the entirety of the earth. Imagine the sharing of breaths across centuries, a living history passing between cultures in an invisible exchange across time. Breaths passed from Mozart to Einstein to Gandhi have been inhaled and exhaled, floating between our voices and bodies without labels of similarities or differences, but as a permeating life force stretching between past and present, powering us in a global future of ever-evolving nonverbal communication.

We do not just communicate with words. With the combined power of our gestures and voices, we harness the air to transfer meaning. When we communicate, it is as if we create our own human wind from the deepest part of the psyche. A wind that is carried by our gestures and emotions, as we express ourselves from the corner office and conference room, to the far-flung regions of the globalized world. Our voices and movements stir the air in rippling and impactful communication.

Performer Mae West once expressed, "I speak two languages, body and English." She was right! Nonverbal communication is often neglected as an optional skill, but is essential to global communication, with particular significance as multinational organizations now exist in the commonplace reality of intercultural situations.

Functioning as another language entirely, nonverbal communication, also known as *paralanguage,* has arisen to prominence as global executives take a special interest in "talking the talk" through *vocalics,* which encompasses techniques for speech volume, speed, and pitch, and "walking the walk" through *body language,* which includes dynamic combinations of eye contact, gestures, and postures.

The key to nonverbal success is, surprisingly, to let go. To think not of control, but of response. As novelist Toni Morrison stated in *Song of Solomon,* "If you surrendered to the air, you could ride it." And this liberation is true of effective nonverbal skills—once we learn to let go, react, and adapt, we arrive at effective nonverbal skills in a globalized network. Nonverbal communication has been shown to share our intentions across the air more than any other form of communication; therefore, the key to nonverbal success is observing patterns of intention.

Essentially, according to many research studies, nonverbal communication transculturally has two functions: *speech addition* and *speech replacement.*

1. Nonverbals can *enhance* a verbal message by either complementing or contradicting it. First, let's say we are giving directions—when we wave our hands, our additional cues *complement* the directions we give. On the other hand, let's say we give a sly wink when speaking that shares a secret message contrary to our words—this cue adds a layered *contrast* to our speech.

2. Nonverbals can also *replace* a verbal message by conveying the same meaning without words. We need only to think of the library and the quintessential action of holding a finger to our lips in order to nonverbally indicate a request for silence.

Nonverbals paint our words with shades of meaning that allow us to more fully share *intention* with one another. Keep in mind that some nonverbals are universal from culture to culture; others are culturally-specific. The key is tapping into *patterns of intention.* We must learn how others *interpret* our intentions and how to nonverbally yet powerfully *communicate* our intentions across the air. When used purposefully, nonverbal patterns of communication ignite our messages with the necessary context to be "heard" all around the world.

In this two-part chapter, we first address how we can harness the dynamism of our *body language* for multicultural audiences in personal, social, and public spaces—such as for presentations, one-on-one meetings, and negotiations. Second, we focus on ways we can power our *voices* for global communication using practical vocal patterns for greater effect and impact. When we expand awareness of our nonverbal voice and body patterns, not only will we arrive at overall well-being and better communication outcomes, we will also ripple a greater global empathy across the world.

4.1 Powering Our Greatest Instrument: The Mind-Body Connection

> *Communication is to relationships what breath is to life.* **—Virginia Satir**

The human breath is our life force and has a special physical and psychological power. Go ahead and intake a breath—feel the power course through your body, exciting each fiber of your being, as every cell within us—from our toes to our fingertips—relies on oxygen to move, express, and live. Then, when we speak, our breaths manifest an elemental force of communication that, when used effectively, expels into the vast mix of headwinds in the world. Fueled by the breaths of those that came before, our bodies shape the air in the act of expression.

Your body is your greatest communications instrument on this planet. This instrument can convey a multitude of emotions using a varied combination of such cues as vocal nuance, proximity, eye contact, posture, touch, and gestures—all of which enhance our communications to produce powerful messages that resonate in the air across cultures, time, and space.

Yet, breathing does more than fuel this greatest instrument for communication; breathing also cultivates *mindfulness*—a term that is now growing with importance in many corporate spaces, from Wall Street to Silicon Valley and beyond. Communication requires a mindful approach—we must be aware and awake to the present moment. Any focused activity can be used to trigger a mindful state, and "focused breathing" is seen as the most effective way to tune our body to this meditative state and to the nonverbals of others.

What does breath have to do with successful nonverbal communication? First of all, breathing stimulates the vagus nerve, the most powerful conduit in the parasympathetic, or "rest-and-digest," nervous system, as compared to the sympathetic, or "fight-or-flight," system. The vagus nerve is the longest and most important nerve in the body and connects the brain stem to multiple organ sites, including your heart, lungs, spleen, fertility organs, stomach, liver, kidneys, neck, ears, and tongue. **Most importantly, when you activate your vagus nerve through conscious breathing, it primes your** *social engagement system.*

Global Nonverbal Tip

Breathe consciously to stimulate your vagus nerve and, in turn, your mindfulness.

In addition to connecting the brain to the body and running through nearly all our organs, the vagus nerve is regarded as being responsible for the *mind-body connection,* which makes its stimulation crucial for nonverbal and verbal communication.

Imagine the vagus nerve as the interpreter of your intentions through breath. If you slow your breathing, it slows your heart rate, sharpening your cognitive focus and ability to respond to new contexts.

Let's suppose someone is crossing their arms while listening to you. Your senses immediately trigger a "fight-or-flight" response, suddenly perceiving this person as being "closed off" or distant. You, then, inconspicuously slow and control your breaths, stimulating the vagus nerve, lowering the stress-inducing adrenaline and cortisol hormones, and composing yourself into a "rest-and-digest" state, which gives you the clarity for decoding context in relation to communication. After all, the other person was actually just nervous or simply cold due to the temperature of the room. The point is that although messages are transmitted through nonverbal signals, those nonverbals cannot be separated from contextual meaning. Mindfulness is needed to decode them.

Be sure to keep in mind that while it is important to observe others' body language to know what they're thinking and feeling, it's not productive to simply memorize gestural meanings for specific situations as if we were storing an encyclopedia of movements in the library of our mind. Instead, *context* remains crucial to decoding nonverbal messages. The key is observing nonverbal patterns of intention.

Examine the following breathing patterns, which research provides as a guide for identifying the nonverbal intentions of others interculturally:

- **Fast and heavy breathing:** May signal high arousal, such as anger, nervousness, fear, love, excitement, or joy.

- **Slow and steady breathing:** May signal low arousal, such as relief, comfort, boredom, hopelessness, or sadness.

Evidently, while the above patterns are useful observational guides, each also requires mindfulness to be practical—the truth depends on the situation. Seeing a coworker inhale a long intake of breath could mean they are exasperated, pleasantly surprised, or just ramping up for a tirade of angry words.

To arrive at a mindful state that paves the path to better nonverbal and verbal communication, we first have to breathe in—and train ourselves to focus on our *own* breaths.

🐱 *Global Nonverbal Tip*

Connect mindfulness with patterns of intention to enhance nonverbal communication.

Culturally, awareness of breath has for a long time held a significant place in both Eastern and Western traditions and has been a core aspect of world views and knowledge systems. Whether we refer to breath as *prana, ch'i,* or *pneuma,* breath is central to well-being in both our personal and our professional lives. **Most importantly, when we focus on our own breathing, a space for patience and compassion is born.**

We have to rethink *breathing* as being a facilitator of health—breathing is also a *practical tool* that awakens our senses. As an *axis* between vocalics and body language, breathing serves as an essential conduit to communication, creativity, and beyond. Chanting, yoga, exercise, even laughter all involve breathing and stimulate meditative states, as well as the vagus nerve.

What is psychologically important to us, in terms of communication outcomes, is liberating ourselves from the idea that breath is only automatic—breath is also *controllable*. Our bodies naturally inhale between seventeen thousand and twenty-three thousand breaths per day on average—however, we always have the ability to engage in the type of breathwork the global business world is embracing, called *conscious breathing*.

Instead of allowing work to dictate erratic adjustments in our breathing patterns, we can breathe *consciously,* which research has shown can lead to improved decision-making on the job *and* deeper connections. Our breath is the only part of our nervous system that we can control, which means that we can easily and practically access this mechanism to shift our thoughts or feelings. We can stimulate our vagus nerve, like strumming a magical harp that has the never-ending power to restore us to equilibrium.

Stimulating our vagus nerve reduces brain anxiety, sends our visceral organs into "rest-and-digest" mode, and heightens our ability to fine-tune emotional responses. Breathing primes us for nonverbal and verbal communication.

When altering our breathing patterns, we alter our state of being. Conscious breathing not only allows us to arrive at clearer thoughts and better decisions, it also allows us to recognize the nonverbal patterns of others and *respond* more effectively to situations, rather than simply react to them.

Our breath allows us to create a new human subjectivity. With breath, we connect fully with our bodies and activate the forgotten language of our gestures and vocal sounds. Breath reminds us that in the act of breathing, we do more than just realize and exhale the past, but also realize and inhale the future that is right in front of us.

Part I: The Body Language Connection

4.2 Communicating the Unspoken: Global Body Language Patterns

> *Art has this long history, predating even language, of expressing nonverbal information.* **—Betty Edwards**

One of the most elusive and fascinating displays of body language is the mysterious smile of the *Mona Lisa.* With her enigmatic smile, she inspires many to wonder whether her smirk is sensual, amused, all-knowing, distant, witty, sly, cold, or sublime. Just like an onlooker of this painting, we spend our professional lives wondering how to decode nonverbal messages.

Indeed, people from all over the world travel to the Louvre in Paris to discover the meaning of this mysterious smile. The painter, Leonardo da Vinci, has given us scant clues and a lot of speculation. Ultimately, without full *context,* after five hundred years, this smile will continue to inspire passionate discussion. For this same reason, body language can never be interpreted in a vacuum, especially in the global workplace. To fully interpret any nonverbal situation, we first need to understand the cultural contexts that shape subtle cues and gestures.

The clear starting point is stepping out of familiar winds, both physically and mentally. Many of us may already work in global teams, virtually or by traveling the world—both scenarios are essential for broadening our mindfulness of cultural contexts. However, we have to go even deeper. Remember, we have to observe *beneath the surface,* connecting what we *see* with what is *intended* to fully integrate an understanding of cultural nuances. We have to expand awareness of what is termed *display norms*—cultural display norms.

Consider this case of misdiagnosis among clinicians in an intercultural situation. In a notable case, put forward by the work of D. Yuhwa Lu, professor at New York University, research has shown that, due to averted eye contact, Caucasian clinicians rated a group of Chinese clients as anxious, nervous, quiet, depressed, inhibited, and lacking self-confidence, while the same clients were rated by Chinese clinicians as adaptable, alert, dependable, friendly, and practical. Viewing this scenario through an intercultural lens reveals that eye contact with a stranger tends to indicate a challenge in East Asian culture, while respect is typically shown when a person looks at your feet. But a clinician who isn't culturally-mindful may inadvertently misdiagnose such a patient.

As global communicators, we must be mindful that the role of body language is fluid around the world. The two aspects of body language communication that we need to focus on are *decoding* (the ability to read the cues of others) and *encoding* (the ability to send our own cues). The goal in every interaction is to fuse observation with mindfulness for effective communication and, ultimately, deeper relationship-building.

The pioneering research by psychologist and nonverbal expert Dr. Paul Ekman and Wallace V. Friesen introduced the world to seven universal emotions: happiness, sadness, fear, anger, disgust, contempt, and surprise. Their landmark findings built on the research of Charles Darwin, who was one of the first to study facial expressions in the context of evolutionary principles and who, along with later researchers, demonstrated that human facial expressions are universal (even among blind people).

One notable study by Ekman and Friesen involved showing participants of differing cultures highly-intensive films. When the participants viewed the films alone—their recorded facial expressions of emotion were identical.

However, when participants viewed films with the experimenter present in the room—some cultures "masked" their negative emotions, by trying to retain a neutral expression or even force a smile. Based on these findings, Ekman and Friesen then coined the term *cultural display norms* to define the range of culturally-acceptable facial expressions of emotion, particularly between Japanese and American societies.

These transformational findings underscore an innate universality. *Our actual facial expressions of human emotions* are universal, with the key underpinning that sometimes our cultures will influence the *display* of those facial expressions and emotions. Results concluded that Western cultures tend to value and sanction outward emotional expressions, while Eastern counterparts may maintain an indirect approach, specifically masking negative emotions in social situations to maintain group harmony.

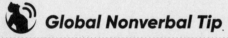 **Global Nonverbal Tip**

Do more than read body language—link observations with awareness of cultural contexts and display norms.

The key patterns of nonverbal intention come from Edward T. Hall, a founding scholar of the intercultural communication field. According to Hall's research, the majority of human communication is nonverbal and functions across two cultural and contextual patterns. In his book *The Silent Language,* he introduced the concepts of *high-context* and *low-context* communication, which pertain to different display patterns of intention—both implicit and explicit. His pioneering work, alongside that of later research in the field, showed that professionals from *high-context cultures,* such as countries in East Asia, Southeast Asia, the Middle East, parts of Eastern Europe, most of Latin America, the Mediterranean, the Iberian Peninsula, and the majority of sub-Saharan Africa, may tend to communicate with implicit messages and look for meaning in nonverbal gestures. Alternatively, professionals from *low-context cultures,* such as in the United States, parts of Canada, Northwestern and North-Central Europe, Scandinavia, and Australia/New Zealand, may tend to communicate with explicit messages and look for meaning in spoken or written words (see Appendix B on *Cultural Contexts*).

As global communicators, we must decode and encode global body language through a lens of critical thinking to understand diversity of expression and communication in all its forms, along with humility, empathy, and respect. As people work, travel, and immigrate worldwide, we are seeing a "human language" of emotions emerge every day.

Initially, David Efron, who first researched gestures of Sicilian and Lithuanian Jewish immigrants settling in New York City, found that distinct, cultural nonverbal expressions disappeared as immigrants became more assimilated into the larger US culture—his work was the cornerstone for research linking culture and gestures. Today, similar findings report that those immigrating from one culture to another tend to integrate the *display norms* of that culture, and then outwardly adapt the expression of their emotions accordingly.

With globalization, the patterns of nonverbal communication overlap and become more apparent every day. We are all capable of identifying and organizing displays of emotion the same way—the key is an expanded awareness of how we choose to manage, express, and navigate nonverbals across cultures.

Whether entering informal or formal business situations, bringing a concerted awareness of cultural trends and connecting inner emotional states to outward expressions can lay the foundation for building more effective global interaction. Global understanding is possible when we are aware of the converging universalities between us.

4.3 Under the Cultural Radar: Unmasking the Seven Micro Expression Patterns

The face is a picture of the mind with the eyes as its interpreter. **—Marcus Tullius Cicero**

We share renowned painter Pablo Picasso's famous question, "Who sees the human face correctly: the photographer, the mirror, or the painter?" The human face gathers the most attention in our relationships. Our brains can recognize facial expressions at the speed of two hundred milliseconds! However, the key to recognizing true emotions is by using a defined set of seven facial *micro expressions,* which last less than half a second. These brief expressions reveal true intentions—before the human face can remask them!

Dr. Ekman and Friesen's research identified these almost-instant flashes of expression (*happiness, sadness, fear, anger, disgust, contempt,* and *surprise*), which have become pivotal in multicultural settings. See Figure 4-1, "The 7 Universal Micro Expression Patterns," for a guide to recognizing these involuntary universal expressions. They closely mirror the seven universal emotions, yet because they happen so quickly as to happen unconsciously, they can supersede even the most disciplined of cultural and learned display norms.

The 7 Universal Micro Expression Patterns

Micro expressions last less than half a second. Learning to recognize these involuntary expressions can help you discern a person's true emotions.

HAPPINESS

- Corners of lips are drawn back & up
- Mouth may be parted, teeth exposed
- A wrinkle runs from the outer nose to the outer lip
- Cheeks are raised
- Lower eyelids may show wrinkles or be tense
- Crow's feet near the outside of eyes

ANGER

- Eyebrows lowered & drawn together
- Vertical lines visible between the eyebrows
- Lower lids are tensed
- Eyes are in hard stare or bulging
- Nostrils may be flared
- Lower jaw jutting out

FEAR

- Eyebrows are raised & drawn together, often in a flat line
- Wrinkles in center of forehead, not across
- Upper eyelids are raised, but the lower eyelids are tense & drawn up
- Eyes have the upper white showing, but not the lower white
- Mouth is open & lips are slightly tensed or drawn over teeth

Figure 4-1a

Overall, micro expressions can reveal a lot about what people are actually feeling, even when people are trying to suppress or conceal their emotions. The landmark efforts from Dr. Ekman and his predecessors even inspired the show *Lie to Me,* specifically his work on decoding the nonverbal messages of the human face.

SURPRISE

- The eyebrows are raised & curved
- Skin below the eyebrows is stretched
- Horizontal wrinkles across the forehead
- Eyelids are opened, white of the eyes showing above & below
- Jaw drops open & teeth are parted, but no tension or stretching of mouth

DISGUST

- Upper eyelid is raised
- The expression you make when you smell something unpleasant
- Lines show below lower eyelids
- Lower lip is raised
- Nose is wrinkled
- Cheeks are raised

SADNESS

- Skin below the eyebrows is triangulated, with inner corner up
- Inner corners of the eyebrows are drawn in & then up
- Corners of the lips are drawn down
- Lower lip pouts out
- Jaw comes up

CONTEMPT

- One side of the mouth is raised (sneering)

Figure 4-1b

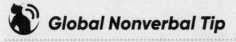

Global Nonverbal Tip

Look for micro expressions, which reveal a person's true emotions—these expressions are difficult to bluff, unlike prolonged facial expressions.

Learning how to recognize these seven facial micro expression patterns is invaluable to understanding others along the global spectrum. Across cultures, the face is one of the most revealing windows into a person's emotions, and these emotions can be "read," not by observing prolonged expressions, but by paying attention to *micro* expressions.

4.4 The Truth Is Out There: The Significance of Eye Movement Patterns

> *Where words are restrained, the eyes often talk a great deal.* **—Samuel Richardson**

Our eyes often move when we think. Therefore, involuntary or saccadic eye movement has the potential to reveal important information about how our business counterparts are responding to our messages—there is even a branch of study dedicated to eye-tracking in the field of web design linking eye gazing patterns to our searches for information online! Since conscious eye movement is very limited, some say the eyes may provide one of the best forms of a human lie detector test. Overall, according to research in eye movements and cognition from Daniel C. Richardson at Stanford University, in collaboration with Rick Dale and Michael J. Spivey at Cornell University, decoding eye movement can provide insight into the cognitive psychology of reasoning and, therefore, contribute to understanding how a person may be processing information.

In this fascinating area of study at the intersection of psychoanalysis, cognitive linguistics, parapsychology, and speculative research in Neuro-Linguistic Programming (NLP), eye accessing cues are continually being studied to determine effective nonverbal communication practices. One of the most interesting theories in the field of NLP is whether subtle "eye cues" that differentiate eye movement patterns can help to determine the way a person is thinking—for example, left eye movement has been associated with *constructing* images and sounds and right eye movement has been associated with *remembering* images and sounds. Additionally, further studies focus not just on how our eye cues may indicate the relationship between thinking and eye movement, but also on how our eye movements may signify the type of mental representational system we are using—namely by indicating our preferred learning and communication styles.

Just think of how an interrogation unfolds in a detective movie, with potential suspects being asked to recount a sequence of events. Professional detectives who are trained in **oculesics** work to interpret eye movement patterns, by searching for inconsistencies between these eye cues and other body language and verbal cues to determine if someone is telling the truth. In another captivating area of study, leading psychologist Dr. Robert Plutchik conducted extensive research analyzing the connection between eye movements and other facial cues in the expression of *emotions*. According to Dr. Plutchik, we must be aware of eye cue dynamics because we often establish meaningful relationships with one another through eye-related nonverbal communication.

For the global communicator, the most important aspect to keep in mind is that eye movement patterns can vary with intercultural patterns—some cultures may have more pronounced and nuanced eye cues than others. As mentioned earlier, many Eastern cultures tend to look down as a sign of respect, whereas in Western societies, direct eye contact often tends to be a sign of trust and confidence. Ensure that you are aware of cultural tendencies and, as Barbara and Allan Pease describe in their book *The Definitive Book of Body Language,* "give the amount of eye contact that makes everyone feel comfortable." Overall, in terms of global communication, they recommend that unless looking at others is culturally taboo, globally "lookers gain more credibility than non-lookers." Direct eye contact can often increase interpersonal influence and connection when speaking.

See Figure 4-2, "Eye Movement Patterns," and consider which eye cues may indicate the degree to which a person may be recalling, processing, and interpreting information across the three sensory styles: visual, auditory, and kinesthetic. While the linkage of specific eye movement patterns (e.g., looking up, peering from side to side, or glancing downward) to learning and communication styles is still speculative, research findings from M. F. Land and Mary Hayhoe have demonstrated that eye movements are connected with moment-to-moment goals and tasks. Overall, when observing global counterparts, your focus is to gain more insight into what representation strategies a person may be using to answer a question, make a decision, or consider a statement.

Eye Movement Patterns

Our eyes often move when we think. Recognizing subtle eye movements can reveal how others process information, by imagining or remembering. *What representation strategies is a person using to answer a question, make a decision, or consider a statement?*

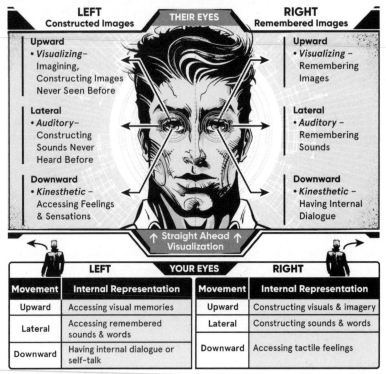

Movement	Internal Representation	Movement	Internal Representation
Upward	Accessing visual memories	Upward	Constructing visuals & imagery
Lateral	Accessing remembered sounds & words	Lateral	Constructing sounds & words
Downward	Having internal dialogue or self-talk	Downward	Accessing tactile feelings

*For many left-handed people, the above chart is reversed (a mirror image). Research regarding eye movement patterns is exploratory and ongoing.

Figure 4-2

4.5 The Three Zones: Bridging the Space between Our Global Connections

> To touch can be to give life. —*Michelangelo*

We can forge stronger connections by understanding **proxemics,** the way we use *space* when communicating. *Proxemics* is how we build intimacy and power, whether we are speaking to one person or a group of people. When we move and gesture, the goal is to connect our body and *messages* to the surrounding space. Additionally, how close we step to others or how far we stand can build important elements, such as trust and respect. See Figure 4-3.

The Zones of Professional Communication

Step forward or step back? The distance we stand from others can build important elements, such as trust and respect. *As a global professional, how do we connect intention to space to enhance global relationships?*

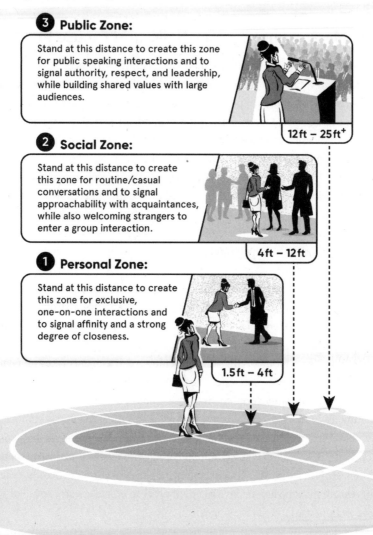

3 Public Zone:

Stand at this distance to create this zone for public speaking interactions and to signal authority, respect, and leadership, while building shared values with large audiences.

12ft – 25ft⁺

2 Social Zone:

Stand at this distance to create this zone for routine/casual conversations and to signal approachability with acquaintances, while also welcoming strangers to enter a group interaction.

4ft – 12ft

1 Personal Zone:

Stand at this distance to create this zone for exclusive, one-on-one interactions and to signal affinity and a strong degree of closeness.

1.5ft – 4ft

Figure 4-3

All our spatial behaviors occur in four key zones of interpersonal distances described by intercultural researcher Edward T. Hall: intimate space, personal space, social space, and public space. Hall's research illustrates how people of different cultures psychologically understand and purposefully use the space around them, including their general comfort level regarding personal space. Our principal body language tips do not include *intimate* space to keep to the most relevant professional contexts in this book.

4.5a Zone 1:
My Personal Space—Hello and Excuse Me

Just think of everyday locations that are bustling with people coming and going, where we have to adjust our preference of personal space. Airports and train stations contend with peak wait times where the boundaries of our personal space are tested every day, while waiting for services—at hospitals, at banks, in elevators, or in theaters with limited "elbow room."

Internationally-recognized environmental psychologist Robert Sommer in his book *Personal Space: The Behavioral Basis of Design* brought the term *personal space* to the mainstream, and not only highlighted how our environment affects our behavior, but also how "we are the environment." Our personal space is the sphere surrounding us that we feel psychologically belongs to us—our "bubble"—which travels everywhere we go, encircling us in every interaction we have.

We usually welcome others into the personal zone to signal an exclusive, one-on-one interaction and, overall, to signal affinity and a strong degree of closeness with others we let into this space. This *closeness* is different from intimacy, and we can use verbal communication more than touch to make that distinction clear, although light social touching, such as handshakes or a pat on the back, may facilitate more effective communication when appropriate.

In global communication, the intrinsic communicative power of touch is a central axis of our personal spaces. Known as **haptics,** touch communication is widely considered essential for social development and is an immensely important consideration when communicating with business counterparts from cultures around the world. Touch can have impactful consequences in specific cultures and must be handled with care in order to create a warm space of welcome and openness to our messages.

The degree of personal touch can vary along a cultural spectrum. For instance, the social nature of *high-context* cultures is steeped in displaying very close personal affection and these cultures tend to prefer the personal zone.

Low-context cultures tend to favor the social zone for business interactions. Keep in mind that some cultures, such as practicing Muslim cultures, usually abstain from personal contact between opposite genders, while also strictly refraining from using the left hand in certain situations.

In the business world, the most important intercultural form of touch is the *greeting,* which has been extensively studied in the authoritative book on international business protocol *Kiss, Bow, or Shake Hands.* Essentially, the greeting is a way to enhance global relationships, and we must grow comfortable managing the intimate and personal zones of conversations with friends, associates, or small culturally-diverse group discussions.

Humorist-philosopher Will Rogers once said, "You never get a second chance to make a first impression." A good handshake, or the cultural equivalent, is widely recognized as one of the most important means of initiating and departing any interaction. This simple gesture is not just proper etiquette for many; it has a cognitive basis for connecting people. While *touching* hands has been shown to psychologically and physiologically establish a shared connection between people, we must also be alert to adapted forms of expressing connections in our technologically- and globally-connected world.

The *greeting* is an all-important opportunity not just for making a good first impression with global professionals, but also for navigating common business interactions with respect and appreciation for cultures around the world. And that *awareness* of common greeting gestures, whether with signs of namaste, waving hands, or air kissing during times of remote adaptability or periods of limited physical contact, can be a defining factor in maintaining global business relationships. As awareness spreads, intercultural etiquette guides have begun to indicate that "greetings vary," as Eastern cultures become more westernized and Western cultures become more aware of Eastern practices. For a visual guide to greeting patterns around the world, see Chapter 2 on *Networking Skills.*

Zone 1

To build *trust* in the *personal zone:*

- Use the power of touch (when socially or culturally appropriate) to show sincerity and to convey positive affection.

- Build a natural rhythm of exchanging eye contact, looking away, and then returning your gaze to gauge comfort level.

- Relax your eyes and dilate your pupils with a limited blink rate.

In a globalized era, where people have grown comfortable with alternate ways of greeting others in social and professional contexts—such as fist bumps, handshakes, waves, and friendly nods—we must remember to train ourselves to recognize Eastern and Western cultural customs for best connecting with others in a personal space. With a better understanding of our global counterparts, we can empathize and work together to better manage expectations and achieve common goals.

4.5b Zone 2:
Our Social Space—Nice to Meet You

> *People may hear your words, but they feel your attitude.* **—John C. Maxwell**

To create the *social zone,* we step back to create a communication space that is four to twelve feet from us—just think of when you are at a networking event. Create this zone to signal that others can join your conversation. Perhaps you want to expand the circle of conversation (or are speaking with someone in the personal zone you want to avoid!). Creating the social zone is very common in the workplace, a restaurant, the classroom, or a conference center.

Remember, *low-context* cultures, such as those in the United States, parts of Canada, Northwestern and North-Central Europe, Scandinavia, and Australia/New Zealand, generally favor the *social zone,* illustrated in Figure 4-3, during business situations. On the other hand, *high-context* cultures prefer the proximity of the *personal zone,* or zone 1. Step backward to create this *social zone,* especially for routine and casual conversations. Creating this zone is an effective way to signal approachability with acquaintances while also welcoming strangers to enter a group interaction.

Zone 2

To convey *respect* and build *trust* in the *social zone:*

- Lead with warm nods and light head movements to convey understanding.
- Reflect an attitude of generosity by maintaining open body language and orienting your body to the other person when listening.
- Show sincerity with open hands, eye contact, and fluid gestures.

Nonverbal communication via gestures and voice takes on a larger role in the *social zone* than in the *personal zone.* Dr. Carol Kinsey Goman, body language expert and author of *The Nonverbal Advantage: Secrets and Science of Body Language at Work,* states that "gesturing can help people form clearer thoughts, speak in tighter sentences, and use more declarative language." Keep in mind that body language is a direct indicator of our intentions and must always support our messaging, particularly in the social space where meaningful global networking revolves around generosity.

One of the prime *social zone* interactions in the business world is professional networking. Nonverbal signals that transmit a desire to *help* others are ironically the key to becoming power networkers, particularly across cultures (see Chapter 2 on *Networking Skills*). Generosity is the feeling we want to project with all nonverbal communication in the *social zone*—just as entrepreneur Keith Ferrazzi said in his book *Never Eat Alone,* "the currency of real networking is not greed but generosity."

To enhance rapport with a global audience, remember to keep in mind the following nonverbal ways to maximize future networking interactions:

- Convey warmth by actively nodding when listening in order to show interest and empathy.

- Demonstrate transparency by showing your hands and by using approachable and fluid gestures in an open manner.

- Foster habits of attentiveness and sincerity in your body language through eye contact and smiles to make others feel comfortable.

4.5c Zone 3: The Public Space—Welcome Everyone

> *The human voice is the organ of the soul.*
> **—Henry Wadsworth Longfellow**

The *public zone* refers to a communication space twelve feet or more from the body and is reserved for large audiences at speeches, lecture halls, and performances. Stand at this distance to create this zone for public speaking interactions and to signal authority, respect, and leadership—particularly when planning for a meeting with your team or to establish a formal or high-profile impression with your audience. Executives and celebrities tend to use this zone, as it is a safe intersection of intimacy and power. This zone is also effective for building shared values with large audiences, as highlighted in Figure 4-3.

Cross-cultural researcher and anthropologist Edward T. Hall highlighted an important consideration in his book *The Silent Dimension*—with more distance between the audience and the speaker, the emotional connection can be lost. Therefore, engage in intentional combinations of body language and vocalics as a dynamic complement to your public speaking for global impact.

The *public zone* is usually reserved for some form of public speaking to large audiences—and audiences across cultures are drawn to coordinated body movements, known as **kinesics,** that guide listeners impactfully toward key messaging. Dr. Kinsey Goman further advises that when presenting two issues, such as comparing the pros and cons of a topic, deliver each piece of information on distinct sides of the stage. In this way our body language marks "sections" and shifts in presentation topics. The use of body language to mark "sections" in a presentation directs global audiences to different message points and vastly enhances communication. Nonverbals should harmonize with what we say, a crucial point for intercultural audiences processing information alongside presentation dynamics.

Zone 3

To communicate *confidence* and guide audiences toward key messaging in the *public zone*:

- Use shifts in *movements* to indicate shifts in *ideas*.
- Spark the attention of audiences by shifting the energy in your movements and by modulating the tone, volume, and pacing of your voice.
- Share an authentic smile with global audiences to make a ready connection.

In the *public zone,* our presentation begins before we speak a word. Audiences form an impression as soon as we enter the room. Convey a warm tone and confident stance that will immediately project your credibility. While confidence is obviously important, a warm tone and a welcoming smile can immediately unite communities in a globalized space.

4.6 The Virtual Zone: Our Digital Sea in a Shell

> *The most important thing in communication is hearing what isn't said.* **—Peter F. Drucker**

Did you know that the simple act of pressing a seashell to your ear holds the secret to powerful nonverbal virtual communication? The quiet roar of waves in a delicate conch may sound as if the shell stored echoes of its past time on other beaches; however, the sound we hear is actually the airwaves rushing around our present environment resonating within the shell's cavity. The shell is a remarkable amplifier of sound! Similarly, when we confer over video calls—our bodies must reverberate much like "shells," using *amplified* facial, hand, and body nonverbal cues to *boost* our meanings and intentions in the *virtual zone*. When online, we must turn up all nonverbals, especially in the era of telework.

Research shows that nonverbals can play a decisive role in online intercultural communication, especially when linked to verbal anchors. This is particularly true when deepening that primal pattern of intention for any global audience—*trust*. The key to amplifying nonverbal signals online is not only harmonizing your gestures with *spoken* meanings, but also harmonizing nonverbals with the feedback you intend to send when actively *listening* as well.

The Virtual Zone

When both speaking and listening, use decisive nonverbals to your advantage to strengthen meaning, resolve discrepancies, and enhance the bond uniting you with others on the screen.

Keep in mind that while people speak, listeners provide cues of understanding through what linguists term **backchanneling,** such as "uh-huh" and "mm-hmm." *Backchanneling* is often not as apparent online, so make sure to heighten your awareness of backchanneling nonverbal cues, especially during intercultural virtual interactions.

- Pay close attention to fast *head-nodding,* which conveys a strong willingness to speak, and slow head-nodding, which conveys understanding/acknowledgment. Taking an audit of others' *backchanneling* signals and auditing your own subtle cues helps shape more effective intercultural communication in virtual situations. Intercultural research even shows that slightly tilting your head while listening builds trust with audiences, while demonstrating willful, vulnerable, and receptive communication.

- The *shoulders* are also a telltale sign of underlying emotions—whether someone displays broad, leveled shoulders commanding respect and confidence or displays raised shoulders indicating uncertainty, doubt, or lack of knowledge. The shoulders serve as a varied cultural bellwether across world societies—be mindful that shoulder display signals common in Western cultures typically receive less acknowledgment in Eastern cultures.

- Finally, remember high-context cultures tend to emphasize *implicit nonverbal elements* of communication, while low-context cultures tend to listen closely for *explicit verbal messages* (see Appendix B on *Cultural Contexts*). So be aware of both contexts when videoconferencing, as it is easy to focus on one aspect of communication more than the other.

Gestures are messages in themselves. Our body shifts have the power to solidify our spoken and unspoken messages in the *virtual zone.* However, this space can be wrought with uncertainty, so make sure to use congruous nonverbals that align with your spoken words for intercultural audiences. Overall, use gestural shifts purposefully to communicate larger shifts in verbal meaning, while also providing backchannel cues to give responsive feedback to the speaker.

The amplified body language of *both* the listener and the speaker impact success in virtual communication. In other words, the listener must participate nonverbally in the exchange just as much as the speaker for successful communication in the *virtual zone.* As interfaces evolve online, both audiences and speakers should be deliberate with nonverbal communication to contribute to a greater future of shared understanding and mutual trust in our global ecosystem.

4.7 From Resonance to Presence: Building Confidence through Vocalics

> *The human voice is the most perfect instrument of all.*
> *—Arvo Pärt*

The human voice is so powerful that with the right tone it can shatter glass. Sound waves have the power to compress air when projected, causing objects to vibrate. When certain tonal conditions are met, the directed sound hurtles through the air at a steady pitch for two to three seconds, building momentum before shattering the glass itself. What often goes unnoticed is that the glass must have microscopic imperfections and a matching resonance frequency, in order to shatter.

In a similar way, the human voice can cause metaphoric breakthroughs. When our vocal tones and messages resonate with crowds, our voices can shatter *inaction* and inspire progressive movements. Our voices also have the power to uplift spirits and encourage dreams to reach greater heights than previously imagined.

How can we tap into this communicative power in business and life? We have to rethink the concept of breathing as fuel. Our vocal chords, which open and close hundreds of times a second, give us resounding possibilities for setting our messages in motion. Our hidden potential arises when we breathe from our diaphragm to shape our voice.

The breath when speaking is a shared communion between us and our subject, channeling meaning and intentionality from one person to the next. As musician Tori Amos once said, "The most important thing to me as a songwriter is the breath. The most important thing I could ever say to somebody is, 'Sometimes I just breathe you in.'"

The vocal features that expressively color our words are what is termed **paralanguage.** Also known as **vocalics,** paralanguage focuses on the subtle signals that speakers use to enhance the meaning of their words. Although paralanguage differs across cultures, it universally highlights our intentions and purpose for speaking. In this chapter, we will cover paralanguage as it relates to Global English, the type of English used for global communication resulting from a multinational movement toward an international business standard of the language (see Appendix A on *Global English*).

When we speak, in addition to the words we say, our vocal cues guide our listeners to how our messages should be interpreted. The most effective vocal patterns for enhancing the transfer of meaning to global audiences resides in the following:

- **thought groups** (phrasing)
- **prosody** (combinations of stress, intonation, and rhythm)

Consider how paralanguage is used around the world for the transfer of meaning; in India, speakers extend volume across multiple syllables to command attention, while in British English, speakers maximize volume in their voices to convey anger. Additionally, Japanese women deliberately raise the pitch of their voices to differentiate themselves from men, and Americans fostered similar voice variations in pitch in a display of power and intimidation.

Tapping into these vocal characteristics is a way for us to greatly enhance our vocal intentions as global communicators, help listeners of other language backgrounds track spoken information, and bring lasting impact.

4.8 Thought Groups: The Hidden Power of Voice Patterns

> *When the whole world is silent, even one voice becomes powerful.* **—Malala Yousafzai**

When we envision "master presenters" delivering powerful conversations and presentations, we often imagine the flow of speech to be as smooth and continuous as a river; however, effective speech is actually made of intricate patterns of starts and stops. These starts and stops are called **thought groups** and are the key vocal patterns that create purposeful speech.

Think of *thought groups* as "phrases of meaning" that occur *within* a sentence. Now, imagine the pauses between thought groups as *stepping stones* on the bank of a shallow river. We often overlook the subtle effects of *thought groups* in the corporate space; however, these individual groupings of phrases remain a powerful speaking tool for conveying our ideas in dynamic and distinct ways.

By dividing *every* sentence into these smaller units of meaning, we evolve our voice pattern, supercharge our messages, and guide our audiences "across the river of speech" and in the uptake of important information.

> ### 🐱 *Global English Voice Tip*
>
> **Divide every sentence into two or more thought groups for impactful phrasing.**

Before covering the guidelines in further detail, first consider how thought group pausing can impact the meaning of a sentence:

> *Ms. Chen / said Alberto / where is the business meeting?*
>
> *Ms. Chen said / Alberto / Where is the business meeting?*

The first sentence demonstrates that *Alberto* is speaking, while the second sentence shows that *Ms. Chen* is speaking. One benefit of thought groups is that spoken speech, unlike written text, cannot be read with punctuation unless the speaker *indicates the punctuation with their voice.*

This is the first indicator of how to form thought groups—each phrase is usually indicated by commas in a sentence (but not always). Generally, thought groups are short, succinct phrases, two to five words in length, and often correspond to grammatical phrases, as indicated below, depending on meaning.

GRAMMATICAL PHRASES	SAMPLES
Prepositional phrases	In a **minute**/at the **office**
Verb + pronoun	**Buy** the parts/then **bring** them
Determiner + noun	My **uncle**/the **broker**
Short clauses	When you **leave**/**call** me
Transition words/phrases (the only case where thought groups can be one word in length)	**First** of all/In **other** words

Note:

- The bold words are suggested *focus words,* which should be said with a pitch change; however, other words may be emphasized depending on the context.
- *Transition words (and phrases)* are called "guideposts" because these signals are responsible for helping listeners navigate the sequence of content, are always their own separate thought groups, and should be said with a pitch change and a pause.

However, thought groups are not always dictated by commas; in fact, we should look for opportunities to create purposeful "breaks" between phrases outside of traditional comma breaks. So, how exactly do we break a sentence into thought groups outside of commas? Compare the sentences below, which have been divided into two different thought group patterns—the first, where the comma would go, and the second, more creatively:

If you want to be a leader / empower others.

If you want / to be a leader / empower others.

Both sentences are effective. We can be creative in deciding the length of thought groups in a sentence—the comma is our guide—but *our meaning* is our primary prism. When giving a speech, it is better for us to use shorter thought groups (two to five words in length) so that we have more time to plan what we are going to say, while also allowing our listeners more time to ingest the information (see Chapter 1 on *Presentation Skills*). For this reason, three types of rhythmic and intonational signals exist to identify the breaks in thought groups indicated in Figure 4-4. In addition to pausing at the end of a thought group, we can make our *voices rise/fall* or we can *lengthen the vowel* in the stressed syllable of the final word.

Thought groups are a way to purposefully group phrases together for meaning and impact. So, keep in mind that *within* each thought group is a **focus word,** which is indicated by a pitch change or slight increase in volume for emphasis. Our ideas determine the *focus word* of choice and how we emphasize the content for impact.

With the example above, possible *focus words* would be "If **you** want / to be a **leader** / **empower** others." We can emphasize the focus word by also adding a pitch change to the vowel of the stressed syllable or lengthening the vowel in the stressed syllable. Ensure that most pitch changes and stretched vowels occur on focus words and that you pause more commonly between thought groups to clearly convey key points.

Thought Group Guidelines

Divide every sentence into two or more thought groups:

- Form two-to-five-word phrases of similar meaning.
- Emphasize a focus word in each phrase.
- Signal the end of each phrase with a pause/pitch change.

Thought Groups

Thought groups are short phrases that express a single idea and are separated by a pause. **How can you use these phrases to create clear and impactful speech?**

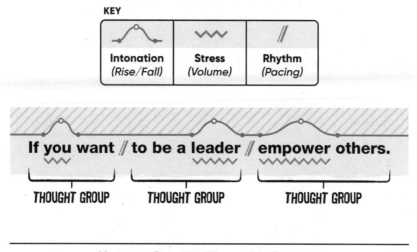

KEY

Intonation (Rise/Fall)	Stress (Volume)	Rhythm (Pacing)

If you want // to be a leader // empower others.

THOUGHT GROUP · THOUGHT GROUP · THOUGHT GROUP

How to Create Thought Groups

Thought groups are 2–5 words in length that form a unit of meaning.

1 **Divide** every sentence into two or more thought groups.

2 **Emphasize** a focus word in the phrase with a higher volume/pitch.

3 **Indicate** the end of a thought group with a pause or pitch change.

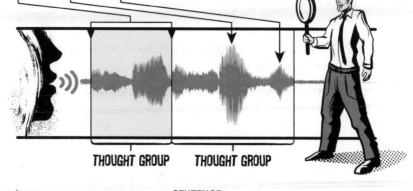

THOUGHT GROUP   THOUGHT GROUP

SENTENCE

Figure 4-4

Overall, thought group patterns contribute to much more than we realize in producing clear speech. Thought groups help both the listener *and* the speaker by supporting purposeful listening and creating impactful phrasing. In linguistics, thought groups are an essential part of spoken English because they enhance comprehension and impact, especially with global audiences.

🐻 Global English Voice Tip

Use clear thought groups to produce clear and effective speech.

These phrases allow us to powerfully structure content with our voice pattern. Awareness of thought groups not only improves our active listening, but also increases our ability to consciously identify and train ourselves to form clear and distinct patterns in our own speech.

Forming our own thought group strategy allows time to plan our content and helps listeners process information. As an important communication tool on the global stage, thought groups are the patterned secret in producing clear and powerful speech.

Activities: "Talking the Talk"

1. **Thought group "breakdown":** Look at the following sentences and (1) make a slash (/) between the most likely thought group boundaries, and (2) underline the *focus word* in each thought group.

    a. Today's news contained a special report on the solar eclipse. *(three thought groups)*

    b. At the next meeting, we'll elect the new chair. *(two thought groups)*

    c. I'd like to introduce my colleague Shakira who manages sales. *(three thought groups)*

2. **Stress power in speeches:** Read aloud these excerpts from President Obama's State of the Union address on January 12, 2016. Remember that there is only *one* focus word per thought group.

Notice the phrase stress in thought groups. Be aware of speech patterns and other discourse intonation elements.

THAT'S / the AMERica / I KNOW / THAT'S / the COUNtry / we LOVE / CLEAR-eyed / BIG-hearted / unDAUNTed by challenge / optiMIStic / that unarmed TRUTH / and unconditional LOVE / will HAVE / the FINAL word / THAT'S / what makes me so HOPEful / about our FUture / I beLIEVE / in CHANGE / because I believe in YOU / the AMERican people / and THAT'S why / I STAND here / as CONfident / as I / have EVER been / that the STATE / of our UNION / IS strong

---

Answers:

(a) *Today's news / contained a special report / on the solar eclipse.*

(b) *At the next meeting, / we'll elect the new chair.*

(c) *I'd like to introduce my colleague / Shakira / who manages sales. (Some focus words and answers will vary depending on context.)*

··

4.9 Voice Identity: Is Your Prosody Music to All Ears?

> *Change the way you sound and the world will change the way they see and respond to you.* **—Roger Love**

If you ever need to provide a form of digital identification, just speak. Like fingerprints, no two voices have the same characteristics, and voiceprint technology has advanced to measure the rhythm and sound of our speech patterns, otherwise known as *prosody,* which is unique to each of us.

Through our vocal quality and variations, we can create the captivating quality of a smooth-talking radio DJ or renowned public speaker. Prosody allows us to convey a broad range of spoken meaning beyond the words we use.

🐱 *Global English Voice Tip*

Our voices matter as much as our words matter.

The next time you are at a conference listening to a successful global executive give a speech or are tuning into a radio announcer or a podcast host, listen closely to how they temper their voice to connect with others when speaking—what you are honing in on is *prosody.* Prosody consists of *volume, tone,* and *pacing*—the qualities of our voice that make our messages more impactful. One way to appreciate prosody would be to imagine its opposite: speech from a robot in one of those electronic monotone voices from TV and film tropes.

🐱 *Global English Voice Tip*

Maximize the three aspects of prosody for vocal power:

- **stress (volume)**
- **intonation (rising and falling tone)**
- **rhythm (pacing)**

Pronunciation experts and linguists champion the undeniable importance of prosody in spoken English. As global communicators, we must *intentionally* tap into these resonant vocal tools, using prosody to deliver meaningful content. These acoustic variations in our voices impact the way we bring attention to new information, indicate what listeners already know, and signal the end of a topic in global business dialogues. Prosodic signals and patterns are essential to facilitate the transfer of meaning in any spoken business exchange.

The following sections explore the three vocal features that comprise prosody—*stress, intonation,* and *rhythm*—along with easy dynamic exercises. Discover ways of enhancing intercultural communication by tapping into these linguistic components, building engagement in speaking situations, and creating moments of inspiration. In addition to supercharging our business calls and client relationships, prosody allows us to deeply connect with global audiences.

4.9a Stress: Supercharging Our Vocal Potential

> *It only takes one voice, at the right pitch, to start an avalanche. —Dianna Hardy*

Vocal power is that sought-after thunder often attributed to seasoned professionals that we can use to bring attention to our messages—how can we harness this power?

In linguistics, the power of our voice resides in the purposeful use of one vocal feature: *stress,* or volume. However, the way to use volume for *vocal power* goes beyond simply trying to be the loudest person in the room. Instead, the key to vocal power is a very nuanced use of stress—an intentional use of volume—to guide the *flow of conversation and meaning.*

In linguistics, our voice quality is a crossroads of two stress parameters: quiet and loud—with variations in volume playing an important role in how our voice can successfully navigate intercultural business situations. The intentional use of volume allows us to shift the direction and purpose of a conversation. When we use voice stress in targeted ways, for example to shift attention toward an agenda item or topic, we can dramatically alter the course of meetings, negotiations, phone conversations, and virtual conferences.

Consider how an intentional use of stress can change the flow and meaning of the conversation below:

The market is **growing.**	Well, it may just be a seasonal fluctuation.
The **market** is growing.	However, our sales are not.

As we covered earlier, stress creates *focus words,* which are essential to emphasizing content words that can change the meaning of a sentence by creating a shift of focus for the audience. In an intercultural negotiation with back-and-forth bargaining of terms and percentages, stress is even more paramount; for example:

We want **two** advertisements for the fall campaign.	You don't want three?
We want two advertisements for the **fall** campaign.	Ah, but not for the spring campaign.

We can increase *vocal power* by opening our mouths just enough to capture our voice in our cheeks and bolster more sound to create a stronger, more resonant, and fuller voice. **Therefore, make sure to create stress with the** *vowel* **of the stressed syllable of a word, not the consonant (e.g., "whAt?" versus "whaT?").** The vowel is where the power of pitch resides.

English features two types of speech stress, **syllable stress** and **word stress,** to achieve clarity and underscore key information for another person.

Take a look at the below two features that help us to supercharge our words:

- **Syllabic stress** is the instinctual way we use volume to create the everyday stress-timed rhythm of English. Every word in English has a stressed syllable, where the vowel sounds of a word (e.g., a/e/i/o/u) dictate its syllabic stress, such as the stressed "o" sound in "hospital." However, in terms of clarity, it is important to distinguish between individual sounds so that a sentence such as "What did you think of the **committee?**" does not sound like "What did you think of the **comedy?**"

- **Word stress,** on the other hand, is where our creativity as a speaker comes in to create "focus words" that we can use to direct the flow of ideas in a conversation. Focus words allow us to *persuade*—harnessing the acoustic energy of our personality, creativity, imagination, and most importantly, our message.

In the following example, consider how *word stress* impacts the listener's potential interpretations of meaning and their associated responses. Also, notice how the focus words intentionally direct the progression of the conversation. It's easier to think of the focus word of a sentence as becoming the *new* thought and the focus word of the previous sentence as becoming an *old* thought, such as "We got the **client.**" "**Which** client?" "The **referred** client."

Using word stress, for comprehensibility and *impact,* can be very strategic because in addition to communication, we achieve persuasion as well—by directing listeners to our intended messaging.

In a presentation, meeting, or negotiation, remember that once the flow of speech has begun, the new thought in each sentence becomes the focus word and should be stressed. Also, while certain words can be stressed for emphasis, shifting to new focus words can also be a strategic way to de-emphasize other words, offers, or concessions in business-specific situations.

Word stress is integral to communication in global interactions, whether in routine meetings or pivotal negotiations. As a result, when we shift *focus words* among sentences, we naturally guide the flow of thought and garner more persuasive power in our messages. Go ahead, give it a try.

Activities: Do You Hear What I Hear?

1. **Warm-up: "syllabic stress pairs":** Practice saying the following pairs of sentences. If any of them sound similar, work further on your syllabic stress and enunciation. The stressed syllable in the target word is indicated in bold.

   a. "Does the reporter like **his**tory?" versus "Does the reporter like his **sto**ry?"

   b. "This contract is **el**igible" versus "This contract is il**leg**ible."

   c. "In the make-up commercial, did the child say **dep**uty?" versus "In the make-up commercial, did the child say the **beau**ty?"

2. **Word stress "match lib":** Practice saying each pair of sentences in the *Statement* column. Make sure to emphasize the bold *focus word* with a volume increase. Note how the differing *word stress* creates different meanings and contexts in the *Complement* column.

STATEMENT	COMPLEMENT
A. **Sales** increased from last year. B. Sales increased from **last** year.	A. However, our profits have hardly moved at all. B. Well, last year was a particularly bad year.
A. We may not get the **whole** contract. B. **We** may not get the whole contract.	A. However, we'll get a good part of it. B. Yes, but someone else will.
A. Please give me **both** medical reports. B. **Please** give me both medical reports.	A. You don't want just one of them? B. So, you need them immediately.

4.9b Intonation:
The Hidden Business Lingo

> *The message behind the words is the voice of the heart.*
> *—Rumi*

Think of a news anchor reporting the latest roundup of stories—if you listen closely, you will notice that they have set "sing-song" melodic patterns with regularized "up and down" movements in pitch to create symbolic distance and an objective tone. On the other hand, trained business presenters purposefully *vary* speech tone to effectively convey messages when speaking in professional situations or in intercultural contexts. This rising and falling "melody" is called *intonation.*

Visualize intonation as "speech staircases" that rise and fall. The next time you watch the news, first follow the progression of intonation in a rise-fall pattern by identifying the "speech staircases" in the news anchor's spoken speech. Then, compare this pattern with a dynamic speaker and notice the differences. You'll likely start to notice the power of intonation everywhere, from daily phone conversations to public announcements.

Intonation patterns communicate the complexities of our perspectives and emotions beyond the words we say. Grammatically speaking (in English), *rising intonation* conveys a question ("That's the new proposal?"), while *falling intonation* signals a statement ("That's the new proposal").

When using intonation in unexpected ways, such as *rising* when we should *fall*, we can convey doubt, sarcasm, or annoyance—"That's the new **proposal!?**" On the other hand, if our voice is flat and lacking an expected rise or fall in pitch, we may come off as bored, uninterested, or disappointed. These vocal nuances in English let global audiences know how we feel toward business proposals, meeting topics, and client affairs.

🐱 *Global English Voice Tip*

Besides indicating questions and answers, intonation creates impact:

- Use *rising intonation* to indicate excitement or that more information will follow.

- Use *falling intonation* to convey confidence or make a neutral statement.
- Use *rising intonation* (when it should fall) to sound doubtful, sarcastic, or annoyed.
- Use *falling intonation* (when it should rise) to sound bored, uninterested, or disappointed.

As you target your intonation goals, also consider how others perceive your speech. Just think of what happens to our voices when we're nervous, particularly in a job interview—our pitch tends to go up at the end of our sentences.

People can involuntarily form a habit of using "uptalk" when nervous by raising the pitch of their voice at the end of a statement as if speaking in questions. This speaking style can indicate uncertainty or a lack of confidence. Just imagine if we heard police officers say the following questions with a rising intonation on the last word, "You're under arrest? You have the right to remain silent?" Law enforcement would have a tough time enforcing the law—all due to uptalk.

The only time to use this speaking style is to signal that we're not quite finished talking yet, especially when speaking on a conference call in order to maintain our speaking turn. To prevent uptalk and keep audiences focused on your message, instead of ending a sentence with an upward pitch, use a falling intonation pattern that returns your voice to its usual conversational pitch toward the end of a sentence.

The good news is that intonation can be cultivated consciously to enhance speaking power. As she progressed in her career, former British prime minister Margaret Thatcher received voice training to lower the octaves of her voice, which was often criticized as being shrill. High-pitched voices can trigger anxiety, detracting from a message, whereas low-pitched voices can be regarded as reassuring and constructive. Continually work to cultivate a speaking voice that further enhances your intended meaning and messaging.

As research shows that the intonation of a sentence conveys upwards of 70 percent of its meaning, this hidden business lingo remains a critical tool for communication in professional intercultural presentations or meetings. Try to use intonation patterns to inject your speech with attitude and to better convey your intentions to a global audience.

Activity: Intonation Switcharoo

Practice saying the phrase below using varying intonation to convey the following meanings (intonation clues are included).

1. Say **"It's official"** to mean <u>"That's a surprise!"</u> *(use rising intonation)*

2. Say **"It's official"** to mean <u>"That's annoying!"</u> *(use falling intonation)*

3. Say **"It's official"** to mean <u>"That's awesome!"</u> *(use varied falling and rising intonation)*

4. Say **"It's official"** to mean <u>"That's a relief!"</u> *(use elongated intonation)*

4.9c Rhythm: Calibrating Your Speech

Just as the wind howls, whispers, and screams in gusts of emotion, so does the rush of air coming from our lips. Many stories associate the wind with having a voice, whether *murmuring* as softly as a breeze one moment or *roaring* as fiercely as a hurricane the next. The wind's voice often complements the bursts of weather it carries, and the rush and gusts of our voices complement our messages and intentions. When we use *rhythm* to breathe life into the words we say, we send messages rushing into the hearts and minds of audiences everywhere.

For many people, public speaking practices are built on the foundation of vocal rhythm or pacing. Varying our rhythm and speed of speaking is a powerful way to keep an audience's interest and hold the pulse of the moment. Compare the following:

> *This is the single most important lesson I've learned.*
>
> *This / is the single / most important / lesson / I've learned.*

Now, keep in mind that vocal pacing works in tandem with other vocal characteristics to paint a complete picture of an intention—it is difficult to separate one element from the other for resonant speaking.

Just as in the thought groups section earlier in this chapter, the pauses between these phrases serve as "voiced" punctuation signals that guide the listener through phrases of meaning. Pauses also guide the listener between periods, paragraph divisions, and other punctuation marks.

On the one hand, English has a stress-timed rhythm; for example, the five-word phrase "I will see you tonight" may become "I'll seeya t'nite." In English, unstressed syllables are reduced and shortened. However, rhythm also comes from focus words and important phrases.

🐾 Global English Voice Tip

Use rhythm and pacing in the following ways:

- *Slow down your rhythm* to emphasize key points by using effective pauses.

- *Speed up your rhythm* to provide additional details, build excitement, or invigorate an audience.

- *Vary your rhythm* to maintain interest and to regain attention.

Pacing, in a larger sense, helps our listeners to understand our words, particularly speakers of other languages, and provides them with "mini-breaks" that give them time to process content, stay attentive, and relate to our expressed meanings. Pacing also gives us time to breathe, and conscious breathing gives us more power and control over our speech.

Always remember to vary the speed of your voice as you speak for dynamism. In general, use rhythm to rapidly shift the energy in the room—speed up to engage audiences and slow down when making your most important points. Deliberate pacing gives messages time to be absorbed by intercultural audiences for maximum impact.

Activity: "Pacing Lines"

Read the following statements aloud and compare them for effectiveness.

1. Identify the statement in this grouping that does *not* work as well as the other two. Why?

   a. The person who never gives up / can never be defeated.

   b. The person / who never gives up / can / never / be defeated.

   c. The person who / never gives / up / can / never / be / defeated.

2. Identify the statement in this grouping that does *not* work as well as the other two. Why?

   a. Leadership / goals / are always / team goals.

   b. Leadership goals / are always / team goals.

   c. Leadership / goals / are always team / goals.

Answers:
(1) C, (2) C

....

4.10 The Global Zone: World Empathy

> *Genuineness requires listening through both verbal and nonverbal channels.* **—Joseph Michelli**

Across cultures, we've historically shared a fascination with how we use our bodies and voices for communication, from ancient Egyptian hieroglyphics, pottery, sculptures, texts, and folklores—to modern plays, paintings, and films. Motivating this obsession is the search for an emotional truth—a human truth that perhaps can be expressed only nonverbally.

Most professionals focus on nonverbal strategies for reacting to others and influencing others—whether through vocalics or body language—but the greater consciousness comes from the pursuit of nonverbal patterns for the larger purpose of better *understanding* others. When we approach nonverbal communication in our human bodies, we should not only be motivated by our own needs, but also seek to uncover revelations about each other in our global human society. Empathy penetrates deeper than the surface of our skin.

Research demonstrates that the primary motivation of human gestures is not just to communicate with others, but to express wordless emotions themselves. This is pivotal. Ways of moving and speaking cannot be separated from ways of feeling. And what each of us feels can be humanly comprehensible to all of us in some way.

It's time that we face toward the wind and breathe. If we step back to see the nonverbal patterns between us, our breathing shifts and our perspective connects us as a human family. Our bodies are instruments capable of a shared music around the world. We all possess five senses. We are all capable of laughing, crying, fear, rage, passion, and love. And in this way, as our breaths lead us into a larger shared communion with others in this global air, not only do we learn to use this greatest instrument of the human body for global communication, we also discover how to use it for global understanding as well.

How do we shift negotiations to win-win outcomes in the age of global collaboration?

Connecting with the World: Negotiation in the Age of Collaboration

> *A wise man will make more opportunities than he finds.* **—Sir Francis Bacon**

As our world grows increasingly more interconnected, the negotiation game is changing. At the center of the global crossroads is an archetypal goddess holding aloft a scale, a universal concept of fairness that is evolving among world communities.

The concept of fairness in a negotiation is no longer a scale tipped in our favor, but a balanced scale between collective interests, now and in the future. The expert negotiators of today no longer see negotiating simply as a *win-lose* proposition, but as a *win-win* opportunity for building trust and relationships. Those that focus on partnerships are the most successful negotiators in the world.

The symbol of the scale dates back to ancient Greece and Egypt. We are very familiar with how in times of trade, physical scales determined how the goods and products of harvests were weighed and measured alongside those of other farmers. However, the scale expresses a concept of balance that penetrates deeper than weights and measurements.

In the past, the distorted view of negotiation that is often displayed in the Machiavellian antics in politics, business, and other high-profile transactions we read about in the news have led some to believe that *power* drives negotiations, when in fact the significance of negotiation is much greater.

Instead, the scale raised by the global goddess represents the wisdom emanating from equal measure or *balanced relationships*. True global collaboration means that we must focus on *cooperative* versus *competitive* interests and approaches. A cooperative mindset in decision-making allows us to see and create new outcomes, as well as turn competitors into partners. In business, we cannot focus only on the "goods" of our market as an outcome, but on *relationships* as key areas of growth. In this way, we become global communicators that not only successfully mediate disputes, but also bring harmony to world exchanges.

Most importantly, a win-win approach is paramount to increasing cultural competence, such as in navigating the two larger cultural communication styles, *directness* and *indirectness,* first identified by renowned anthropologist and scholar Edward T. Hall (see Appendix B on *Cultural Contexts*). Cultures that prefer a **direct communication style** value truthfulness and efficiency in negotiations. These cultural interaction patterns tend to be *task-oriented*, and success is viewed as an accumulation of completed tasks and achievements (indicative of Western cultures). On the other hand, cultures who favor an **indirect communication style** value handling negotiations with tact and discretion. These cultural patterns tend to be *relationship-oriented,* and the accomplishment of goals is viewed through group harmony, cooperation, and relationships (indicative of Eastern cultures).

A win-win approach completely changes the interaction of these two communication style preference patterns. With a win-lose approach, global negotiators may be driven in commitment toward one goal and may not take time to be aware of diverse communication styles, nor try to adjust their own style when honing in on a power agreement. However, research shows that negotiators with a win-win approach tend to be more flexible in communication styles. With this approach, **direct negotiators** often learn to soften statements, enter into topics gradually, read "between the lines," and become patient with gentle follow-up requests for decisions. Similarly, with a win-win approach, **indirect negotiators** learn to reassure the other party with sincere and direct answers over a "gentle letdown," while also learning to view direct questions not as a challenge but as a useful indicator of unease that can be reassured by giving a specific time frame when an answer cannot be provided. Essentially, a win-win approach leads to *adaptability,* which creates greater trust, cultural understanding, and collaboration.

The larger picture is that, as our world moves increasingly toward a global community, mutual understanding is important, not just for productive outcomes related to business, but for a stabilized future of diplomacy and world peace. The priority in global negotiations is not one party's accomplishments but maintaining professional and human relationships. If you are a *task-oriented* negotiator, you must make time for relationship-building. If you are a *relationship-oriented* negotiator, you must make time to include explicit communication regarding your proposals and decision points. Above all, we must trust the power of a win-win and mutual gain approach, whether or not the other party uses the same approach. Global influence first begins with each of us. Only then can we move beyond positional bargaining and arrive at a shared respect and understanding across cultures.

Traditionally, in the past, we prized the hard negotiator who was simply focused on winning by making demands and prioritizing their own principles. However, these negotiators lost sight of the opportunities that can be discovered when arriving at an impactful outcome benefiting both parties. Today, the successful global negotiator is not a hard or soft negotiator—but a *creative* negotiator, focused on cultivating relationships that create present and future benefits for all involved. As notable philosopher and statesman Sir Francis Bacon said: "A wise man will make more opportunities than he finds." You never know what future opportunities a partnership can bring.

In this chapter, we will explore how to become an intercultural creative negotiator, incorporating patterns of behavior that look for agreement, mutual gain, and long-term partnerships. At the same time, we will cultivate a strategic approach to building collaborative environments, handling conflict, and arriving at joint ways to influence outcomes in the interest of both you and the other party. As an essential skill of the modern business professional, becoming a creative negotiator can be developed and perfected to achieve trust and positive results at the global negotiating table. Let's begin.

5.1 The Crossroads of Negotiation: From a Path of Competition to Cooperation

> *To every problem, there is a most simple solution.*
> **–Agatha Christie**

Standing at the crossroads of a negotiation, we are faced with the "negotiator's dilemma" as we choose between pursuing the path of a competitive or cooperative approach. The proverbial scales peer at us from the apex of these crossroads, awaiting our decisions. Will we tip those scales in our favor? Or will we use the scales to achieve balance?

We are constantly searching for a sense of balance in everything we do—ways to balance our relationships so that we are equal partners and ways to balance our spending so that we don't spend more than we earn. In terms of negotiation, if we can shift our perspectives to bring that same concept of balance to our negotiation outcomes, then we'll be well on our way to impacting cultural audiences as global communicators. The approach to take at this crossroads is the *cooperative* route.

Every negotiation is a combination of two basic approaches: **distributive** (win-lose) and **integrative** (win-win). Both approaches get their fair share of attention in negotiation decision-making; however, in intercultural negotiations, integrative approaches are the primary part of the negotiation process, as they lead to successful intercultural communication and understanding.

At the negotiation crossroads, it's tempting to take the detour around rapport and relationship-building to set sights on only one outcome—to gain independent advantage and get the best possible deal (such as in private sales, at the customer service counter, or while online discount shopping). Other times we may pursue an imbalanced conflict resolution, where one team aims to win and cause another one to lose (think of custody battles, warranty disputes, or compensation discussions). These forms of negotiation, commonly referred to as **distributive bargaining,** or win-lose, are encouraged as "bargaining" in some cultural communities, even though modern negotiation theorists emphasize the importance of mutual gain in successful intercultural negotiations. A "win-lose" form of bargaining is tempting because in a high-stakes dispute, especially if "the pie" (the value of an outcome) seems fixed, such conflicts appear resistant to a joint resolution.

However, every "piece of the pie" can be expanded—each party can be given more of an equal share in the negotiation process. Every negotiation can be turned into an **integrative bargaining** situation, or win-win situation, with the right approach and perspective. A negotiation is about more than getting "the most" from the other party, especially in an intercultural context—to be global negotiators, we must keep a cooperative, open-minded mentality going into every interaction with a range of win-win outcomes. An integrative approach allows us to expand our vision into multiple viewpoints at once and find balance in the flow of every dialogue.

As we walk down the integrative path toward negotiation, remember that the ultimate goal is finding common ground on a particular issue and preserving relationships to bring about unity between parties. Awareness transforms our needs and wants until we begin to see an abundance of opportunities within every choice. This goal requires a tremendous but rewarding cognitive *shift* in perspective.

Global Negotiation Tip

See every negotiation as a partnership opportunity and you will discover new and better solutions than you or the other party previously conceived.

Part I: The Framework for Successful Intercultural Negotiation

5.2 Patterns of Collaboration and the Win-Win Mindset

> *Identify your problems but give your power and energy to solutions.* **–Tony Robbins**

When every negotiation situation is seen as a partnership opportunity, new solutions emerge. In other words, new options for mutual gain come to light as *similarities* between parties dominate the minds of negotiators. The *integrative negotiation* practice is the approach of the most successful intercultural negotiators—and not only creates better relationships and more effective communication, but also results in the unique benefits of a joint problem-solving approach. This mindset has a powerful impact on decision-making. To illustrate the power and importance of this shift in perspective, let's consider the following tale of two cooks and a lemon.

5.2a Two Cooks and a Lemon: An Integrative Case Study

> *The best move you can make in negotiation is to think of an incentive the other person hasn't even thought of—and then meet it.* **–Eli Broad**

Imagine that two cooks are fighting over the last lemon remaining in their restaurant kitchen. Both cooks desperately need the lemon to fulfill time-sensitive orders. The ultimate dilemma they face is, How should they decide which cook gets the lemon and which does not? Based on what? What would be the fairest way to resolve the dispute?

A distributive win-lose negotiator would search for a way to win the *whole lemon,* either by force, demand, manipulation, or even threat. Indeed, the first cook tries this approach. However, when we inadvertently overlook the other party's interests in a negotiation, we can end up focusing simply on *short-sighted goals* and *missing alternative outcomes*—in this case, the cook only envisions getting the lemon, and in this win-win perspective, no other option seems viable. Also, with waiting customers outside, walking away is not an option either.

On the surface it may seem that there is only one other alternative—perhaps the fairest resolution would be to divide the lemon in half. However, this would not be optimal for either cook as their recipes call for more than half a portion of a lemon. This is a dilemma indeed!

So, what other options are there? What would an integrative win-win negotiator do? Well, *trust* can seem anathema to the competitive and distributive negotiator—but to the integrative creative negotiator, trust is the building block of success (from bargaining cooks to executives). The second cook takes this win-win approach. And by recognizing that he must integrate the other cook's goals alongside his own goals—he focuses on the *long-term objective* of arriving at an outcome that benefits both parties and their stakeholders (in this case, their customers). He then begins to think beyond immediate options and begins to ask questions in order to reveal creative solutions.

And the turning point for him is this: *What if we approach the negotiation by* asking *instead of demanding?*

In other words, what if one cook asks the other cook what he wants the lemon for?

As it turns out, the first cook needs the *fruit* of the lemon to make lemonade. The second cook needs the *peels* to make candied lemon peels. Since they both need different parts of the lemon, they can both "win" if the situation is resolved as an integrative win-win bargaining situation. All it takes is a different approach and perspective to negotiating.

See Figure 5-1 for an example of the creative solutions that emerge when we share a win-win mindset with our negotiation partner. This simple scenario illustrates, cognitively, the opportunities that melt into focus when choosing an integrative win-win negotiation over a distributive win-lose negotiation as a dominant strategy. When we "expand the pie," or boundaries of the negotiation, we allow both ourselves and the other party to create new value and satisfy needs. The "pie" may be an object, or it may even simply be the *information* pertaining to the negotiation situation. The solution to a dispute usually has less to do with the *object* of the dispute and more with the *desires* involved in the dispute. For example, cutting the lemon in half may have seemed fair, but it was not the ideal outcome for either cook.

The story of two cooks and a lemon reveals how a win-win mindset can uncover new solutions neither party had previously imagined.

Figure 5-1

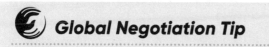 **Global Negotiation Tip**

The most powerful win-win negotiation strategy is not making the right statements but asking the right questions.

Exchanging *demands* in a negotiation inhibits creative thought processes. However, creative solutions emerge when we treat all possibilities as viable, while also being willing to explore and generate new joint options.

Across cultural contexts, patterns of behavior change when we focus on different outcomes. The practice of a *hard* negotiator is competitive, and a *soft* negotiator is accommodating—however, the *creative* negotiator is *collaborative*. This scenario illustrates the importance of *information-sharing* in negotiation and the importance of trust in, ultimately, arriving at a successful win-win integrative negotiation outcome.

···

Activities: Negotiation Creativity

1. **Turn it around:** All distributive (win-lose) negotiation situations can be turned into integrative (win-win) negotiation outcomes. Examine even the most common win-lose bargaining situations, such as private sales, customer-service-counter interactions, online discount shopping, custody battles, warranty disputes, and compensation discussions. What are ways each of these scenarios could be turned into win-win situations? Then, think of a specific bargaining situation you are facing right now in your own life. Why does it feel one-sided? Has all the information been shared? How can a win-win approach help? What new opportunities or solutions come to mind when adopting this perspective?

2. **Perspective shift:** Becoming a creative negotiator involves a deep *shift* in perspective—namely a shift in the attitude that directs your behavioral pattern. See if you can divide the following behaviors into the correct columns below that correspond with the characteristics pertaining to the two types of negotiation styles, *integrative (win-win)* and *distributive (win-lose)*.

NEGOTIATION BEHAVIORS: INTEGRATIVE VERSUS DISTRIBUTIVE			
Applies pressure	Is open about interests and uses fair principles	The goal is victory	Is diplomatic and favors collaboration
Is aggressive and demands concessions	Participants are competitors	Is misleading and purposely omits details	Insists on opinions and point of view
Appeals to reason, creativity, and principle	Seeks win-lose opportunities	Prioritizes interests over positions	The goal is collective agreement
Seeks win-win opportunities	Insists on impartial standards and integrated perspectives	Participants are partners	Emphasizes position and inflexibility

Determine which behaviors correspond with integrative (win-win) negotiation versus distributive (win-lose) bargaining, and write the above behaviors in parallel, placing each in the two corresponding columns that follow. The first set of parallel items have been done for you.

INTEGRATIVE NEGOTIATION	DISTRIBUTIVE BARGAINING
1. participants are partners	1. participants are competitors
2.	2.
3.	3.
4.	4.
5.	5.
6.	6.
7.	7.
8.	8.

Answers:
The numbers below refer to parallel pairings.

Integrative negotiation:
(1) *participants are partners,* **(2)** *the goal is collective agreement,* **(3)** *is diplomatic and favors collaboration,* **(4)** *prioritizes interests over positions,* **(5)** *is open about interests and uses fair principles,* **(6)** *insists on impartial standards and integrated perspectives,* **(7)** *appeals to reason, creativity, and principle,* **(8)** *seeks win-win opportunities*

Distributive bargaining:

(1) *participants are competitors,* **(2)** *the goal is victory,* **(3)** *is aggressive and demands concessions,* **(4)** *emphasizes position and inflexibility,* **(5)** *is misleading and purposely omits details,* **(6)** *insists on opinions and point of view,* **(7)** *applies pressure,* **(8)** *seeks win-lose opportunities*

Final reflection:

Finally, examine which of these behaviors you want to change, and most importantly, which behaviors you want to integrate into your own negotiation practice. How can win-win negotiation practices become more habitual in your thoughts and actions? How can creative behaviors help you discover opportunities and solutions in your next negotiation situation?

....

5.3 Partnership Bargaining: Concessions and the Satisfaction "Trade-Off"

> *The basis of social relationships is reciprocity: if you cooperate with others, others will cooperate with you.*
> **—Carroll Quigley**

How do we strategize the "give-and-take" process? In the heat of a negotiation, patterns of behavior can mentally start to resemble a sports team's playbook containing a collection of a coach's strategies and game plans, where core strategies are depicted as "X's" and "O's," to create an array of converging offensive and defensive patterns in hopes of reaching a shared goal. Just as every coach in a sports scenario mentally reviews a steady rundown of possible plays, as negotiators, we must also often consider sets of strategic moves in each negotiation scenario.

However, when approaching negotiations from a cooperative standpoint, we must broaden our viewpoint from a negotiating playbook. Instead, we must use a creative perspective to shift the ebb and flow of *competitive* decision points toward *cooperative* ones.

First, we have to expand our definition of relationships, as *a partnership where the meaning of the relationship between parties extends from the present to the future in a way that influences all current interactions.* This definition incorporates the history and future of the relationship, as well as a greater collective meaning than what each individual party brings to the partnership. With this definition in place, the concept of concessions changes in a substantive way as these "trade-offs" relate to the present and future relationship.

Now, keeping the larger win-win approach in mind, even if we are entering a negotiation from a creative perspective and not a competitive standpoint, some form of "bargaining" behavior is always involved. Bargaining, while common in many parts of the world, often involves the discussion of price and is driven by an overlapping of goals and perspectives between parties. But the method changes with a shift in perspective and goal. So, just how does a creative negotiator who favors win-win outcomes even begin to approach bargaining situations?

Even to find the best win-win solution, all negotiations, regardless of professional or intercultural contexts, require making offers and counteroffers—bargaining remains a critical aspect of any "trade-off," whether negotiating through written correspondence or orally.

But as creative and global negotiators, we must differentiate our exchanges during the "give-and-take" process from *haggling*—a term for a stern negotiating game where the exchange of rigid offers forces the other party to compromise. While patterns of haggling are practiced in many areas of Asia, Latin America, the Middle East, and North Africa, and are often regarded as a welcome pastime to see who can best the other person, to the global negotiator, the objective instead is goodwill and reciprocity, even when making concessions.

As creative negotiators, especially when negotiating in intercultural contexts, we must identify opportunities for concession that move beyond immediate gains and create solutions where both parties share in the promise of joint gains (shared mutual opportunities of value). To do this in a win-win integrative bargaining situation, you must get to know the other party by finding out their true interests and what they value the most.

A **concession** is an offer of equal or lesser value that is made during the negotiation process. However, what many don't realize is that concessions can help us enhance our position, while at the same time encouraging the other party to consider a "trade-off" that likely brings both parties closer to an agreement. Even if either or both parties begin a negotiation with high and low offers, relationship parameters in a win-win approach can bring all teams to a middle ground with new accommodations very quickly.

As a key strategy, according to Bill Scott, author of *The Skills of Negotiating,* when preparing for negotiation concessions, first identify what the other side will be happy to gain and then *concede what is low-cost to you yet valuable to them.* In other words, if the other party feels that they are winning concessions, they will, ultimately, be more likely to concede on issues that are important to you.

However, keep in mind what Gavin Kennedy, author of *The New Negotiating Edge,* advises: we must not get trapped in the extremes of giving-and-taking behavior in negotiations. Instead, we should engage in patterns of *authentic* trading behavior and focus on people as they are, not as how we want them to be. When we focus on agreement as a broad principle, we are more likely to arrive at a consensus that both sides feel is to their advantage.

5.4 Creating Your Flow: How to Build Team Synergy in Negotiations

> *Strategy is a pattern in a stream of decisions.*
> *—Henry Mintzberg*

In the game of chess, with each chess piece we slide into position across the chessboard, we must *think* several moves ahead in anticipation. In fact, grandmaster chess players are said to think an astounding twenty-five to thirty positions in advance! Similarly, effective team negotiators must trace patterns of logic together on the in-person or virtual chessboard. As our remote teams expand globally and our communication cues evolve, our team synergy in-person and online must be connected to a deeper understanding of the fundamental stages of a negotiation.

Every effective negotiation starts with a negotiation success plan; however, even more important in intercultural negotiations is understanding the customary stages in the actual *flow* of the negotiation. Whether negotiating individually or in teams, navigating this flow is essential to influencing intercultural interaction once the dialogue begins.

Modeling the actual negotiation stages should not be prescriptive. Rather, when preparing for intercultural negotiations, we must first forge our team synergy from a series of stages that allows us to jointly *anticipate* and act upon next moves, while remaining flexible in the process. Especially online, negotiation is driven by team decision-making, and a framework allows us to set clear goals and a strategy for reaching those goals. Subsequently, this team synergy must also be adaptable within the negotiation cycle and go deeper than the subtle in-person or virtual cultural cues in the conference room or in cyberspace.

5.4a The Six Intercultural Negotiation Stages

Use the intercultural negotiation model depicted in Figure 5-2 to launch a team synergy toward a shared goal. This general blueprint of steps highlights the cultural dimensions associated with preparation, analysis, and execution in intercultural negotiations. First train yourself and your team to think in this larger sequence. Remember that an intercultural negotiation is not about a climactic "showdown," but about mutual agreement. You and the other party are connected by shared interests; therefore, always keep the "give-and-take" process focused on *mutual gain.*

The Six Intercultural Negotiation Stages

Stage 1: Start with a profile.

- Internalize cultural research regarding values, goals, and identities.

- Identify shared interests, joint principles, and points of collaboration.

Stage 2: Build relationships.

- Build trust around shared interests and get to know one another.

- Note cultural preferences related to relationship- and task-orientation.

- Lay a strong foundation for the success of later stages, such as allowing new mutual solutions to surface.

Stage 3: Exchange information.

- Learn about and evolve individual positions toward aligned interests.

- Create and discover shared value among all parties.

- Observe cultural propensity toward logical, emotional, and ideological appeals.

Stage 4: Exchange offers.

- Start the "give-and-take" process focused on satisfying mutual interests.
- Observe cultural propensity for making extreme or moderate offers based on relationship- and task-orientation.
- Recognize cultural perspectives, avoid rigid positions, be flexible, pose questions instead of statements around disagreements, and create value to nurture trust.

Stage 5: Confirm agreement.

- Confirm points of agreement and jointly fulfilled interests.
- Note cultural nuances regarding oral and written confirmations of agreement.
- Prepare written contract of appropriate length:
  - A *brief* contract emphasizing trust is relationship-oriented (high-context cultures).
  - A *lengthy* contract with precise terms is task-oriented (low-context cultures).

Stage 6: Expand the global partnership.

- Implement formal agreement, honor commitments, and maximize joint returns.
- Note cultural negotiation goal and process (e.g., signed contract or new relationship).
- Expand value, address new shared interests, and initiate the next negotiation opportunity.

The 6 Intercultural Negotiation Stages

Every successful negotiation starts with planning, especially virtually. Train yourself to think in the larger negotiation sequence. Remember, some intercultural negotiations may linger more in certain stages than others depending on *high-context* or *low-context* cultural dimensions.

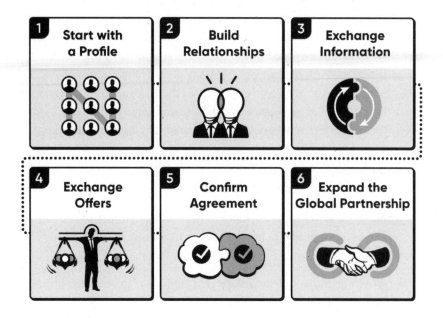

Build Linguistic Patterns

Use **adjacency pairs** to effectively structure a negotiation and build a conversation toward intended outcomes.

Figure 5-2

5.4b **Adjacency Pairs**

Successful negotiators also build strategy linguistically through the *dialogue* itself. In the chess game of negotiation, the process is also a game of words, so learn to isolate the most basic linguistic pattern—the **adjacency pair.**

These basic coupled sequences in a dialogue range from *question-answer* to *instruction-compliance* to *statement-acknowledgment.* The idea is to think at least three conversation turns in advance. Just think about when you ask the question "How are you?" and expect the usual response of "Fine—and you?" By anticipating your future response, you are already thinking three conversational moves ahead to where you want to guide the dialogue. Once you learn to break down a complex negotiation into these paired sequences or *conversation turns,* you can deliberately build conversations toward intended outcomes.

> ## Thinking in Adjacency Pairs
>
> As highlighted in Figure 5-2, learn to work with *adjacency pairs* in an international negotiation (remember, each pair should be conditionally relevant):
>
> - When giving an *opening statement,* already plan your response to possible *return statements.*
> - When giving a *question,* prepare to follow up on possible *answers* you could receive.
> - When giving an *offer,* plan potential responses to the *acceptance/refusal/counteroffer* you may receive.
> - When giving a *concession,* plan for additional replies to the *acceptance/refusal* you may receive.

The concept of *adjacency pairs* is merely a framework—however, it helps shape expectations, understanding, and actions. This is true especially among pairs where the first part *isn't* followed by the expected second part. Contrast the expected *adjacency pair* below with one that is not—what conclusions can be made?

EXPECTED ADJACENCY PAIR	UNEXPECTED ADJACENCY PAIR
A. Do you agree with the new policy? B. Yes.	A. Do you agree with the new policy? B. In what respect?

An unexpected *adjacency pair* can also allow you to notice important attributes of the exchange, such as inferred agreement, cultural dimensions, and disposition. Train your mind to think linguistically in terms of *adjacency pairs* and witness your strategic thinking evolve, especially in the six larger intercultural negotiation stages. Overall, global teams must be able to recognize patterned choices on the global chessboard. Once we link awareness with planning, then we truly begin to develop the progressive decision-making skills that are vital to effective intercultural negotiations.

5.5 Effectively Structuring the Negotiation Process: Starting with the Big Picture

> *You never really understand a person until you consider things from his point of view.* **—Harper Lee**

So how exactly does the structure of a win-win integrative negotiation differ from a win-lose competitive negotiation? Well, win-lose negotiations tend to be *single-issue* negotiations committed to distributive outcomes that are beneficial for ourselves, whereas win-win negotiations tend to be *multiple-issue* negotiations committed to organically creating packages that are mutually beneficial and ideal for all parties.

Let's look at two versions of the same call in Figure 5-3, where Vista Hospital, a research medical institution located in Porto Alegre, Brazil, is negotiating with New York–based Sunnyside Hospital in the United States over the purchase of new portable diagnostic devices. Although both win-lose and win-win negotiations contain the potential for agreement, the win-win negotiation is more effective in the organic creation of a mutually-beneficial outcome, because Vista Hospital approaches the interaction from a standpoint of "*Why* do you want this?" instead of asking "*What* do you want?"

Case Study: 2 Negotiation Approaches

Two hospitals negotiate over the purchase of new portable diagnostic devices. Compare two versions of the same call – a **"win-lose"** approach versus a **"win-win"** approach.

Distributive Negotiation
(Win-Lose)

VISTA HOSPITAL
Porto Alegre, Brazil

SUNNYSIDE HOSPITAL
New York, NY, USA

CALL OPENS ······▶

Offer to buy 40 portable diagnostic devices if *Vista* can give you a good price.

Ask
What
models they want.

You seek to purchase 40 new portable diagnostic devices with mobile medical application.

Say that your prices vary due to demand and need.

Ask for a discount.

Say a discount could be possible if **Sunnyside** agrees to pay for shipping costs.

Tentatively agree.

Offer 4% discount.

Ask for 8%.

Unfortunately, you can't agree unless **Sunnyside** pays for the data software package upgrade.

Suggest an adjournment to consider the offer.

Confirm adjournment.

······▶ **CALL ENDS.**

Figure 5-3a

How does the approach influence the outcome?

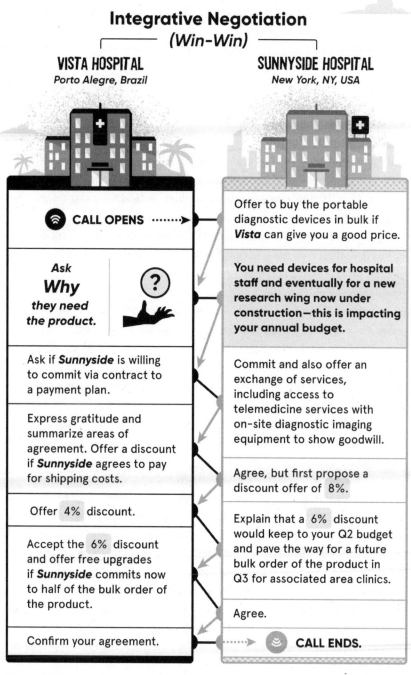

Integrative Negotiation
(Win-Win)

VISTA HOSPITAL
Porto Alegre, Brazil

SUNNYSIDE HOSPITAL
New York, NY, USA

CALL OPENS

Offer to buy the portable diagnostic devices in bulk if **Vista** can give you a good price.

Ask **Why** they need the product.

You need devices for hospital staff and eventually for a new research wing now under construction—this is impacting your annual budget.

Ask if **Sunnyside** is willing to commit via contract to a payment plan.

Commit and also offer an exchange of services, including access to telemedicine services with on-site diagnostic imaging equipment to show goodwill.

Express gratitude and summarize areas of agreement. Offer a discount if **Sunnyside** agrees to pay for shipping costs.

Agree, but first propose a discount offer of 8%.

Offer 4% discount.

Explain that a 6% discount would keep to your Q2 budget and pave the way for a future bulk order of the product in Q3 for associated area clinics.

Accept the 6% discount and offer free upgrades if **Sunnyside** commits now to half of the bulk order of the product.

Agree.

Confirm your agreement.

CALL ENDS.

Figure 5-3b

Overall, Vista Hospital focused on underlying interests to better position their offer and incentivize Sunnyside Hospital to commit to a bulk order of the product with the added value of free data software package upgrades on their order. Furthermore, Sunnyside Hospital created value by offering access to telemedicine services with remote on-site diagnostic imaging equipment as a show of goodwill. As a creative negotiator, moving away from competitive elements, such as a focus on price, and toward other incentives can lead us closer to negotiation and integrative success.

Vista Hospital saw the potential for collaborative negotiation by arriving at a fair agreement and satisfying the needs of both parties. Instead of being rigid and tactfully issuing threats, the win-win negotiator seeks information to determine motives, preserves open-mindedness, and taps into creativity to invent options that will satisfy the key interests of both parties. All it takes is this shift in perspective to uncover joint solutions and to build long-term relationships.

As creative negotiators, we must frame a bargaining situation collectively, as in the outcome of the win-win hospital negotiation in Figure 5-3. Additionally, an integrative approach opens possibilities for negotiating in *parallel* versus negotiating each point as items in a series. When we negotiate in parallel, we put all issues on the table at once, instead of going through items in sequence or in a list. The upside to this way of negotiating, as opposed to alternating between items in succession, is our ability to effectively create a larger negotiation picture by *trading* between issues we believe are most important, creating joint flexibility in a shared approach, and accelerating the bargaining process toward value-creating by jointly keeping this "big picture" in mind throughout the negotiation.

Again, being a creative negotiator doesn't mean we are *soft* negotiators. A win-win approach doesn't mean that we must sacrifice our own interests, but that we are clear about *what* we want and *why* we want it—while also establishing *what* the other party wants and *why* they want it. When done successfully, a creative negotiator uses this information to create high-value solutions for the benefit of both parties. In the global marketplace, this integrative approach to bargaining cultivates respect and results in establishing more effective relationships, solutions, and communication.

We must also consider how culture affects bargaining displays in every country. For example, *Harvard Business Review*'s "Negotiating Across Culture" series concludes that out of respect, many collectivist cultures across regions of Asia, South America, Central America, and Africa will appear to say yes when they really mean no. Or, at times, these cultures will say "We will try our best," which often translates to "No, it's not possible." These cultural nuances are quite the opposite in individualistic cultures like the United States, parts of Canada, Northwestern and North-Central Europe, Scandinavia, and Australia/New Zealand (see Appendix B on *Cultural Contexts*).

Overall, global negotiations require that we understand and adapt to intercultural conversational styles in the creation of mutually-beneficial outcomes. Doing so will demonstrate our respect for values and our commitment to solutions. Therefore, to effectively structure a negotiation, include room for *information-gathering* to inform decisions and guide intercultural dialogues. Avoid yes/no questions (closed questions) and, instead, ask more open-ended questions. Always find other ways to interlink goals.

5.6 Taking Off the Fighting Gloves: Handling Conflict

> *You cannot shake hands with a clenched fist.*
> **—Indira Gandhi**

Conflict is sometimes unavoidable on the negotiation path, but there is always an alternative route toward solutions. Do opposites attract? Well, that depends on whether you are talking to a physicist or a communications expert. We see this phenomenon happen when we bring two magnets together. If you place the north pole of a magnet near the south pole of another, the magnets attract each other. But, flip one end so the north pole of a magnet is near the north pole of another, and you'll have yourself in an uphill battle with the repellant forces in basic physics.

Negotiations—especially on the global scale—function in similar ways, where we feel that we have entered a *cultural* magnetic field only to feel like we are struggling to connect in meaningful ways. Sometimes all we have to do is reorient ourselves. This magnet metaphor can explain why in some of our intercultural negotiations we must always be open to trying new approaches when the going gets tough.

Conflict can lead us to a sudden breakdown of negotiations, but with the right communications approach, conflict resolution is always possible. Even if an agreement seems unimaginable, focusing on the partnership can salvage most negotiations, according to Gavin Kennedy in the *Pocket Negotiator.* When conflict arises, try appealing to the relationship and emphasizing the loss to both sides of not reaching an agreement, whether through inventing new options for mutual gain or changing the "negotiation package." If necessary, adjourn to think and reflect, change location, change lead negotiators, or bring in a third-party mediator (otherwise known as an arbitrator). Your goal is to get the negotiation back on track and have both parties' magnetic fields align to get the conversation moving forward.

But reducing conflict doesn't mean that we instinctively give up on tough negotiations. As mentioned, some cultures even welcome healthy debate. Skilled communicators negotiate as long as possible until reaching their Best Alternative to a Negotiated Agreement (BATNA)—a result of careful planning and outcome preparation. The term *BATNA*, made famous by Roger Fisher and William Ury in their book *Getting to Yes*, refers to your *leverage*, the power that you have to influence the negotiation. Leverage comes in many forms—usually as information—and can be used to sway the other party to concede on particular issues holding up the negotiation. For example, if we are negotiating our salary, our BATNA may include having another job offer. Likewise, in a rent dispute during a lease renewal contract negotiation, the BATNA could be having another apartment option in reserve.

Let's take a closer look. In high-conflict negotiations, such as in diplomatic affairs involving territorial disputes and disarmament, negotiators can find themselves in a standoff, either because they want to wait as long as possible before revealing their BATNA or because they haven't adequately prepared their BATNA. For Eastern cultures that are indirect and relationship-oriented, disclosing a BATNA, or "make or break" point, may take a long time, while for Western cultures that are direct and task-oriented, revealing their BATNA earlier may appear strategic depending on the direction of the negotiation. Overall, while the distributive win-lose negotiator may reveal their leverage as a last resort, a threat, or even a last-ditch effort, the creative negotiator handles their BATNA differently.

🌀 Global Negotiation Tip

Reveal your BATNA only when it creates leverage and the power to make your request fully heard by the other party.

The creative negotiator regards their BATNA as a natural part of an honest series of dialogues consisting of offers, decisions, rejections, counteroffers, and compromises—collectively referred to as **the bargaining mix.** This straightforward approach encourages a willingness from the other side to participate in an open exchange of information and interests to create shared value, and ultimately reveal where there is potential for resolution in claiming a "piece of the pie." Now, who wouldn't want that? Otherwise, we think of our leverage in a distributive way, simply as a final key planning strategy, so that we can go into a negotiation situation with the confidence that we have nothing to lose. However, we never want to lose the relationship, which is why the BATNA should be handled with great care.

As negotiations unfold, even if you have to take a break before coming back to the topic, always summarize progress and areas of agreement with the other party. This intercultural best practice will help you stay focused on win-win outcomes and will put the other party at ease. Remember, walking away from the partnership should be a last resort.

Part II: The Axis of Negotiations: Relationships

5.7 The Intercultural Connection: Deal-Making and Partnerships in Global Negotiations

> *Language and culture are the frameworks through which humans experience, communicate, and understand reality.* **—Lev Vygotsky**

In order to forge intercultural agreements with others, we must develop an awareness of the intricate communication patterns underlying the unique cultures of the world. Like an infinite mosaic of colors and shapes coming into focus when we look through a kaleidoscope, the background of cultural nuances may be unconsciously overlooked in the foreground of negotiations. However, building our dialogues with an awareness of varying communication styles among the mosaic of interactions will result in larger gains and a greater intercultural perspective.

Today, to be a global negotiator is to acknowledge that cultures are constantly being shaped and molded by shared influences and so, too, is our understanding as circumstances change. As our exchanges become more globalized, the world will continue to become more integrated—and an intercultural perspective will become the unifying characteristic for succeeding as a global negotiator. We just have to train ourselves to become more aware of the overlapping style patterns in our intercultural conversations. After all, in terms of finding the intersection points of cultural information and cultural universality—it's all in the details.

The global negotiator not only bridges gaps in communication, but bridges cultures as well. Negotiations have moved beyond being a simple business process to a much deeper level of human and cultural interaction. Sure, in our technological age, data-techies are seeking to uncover the harbored "secret negotiation formula" found within patterns, trends, and associations. Poring over data sets, some people hope to find the blueprint for the perfect and quintessential negotiation plan. After all, who wouldn't want a negotiation "recipe" for perfectly matching their goals across any distance to another company's goals?

However, the answer won't be found in digital platforms and algorithmic code. Instead, negotiation strategies that are rooted in deeper levels of human interaction are essential to understanding intercultural norms and developing a culturally-responsive negotiation strategy. The real question is how to peer into the minds of other cultures and gain a deeper understanding of their inner motivations and behaviors. In order to be a creative negotiator that is a global communicator, we must be able to navigate cultural dimensions as naturally as walking, with an open mind and purposeful step.

In order to develop a more informed *international perspective,* our primary axis point in intercultural business is the overlap and shift of **cultural dimensions** identified by Dutch social psychologist Geert Hofstede in his extensive research on national cultural values. These characteristics are based on the complex system of decision-making patterns of the international business world that continue to evolve across diversity at the individual and cultural level.

In intercultural negotiations, cultural norms and values play an integral part not only in influencing communication—but also in influencing negotiation outcomes. A global negotiator must instill an awareness of Hofstede's five *cultural dimensions,* outlined in his influential work, *Cultures and Organizations: Software of the Mind,* before arriving at creative solutions that respect the deeper characteristics of the cultures in the world and enrich the negotiation process for all involved (see Appendix B on *Cultural Contexts*). Look at the five decision-making influences in global negotiations adapted from Hofstede's work, as indicated in Figure 5-4. When in an intercultural negotiation, identify these underlying values that influence decision-making in the negotiation. Focus on observable patterns of behavior. Then, use your observations to arrive at win-win outcomes. Keep in mind that influences may vary by individual and occupation as well as culture.

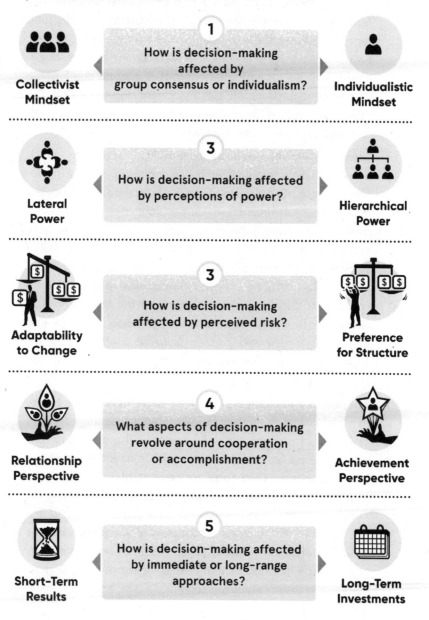

The 5 Key Decision-Making Influences in Global Negotiations

Identify the underlying values that may influence decision-making in intercultural negotiations. Focus on observable patterns. *How can your observations create win-win outcomes?*

1 How is decision-making affected by group consensus or individualism?

Collectivist Mindset — Individualistic Mindset

3 How is decision-making affected by perceptions of power?

Lateral Power — Hierarchical Power

3 How is decision-making affected by perceived risk?

Adaptability to Change — Preference for Structure

4 What aspects of decision-making revolve around cooperation or accomplishment?

Relationship Perspective — Achievement Perspective

5 How is decision-making affected by immediate or long-range approaches?

Short-Term Results — Long-Term Investments

Figure 5-4

Decision-Making Parameters

- **Collectivist mindset/individualistic mindset:** The degree to which decision-making is linked to group contributions or individual positions. Negotiators with a **collectivist mindset** may favor rapport with the same negotiating parties over the long term, prioritizing the relationship when completing the deal. *Style preference pattern: Eastern or high-context cultures.* Negotiators with an **individualistic mindset** may be comfortable switching negotiators mid-process, prioritizing the task in the interest of successfully completing a deal. *Style preference pattern: Western or low-context cultures.*

- **Lateral power/hierarchical power:** The degree to which decision-making is influenced by viewpoints of power distribution among parties. Negotiators with a **lateral power** worldview tend to distribute decision-making authority evenly across team members, expediting the negotiation process. *Style preference pattern: parts of Northwestern and North-Central Europe, most of Scandinavia, the United States, parts of Canada, and Australia/New Zealand.* Negotiators with **hierarchical power** tend to concentrate decision-making authority at the highest level of leadership, resulting in a lengthier negotiation and approvals process. *Style preference pattern: East Asia, Southeast Asia, the Middle East, parts of Eastern Europe, most of Latin America, and the majority of Africa.*

- **Adaptability to change/preference for structure:** The degree to which decision-making is influenced by comfort level in ambiguous situations. This influence may also pertain to how decisions are affected by perceived risk in negotiations. Negotiators **adaptable to change** are comfortable in unstructured situations and flexible parameters. *Style preference pattern: the United States, the United Kingdom, parts of Canada, Australia, and Chinese and Nordic cultures.* Negotiators with a **preference for structure** are likely to avoid vague scenarios and prefer clear parameters in the negotiation process. *Style preference pattern: Eastern and Central European countries, Japan, and Latin American countries.*

- **Relationship perspective/achievement perspective:** The degree to which decision-making is influenced by values favoring relationship-oriented outcomes versus goal-oriented outcomes. Relationship perspectives favor quality of life and lasting connections with others, whereas achievement perspectives favor assertiveness and tangible success. Negotiators with a **relationship** worldview may practice more empathy and concessions during negotiations. *Style preference pattern: Nordic countries, the Netherlands, some Latin countries (such as Spain, Chile, and Portugal), and some Asian countries (such as Thailand and Korea).* Negotiators with an **achievement** worldview may practice a results-oriented and value-claiming approach. *Style preference pattern: Eastern and Central European countries, Japan, some Latin countries (such as Mexico and Italy), and the United States and parts of Canada.*

- **Short-term results/long-term investments:** The degree to which decision-making in the face of change adheres to preferences for **short-term** approaches based on tradition or *familiar* present parameters, versus long-term approaches, which focus on adapting to *new* parameters and future outlooks. Negotiators with a short-term worldview focus on personal stability and immediate return on investment. *Style preference pattern: the United States, Australia, Latin America, the Middle East, North Africa, and parts of Southeast Asia.* Negotiations with a **long-term** worldview may focus on strengthening relationships via long-range planning and strategic investments. *Style preference pattern: East Asian countries, Eastern Europe, and Central Europe.*

You may be thinking that these five *cultural dimensions* also provide important information about how societies organize themselves. Well, these dimensions not only aid us in responding to cultural patterns in a negotiation, but also provide a greater understanding of cultural contexts. By keeping these attributes in mind, we can discover additional ways to manage communication in order to co-create options that fulfill both parties' underlying values and interests.

Just as a painter adds new colors to the palette, as global negotiators, we must integrate all these cultural dimensions into our negotiation toolkit in order to orient ourselves within intercultural interactions. In this way, we can push past *competition* and *conflict* in order to arrive at *cooperation* and *opportunity*.

Now, integrating these cultural dimensions into our negotiating reality takes discipline, preparation, and skill. But once we take this approach, we enter another level of creative negotiation—where, instead of focusing on *planning* for concessions and counteroffers, we shift the dialogue toward *initiating* a joint solution to the issue at hand. Additionally, research and information-gathering are the two primary tools at our disposal for better understanding the other party and arriving at a win-win negotiation. And in this way, we begin to build the authentic trust needed to foster long-term and beneficial relationships.

....

Activity: Intercultural Self-Assessment Quiz

Take the following intercultural self-assessment quiz. Circle T for true and F for false. Then, use the final reflection to explore further ways to expand intercultural awareness and practices.

INTERNATIONAL NEGOTIATION—INTERCULTURAL SELF-ASSESSMENT	
T/F	1. When negotiating a business deal with your client in Saudi Arabia, you may need to be prepared for a very lengthy decision-making process and allot plenty of time for the drafting of contract terms, as contracts in that region are expected to include many details.
T/F	2. When you negotiate with your Russian client, they appear to become aggressive, which might signify that they do not feel positive about how the negotiation is going nor about your partnership.
T/F	3. A business partner that you meet in the United Kingdom informs you that she doesn't need approval from the executive board to close the deal. Upper management typically does not need to approve final terms and decisions.
T/F	4. A Brazilian colleague that you are scheduled to meet with next week will likely want to read through the entire contract and carefully consider all of the details of the deal before making a decision.
T/F	5. An Israeli negotiator may keep quiet at certain points during the negotiation because she wants to use silence as a pressure technique to push the other party into making additional concessions.

INTERNATIONAL NEGOTIATION—INTERCULTURAL SELF-ASSESSMENT	
T/F	6. In your next round of negotiations with your counterpart in Japan, you expect your client to increase or decrease their offers by no more than 5 percent from their initial offer, even over the span of multiple counteroffers on the way to final agreement.
T/F	7. In India, a business negotiation reaches a point of high tension due to diverging goals. The right thing to do is to avoid eye contact because eye contact in this context could be interpreted as disrespectful and aggressive.
T/F	8. In order to settle an argument during a negotiation with Mexican colleagues, consider that talking about common interests and appealing to your relationship may resolve the conflict.
T/F	9. On a conference call, your German client confirms a deal with a simple "Approved." No written contract is needed because under German law oral contracts are legally binding.
T/F	10. Save time and skip exchanging introductory information with your Chinese client—they often want to get started right away with the negotiation process and don't want to lose time exchanging personal information at the outset.

Answers:

(1) *False,* (2) *False,* (3) *False,* (4) *False,* (5) *False,* (6) *False,* (7) *False,* (8) *True,* (9) *True,* (10) *False*

Final reflection:

After taking the quiz, engage in self-reflection. How did your results surprise you? What intercultural objectives can you identify and integrate? What awareness can you build for future interactions?

5.8 Building Relationships across Cultures, Not Walls: Strengthening Your Negotiation Bond

Relationships of trust depend on our willingness to look not only to our own interests, but also the interests of others. —Peter Remnant

As legend has it, King Arthur and the knights of the roundtable might have provided one of the best models for collaborative relationships. As a medieval equivalent of today's "boardroom," the *roundtable* embodies the belief that the contributions of those seated around it were equally valued. This model was ahead of its time with its concept of equality in group endeavors. Even today, it reminds us that, in intercultural negotiations, every relationship and point of view should be met with a commitment to respect and equity that, ultimately, strengthens communicative bonds and the fulfillment of mutual goals.

The roundtable model is an important metaphoric tool. Once we develop the critical mental shift in perspective toward a collaborative negotiation, we not only constructively evaluate our current relationship with the other party, our future negotiating partner, we also gain introspection into our own values, culture, and motivations in the negotiation. Only then can we truly begin to engage in the profound relationship-deepening and the joint solution-building that would benefit both parties in the long-term.

The overall objective of engaging in this level of analysis and negotiation behavior is to also enrich our understanding of our own emotional and cultural triggers. For when we recognize the common ground and long-term benefits of a relationship, the resulting outcomes and challenges become opportunities to find solutions together with the other party.

🌀 *Global Negotiation Tip*

The more time you spend researching relevant cultural informa-tion and identifying the interests of the other party, the better you can assess the negotiation situation and arrive at a mutual partnership.

According to Chester Karrass, author of *The Negotiating Game,* the effective negotiator engages in strategic planning that is concerned with long-range goals and values. In other words, the more we invest in researching our cultural counterparts and identifying interests and positions, the more effective we are at assessing the negotiation situation, arriving at successful outcomes, and forming mutual partnerships.

When you think about it, the world operates in a constant back-and-forth flow of shared information, and negotiations are no different. The negotiation process, both online and in-person, affords us the chance to engage in information-sharing and information-trading of our own, in order to create stronger rapport, communicative bonds, and emotional acumen.

As creative negotiators, we must use *information* to empower our decisions by helping us nurture strategies for creating open communication, ultimately building trust within cultural negotiations. To do so, there are three interlocking components that every negotiator should cultivate to enhance their portfolio of relationship-building practices in a negotiation.

5.8a Shaping Rapport across Cultures: Conveying Value in Relationships

> *Unless both sides win, no agreement can be permanent.* **—Jimmy Carter**

Relationships depend on meaningful interactions and this includes negotiations. We do this through building *rapport,* the dialogic process of deepening our connection with the other party. A chief way to do this in intercultural dialogues is to employ *active listening* to deepen the negotiation exchange. While this concept is commonly used as a strategy in music collaborations and acting improvisations, ultimately our goal as a global negotiator is to meaningfully integrate new information into our offers to indicate to the other party that we are listening and responding to their needs and wants.

Safe environments contribute to building rapport. According to Dr. Margaret Paul, author of *Healing Your Aloneness,* people open up and take more risks when they feel safe. It has become increasingly crucial at the initial exploratory stages of a negotiation to first begin by building a congenial relationship with the other party. Then, we should determine in what ways the other side shares our values and priorities, as well as meets our standards for forming a partnership (see Chapter 2 on *Networking Skills*). After all, we wouldn't be in the negotiation if we could achieve the task by ourselves.

The importance of trust is universal across all cultures. Trust is the only true building block of a relationship. And once we meet a set of implicit expectations and priorities—confidence is increased, and common ground is discovered. When trust is established, we find that much needed common ground for the negotiation to take off in the right direction. Instead of the other party believing that they are exposing themselves to risk, they are secure in the certainty that we are now on a journey together in a partnered venture to joint solutions. Building a complementing pattern of rapport interculturally can increase loyalty and help the other party appeal to you as a potential long-term partner who genuinely cares about their needs.

Global Negotiation Tip

Gain power and trust by asking open-ended questions instead of yes/no questions, then create value by weaving this information into offers and counteroffers. *Focus on "give-and-take" efforts that bring more solutions to the table than concerns.*

An easy way to establish rapport and create value interculturally is by asking open-ended questions rather than yes/no questions. When we do so, we are able to gather more information to weave into a broader "package" of complex bargaining offers and counteroffers that meet the other party's competing demands. This is a surefire way to jumpstart any intercultural relationship. When we concentrate on "give-and-take" efforts and try to bring more solutions to the table than concerns—we, in turn, gain more power and trust in the negotiation.

5.8b Reciprocity in the Global Community: Sharing Value in Relationships

> *Reciprocity is a deep instinct; it is the basic currency of social life. —Jonathan Haidt*

The one concept that unifies parties the most when seeking to form a mutual bond in a negotiation situation is *reciprocity,* the concept of interaction for mutual gain. Reciprocal negotiators gain much more over time than hard, win-lose negotiators who only achieve gains in short-term ways. The goal is to practice *active listening* in order to interlock goals and form a mutual bond. We can often become distracted in the complexity of negotiation conversations, but keep in mind that active listening must be both an *internal process* and an *external display.*

Let's envision this process. First, begin with small steps within the general exchange of pleasantries—acknowledge and exchange compliments or statements of goodwill (see Chapter 2 on *Networking Skills*). Even offering to make meeting arrangements can go a long way toward affirming how much you value and respect the other party. These polite acts can contribute to the long-term objectives of creating strong bonds of interdependence, where the other party really needs us to fulfill an aspect of a future partnership.

If you find that the other party is not reciprocating your offers, become appropriately explicit with significant proposals, such as "I've just offered this concession; now, are you able to . . ." The key to strengthening reciprocal bonds is to continually evaluate the other party's responses, monitor their comfort with risk, and gauge their trust after each exchange. Be patient and transparent with your demands and intentions, and the other party is bound to reciprocate the gesture.

As we shift our focus to how we can meet and deliver on the expectations of the other party before meeting our own expectations, people are likely to notice and reciprocate as well. When this is done in increments, we can position ourselves for win-win outcomes and a thriving partnership in the future.

Global Negotiation Tip

Continually practice reciprocity with the other party. Be patient and transparent with your demands and intentions, and the other party is bound to reciprocate the gesture.

5.8c Leading with Cultural Empathy: Prioritizing Value in Relationships

> *Our feelings are our most genuine paths to knowledge.*
> *—Audre Lorde*

The secret to developing what has been termed emotional intelligence is seeing emotions as *information* that we and our counterparts can use to manage an interaction. While international exchanges have rapidly increased over the past twenty years due to globalization, no single universal cultural pattern governs the expression of emotions. Yet, the seven *universal* human emotions have been identified (see Chapter 4 on *Nonverbal Skills*); however, the cultural "display norms" regarding these emotions are complex. Cultural norms, which influence how much we *show* of our emotions, play a significant role in the negotiation and trust-building process.

Some Eastern countries discourage the expression of emotions, instead valuing moderation and self-control, while some Western countries encourage emotional expressiveness, valuing openness. Then, within those cultures, there are individuals with differing preferences in terms of emotional display (see Chapter 3 on *Effective Emailing*).

Emotional intelligence is considered the art of "reading," reasoning with, and managing emotions—both of ourselves and of others. So, how are we to arrive at an intersection of cultural and emotional intelligence, especially when in an intercultural negotiation situation? This topic has always fascinated business leaders and entrepreneurs in terms of contributing to a positive negotiation process when interacting in online or in-person environments. In terms of the creative negotiator strategy, the main principle is quite simple: we tend to trust people who are like us and are fair to us. This type of reciprocity holds true when reflecting back the same language, generosity, and expressions of our intended audience.

In some cultures, an abundance of expression reflects positively in communication and is perceived as honesty, while other countries can regard such expression as a sign of immaturity since it doesn't clearly indicate objectivity. However, our goal is not to hold on to cultural preconceptions. Our goal with emotional intelligence is to continuously *perceive, reflect on,* and *manage.* **We must actively *perceive* verbal and nonverbal emotions, reflect on emotions to *prioritize* thinking, and most importantly, *manage* our and the other party's emotions to promote joint gains.**

Positive emotions, such as contentment, joy, and interest, tend to steer negotiations toward integrative outcomes, while negative emotions, such as aggression, fear, and frustration, can redefine a situation as distributive and competitive. Cultivating positive emotions in the negotiation process can lead to increased ability to analyze the situation, to successful win-win agreements, and to deepening partnerships.

Like building rapport, acting on emotional intelligence goes a long way toward building trust. Creative negotiators who are emotionally intelligent are often regarded as charismatic, another key factor within intercultural emotional contexts. As researched by Dr. Ronald E. Riggio for his book *The*

Charisma Quotient, charisma consists of a combination of emotional intelligence and social intelligence that contributes to a deep connection with another party. Applied to negotiation, the global and creative negotiator must constantly reflect and act on the other party's complex social and emotional triggers to build the "web of communication" that interlocks goals, interests, and objectives.

Emotions can be tricky, but one thing is certain—people are drawn to others that share the same interests, looks, and behaviors. As a principle, remember that emotions convey useful information—about us and the other party. Reflect upon this information and then integrate your understanding of these emotions as you mirror the communication style of the other party (see Chapter 3 on *Effective Emailing*). Generally, maintain formality when interacting with other cultures before personalizing the conversation—some cultures prefer formality over informality.

Global Negotiation Tip

Emotions convey information—about yourself and the other party. Reflect on this information and apply it when mirroring the communication style of your counterparts.

All of the above relationship-building practices demonstrate the importance of information-gathering in order to allow trust to emerge and progress the relationship toward full partnership. In order to be a creative and global negotiator, we must recognize that there are competing priorities between people and groups that are dictated by cultural beliefs and attitudes. However, once we adjust our perception to a focus on responsiveness—we arrive at a place of trust.

The key to finding common ground and building trust among intercultural communities is to encourage others to move beyond their own interests and collaborate with you. For example, this act can be as simple as making a first concession to put the other party at ease and underscore your good intentions for a fair negotiation. A concession that demonstrates your honesty, goodwill, or an act of good faith will help to inspire trust from the other party and also build your credibility in the process.

So, now that we've covered ways to build a relationship, let's explore how to deepen the trust that is essential to maintaining a relationship.

5.9 **The Golden Rule: Building Trust**

Vulnerability is not about winning, and it's not about losing. It's about having the courage to show up and be seen. Vulnerability is the only bridge to build connection. —Dr. Brené Brown

So how do we get someone to trust us? Trust shares a delicate balance with risk, and to build trust we have to be willing to engage in a combination of useful strategies that includes exposing our vulnerabilities.

The combination of building rapport, establishing a long-lasting bond, and acting on emotional intelligence leads to inspiring trust from the other negotiation party. Trust must be present for any relationship to thrive, but first we have to release it from the layers of other emotions that guard it. We all have mental "checklists" of behavioral expectations surrounding trust, some cultures with greater expectations than others. And we all know that trust is earned, but like most things in life—it's a choice, and everyone has a varied set of criteria before rolling out the welcome mat.

According to Dr. Brené Brown at the University of Houston, vulnerability is the "core of all emotions," and although vulnerability is our greatest risk, it is what connects us with others. In other words, relationships really only start when we allow ourselves to inspire trust through taking a vulnerable position in the negotiation.

But the question we struggle most with, even after deciding to reveal our vulnerabilities, is *when* to do so. When is too soon to risk? And when is it too late? First, we must establish our expertise and reputation before revealing a vulnerability by initially sharing our past credentials and successes that matter most in the negotiation situation. Remember, first impressions are essential! So is your smile, which usually contributes to building cooperation with the other party (see Chapter 4 on *Nonverbal Skills*).

Vulnerability is usually considered a weakness, but when building trust in a negotiation it can be our greatest asset. After establishing credibility, use your vulnerability as a means to show transparency and inspire the first stages of trust at the negotiating table. Pay close attention to how the other party responds, both in acknowledgment and in what they reveal in turn. Remember, as Dr. Brown mentions in her book *Daring Greatly,* "being vulnerable connects us with others," regardless of cultural background.

When faced with your next negotiation, take a breath and stop thinking of vulnerability as a bad thing. While on the surface it may seem that some cultures consider vulnerability to be a weakness, in actuality, it is what brings about the truth of everyone's intentions in negotiations. All countries seek trust as a means to build a mutual partnership, and the truth is a crucial factor in this process.

Make no mistake that every negotiation is sure to have a fair share of inescapable uncertainties and risks, but how we handle trust in the negotiation with a cultural counterpart has the potential to fulfill a partnership and unite on all fronts to achieve success.

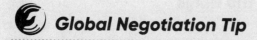

Global Negotiation Tip

In your next negotiation, take a breath and rethink vulnerability, viewing it as a strength. Trust brings out the truth of everyone's intentions in negotiations. All countries seek trust for partnership-building.

5.10 Nurture. Grow. Repeat: Building a Lifecycle in Every Negotiation

People first, then money, then things. **—Suze Orman**

All negotiations are only as strong as the shared commitment of the individual parts. You may be thinking that once trust has been established in a relationship, you must turn your attention to the real negotiation focus. Not a chance. Now is not the time to kick back and invest all of our time on the negotiation topic. You must nurture and grow the relationship throughout the negotiation process, be it online or in-person. You need to continually inspire the other party to strengthen the trust that you have established. In this situation, remember this mantra for all of your relationships—**nurture. grow. repeat.**

We have you covered—below are some relationship "encouragers" to help you deepen any negotiation relationship.

RELATIONSHIP "ENCOURAGERS"	
Commonality	Finding shared features or attributes
"Showing an interest"	Demonstrating a genuine willingness to know the other party
Flattery	Sharing consistent praise in a meaningful and sincere way
Generosity	Being thankful and appreciative
Personalization	Meeting personal needs more effectively

5.11 Stepping Out of the Shadow Negotiation: Establishing the Rules

> *The quality of your communication is the quality of your life.* —*Tony Robbins*

As the world moves toward a global community, the scale as a symbol and concept of balance is central in the vast interconnected process of human interaction. In global affairs, **the focus on *balance* demonstrates the true benefits of win-win outcomes and relationships—which have a significant impact in the age of global collaboration.**

Relationships are not just the most significant element of any successful negotiation—in fact, they are the most rewarding aspects of our common humanity. We all exist in this world with personal and common interests. However, the way that those interests interlock and build bridges instead of conflict is up to us—up to the commitment of our minds and hearts.

True, every relationship has a secret language. Can you recall those unspoken moments where you began to guess the other person's next words or reaction to a situation? Communication is about connectedness, both stated and implied, in our own culture or abroad. Our ability to exchange information, invest in our relationships, and interact in collaborative ways will always strengthen our diverse partnerships and, ultimately, the success of our decisions in cultural negotiations.

In the negotiation process, these unsaid aspects are often referred to as the "shadow negotiation"—the unspoken elements that are influencing and guiding the discussion but are difficult to recognize on the surface. And what is your goal as a creative and global negotiator? To step out of the shadow negotiation and into the light of productive dialogue and interaction with our cultural counterparts. This goal is a shared task.

We want to get to that rewarding point in the relationship where the other party feels connected—sharing in our every expression and intended meaning so that we continue to traverse a common bridge of understanding. This forging of commonality is especially important at the outset of a negotiation in a win-win framework. One way to do this, in addition to establishing commonalities, is to establish clear and helpful rules of the negotiation—rules that do not limit, but rather guide and create clear parameters for the interaction. Many people forgo discussing the "rules" of the negotiation, which often leads to unspoken and assumed misconceptions. Without the transparency of these unspoken "guidelines" and other interests, the relationship can suffer from mishaps of communication that can be detrimental to any negotiation, especially intercultural negotiations.

Instead, take hold of the relationship on a human level and collaborate with the other party to establish jointly-beneficial terms for how you both envision the negotiation (e.g., length, deadlines, conflicts of interest) to better manage expectations, the overall relationship, and impact on the process.

At a global level, negotiation skills may be the key to bridging differences and arriving at an evolved exchange of ideas and values between people. Remember, those that focus on relationships and partnerships are the most successful negotiators in the world. When we are creative negotiators that look for agreement, mutual gain, and long-term partnerships, we will arrive at successes that we, and the human race, can build on for many future negotiations and global conversations to come.

How do we connect with our readers by using meaningful patterns in our writing?

Connecting with the Mind: Strategic Writing in the Global Space

> *The best thing we have going for us is our intelligence, especially pattern recognition, sharpened over eons of evolution.* **—Neil deGrasse Tyson**

The dream of every writer is to dive into the mind of the reader—so what is the secret of human thought? *Pattern recognition.* We all have had experiences where seeing a pattern has completely changed our lives. The world suddenly melts into focus, and chaos becomes order, much like seeing a constellation for the first time.

Pattern recognition is the human trait that has given us the evolutionary edge on this planet since the dawn of time, whether through the pursuit of scientific or artistic aims. Our minds are hardwired for patterns, and as writers, identifying the patterns between us leads to greater global communication.

The most influential place we have ever searched for patterns, along with our ancestors, is not the earth, but across the sky—plotting patterns that continually alter the course of our lives. Gazing upward across the star-studded heavens, our perspectives have connected the stars in a myriad of ways, not just forming a rich tapestry of stories and meanings, but also recognizing patterns between the stars and Nature that enabled us to write a calendar in the sky.

The stars whispered messages to our forefathers and foremothers about the coming rains, storms, and weather, as well as when to camp, hunt, and migrate. Additionally, when we found a connection between the motions of the stars and the seasonal cycles of life on Earth, we told campfire stories of gods beneath the night sky, that we later wove together as written patterns of cosmic influence.

Over time, our constellations have risen and faded, some ancient myths forgotten, other stories reworked, then blended together—however, this human quest for patterns remains. For a ready example, gaze up at the *Big Dipper,* the most culturally-universal *asterism,* a recognizable pattern of stars that form larger constellations. According to research by astronomer and data scientist Nadieh Bremer, although this asterism has many names across cultures, we universally *see* the same "cooking pan shape" as a standalone form that makes up other figures based on the overlapping of various cultural frames in the biggest game of "connect the dots."

Our ability to identify star patterns, even with different cultural references, transcends culture—pattern recognition is a human trait. Stars hold many names across time and cultures. But even though our perspectives tell richly-different stories, our eyes are filled with awe at the same object. And, since every ancient human culture, somewhere between these stories, perspectives, and constellations is the truth humanity has framed, an unanswerable wonder we all share.

Similar to how we mentally connect stars to arrive at meaningful information, we must help readers comprehend ideas and messages in our writing by organizing information into recognizable and meaningful patterns. In this way, we achieve a specific yet greater purpose. As our audiences learn to see the world with new eyes, we learn to see the world with new eyes as well.

In this chapter, we will examine the strategic and organizational patterns of writing that allow us to connect with professional audiences from all over the world. More specifically, we will explore how to tap into preexisting patterns that are standard in many types of business writing and how to combine these patterns in new intercultural ways that build further engagement with our content.

Patterns exist at the paragraph level and document level, as well as in the practice of "framing," a communication technique that effectively places information within a field of meaning. The strategies we focus on will be applicable to various forms of print and digital business writing, including informational, persuasive, and engaging writing types. When we use patterns more purposefully in our writing, we more powerfully build comprehension among our audiences and create a space for greater innovation across the globe.

6.1 The Adjacent Possible: Where Innovation Comes From

> *Innovation is taking two things that already exist and putting them together in a new way.* **–Tom Freston**

What role does writing play in innovation? Imagine for a moment all of the modernizations in the world that have resulted in evolutionary success for the human race. The faces of innovators may flash across your mind, from Albert Einstein to Steve Jobs. So, where does innovation come from? Pattern recognition—whether of trends that are on the horizon or trends that have yet to materialize. As professional ice hockey player Wayne Gretzky once said, "Skate to where the puck is going to be, not to where it has been."

Innovation is collaboration that occurs across time, cultures, and history. It is the result of taking a deep look at the world, bringing yourself into the connecting threads of possibility, and finding patterns never before seen in the evolving motivations, needs, and imaginations that have converged from human history into the present moment.

What is exciting is that the writer has a unique place on this path. We often believe that we have to be at the right place at the right time. However, with the right strategies, we can use pattern recognition, not just to see trends before anyone else can see them, but also to *communicate* the trends that make global innovation possible. Our audiences seek to collaborate with our ideas in order to expand the criticality that will open new paths for thinking and doing. We stand at the crossroads, merging history and imagination—and when we make framed combinations to reinvent the present—we are experiencing the "adjacent possible."

Originally describing the process of the *adjacent possible* from a biological perspective, environmental theoretical biologist Stuart Kauffman explained how biological systems evolved through small incremental connections alongside other systems to reach more progressive and sophisticated systems. How does this apply to writing? Well, as writers, we not only have the power to shift perspectives, incrementally, person by person. We also have the power to transculturally create writing that *connects* multiple perspectives and then evolve new viewpoints from those perspectives.

We live in a globalized world of adjacencies, and just as there can be multiple patterns that lead us to a singular new perspective and innovation, we can incrementally shape frames of reference on a given topic and arrive at a renewed perspective relative to past information. In writing, we can redefine or reframe preexisting knowledge and sculpt it for audiences to discover new angles, thus providing new processing patterns for global counterparts to arrive at a fuller perspective and spectrum of solutions.

The global exchange of culture has more in common with the *adjacent possible* than we may think. We often view cultures as separate when we focus on differences; however, when we imagine the possibilities and opportunities that each culture brings to the world as part of the larger fabric of humanity, we can see the interwoven combinations among us that have opened the path toward many advancements. A global outlook changes everything.

💡 *Global Writing Tip*

Collaboration across cultures is the key to innovation.

What is often left out of our cultural frames is that there was always a preexisting cultural point of reference prior to each human innovation. Europe served as an adjacent influence to North America, inspiring new cultural elements and societal structures that combined Old World traditions with New World hopes. Indirectly, the American West became a third iteration of this adjacent possible concept, by bringing more renewed ideas and perspectives first removed from America's colonies and second removed from European societies. How do we recognize these trends? The secret is *associational thinking*. To get ahead, we just have to connect unrelated topics.

Innovators count on this skill, which is sometimes simply called "associating." In *The Innovator's DNA* by Clayton Christensen, Jeffrey Dyer, and Hal Gregersen, research on nearly five hundred innovators as compared to five thousand executives identified five behavioral skills that distinguish innovators from the rest. The skills are **asking questions** ("If we challenge the status quo, what could happen?"), **observing** ("What are new ways we can do things?"), **networking** ("What new perspectives and ideas do people offer?"), and **experimenting** ("What new experiences and experiments can I create?"). As a writer, see if you can dip into the world's cultural reservoir to do this. An American poet may look at a French surrealist painter's work for phrase inspiration. A Korean pianist may study a Spanish guitarist's music to evolve new musical styles. Western executive business coaches may study Eastern meditative practices to create an industry around "conscious breathing in the workplace" (wait, that has already happened!).

As a writer, you too can engage in "associational writing" that generates novel business ideas and global innovation. The first step is to train your mind to look for new patterns across cultures and activities—integrate ideas from other mediums and cultural situations and apply them to your own medium and cultural context.

Let us refer back to the *overview effect* from the introduction of this book. If we remove the "them" from the "us and them" binary mentality created by a focus on cultural differences, we can see the larger picture and shared perspective that there is only "us" on this planet—a humanity that shares goals in an interconnected system. When we see ourselves as part of this shared perspective—we see the adjacent possible riddled among the pathways to many processes, objectives, and strategies.

We then begin to see new potential and possibilities when thinking about how we may have culturally arrived at and informed a specific approach. We have borrowed from and been inspired by other cultures, just as we have done with other disciplines to invent "the new." The question to ask ourselves is how our culture and experiences continue to frame how we perceive and act in the world around us, especially as we take part as innovators in the largest business meeting—the global economy.

....

Activities: Finding the Next Big Idea

1. **Connect the unconnected:** How can you "connect the unconnected" in your global writing? Try to write down as many questions as you can about your topic or innovation goal. Then, see if you can enhance the path of your questions with solutions from other industries and markets.

2. **Writing transculturally:** Write "transculturally" about unrelated topics often—connect your written observations with cultural information from all over the world. Brainstorm domestically, abroad, and with everyone you meet in between. Experiment often with written ideas that globally "connect the unconnected."

....

6.2 **Global Writing: Shared Passions and Purposes**

> *The way in which the world is imagined determines at any particular moment what men will do.*
> **—Walter Lippmann**

Just as the stars burn with a purpose vital for life to exist, every piece of writing has a purpose. The sun's purpose is light and heat; however, the formula for life also depends on the earth orbiting the sun's rays at an ideal distance, allowing for the atmospheric filter to support biological life. Similarly, writing is only half the equation for effective communication—the audience filtering in our ideas is the other half.

We commonly think of a writer's purpose as *exploratory,* where the page becomes a mirror for discovering ourselves. However, in the global workspace, writing is *transactional,* where you bridge ideas to a larger audience. In the global context, we do not simply write to express ourselves—we write to communicate. We write to move the world. The act of global writing helps us develop a greater sense of who we are—not just to ourselves, but in relation to others. We write to negotiate meaning in social, professional, and cultural contexts.

💡 *Global Writing Tip*

When writing globally, we never just write for ourselves, we also always write for our audiences.

In a globally-connected world, every act of writing is a form of interpersonal communication. **The three writing purposes are to *inform,* to *persuade,* and to *entertain* our audiences.** If you are writing to *inform,* the goal may be to describe, define, instruct, or advise. If you are writing to *persuade,* the aim may be to convince, influence, or recommend a course of action. And if you are writing to *entertain,* the goal may be to engage your audiences, often in combination with one of the other two purposes.

Our audiences bring their own purpose to the page, which is usually to be entertained. Their goal for being *engaged* could range from wanting to be notified, to feel unity, to receive instruction, to hear advice, to be inspired, or to think critically.

The common thread between both purposes of informing or persuading is *better decision-making*. Once you've determined whether your purpose is to inform or persuade, try to infuse that with the audience's purpose for engagement. Combining purposes is the key to creating more successful intercultural communication outcomes.

6.3 "Give Me the Facts" versus "Sell It to Me": Writing to Inform versus Writing to Persuade

> *If you would persuade, you must appeal to interest rather than intellect.* **—Benjamin Franklin**

In the digital and print world of global business writing, mounds of data and articles implore us to rely on trusted sources for the facts and opinions that will impact one thing—*our decision-making*. Yes, some global industries just need the facts via a trusted source before making a pivotal choice. Others seek a reliable expert for opinion and perspective prior to a course of action. The key when "writing to inform" and "writing to persuade" is to consider how our structure and style will impact the *decision-making* of our audiences.

- **Writing to inform** deals primarily with *facts*. In order to connect with fact-hungry audiences seeking to make more informed decisions, focus on conveying information in a structured and methodical way. Look at the style of daily newsletters or alerts that ping our smartphones and provide a snapshot of need-to-know information to start our day. Imitate the style of instructional textbooks, how-to guides, meeting minutes, negotiation summaries, or the encyclopedia articles you've read. If your information is clear, concise, and uncomplicated, it will pave the way for engaged audiences and informed decision-making.

  Key tips when writing to inform:

  - Focus on specificity over generalizations.

- Explain details in chronological and logical steps.

- Contextualize facts with an objective tone.

- Include data, charts, and statistics to support and reinforce factual claims.

- Assume skepticism of audiences and present information accordingly.

- Use technical terms and specialized jargon as appropriate.

- Refer to the *Analytical* style as a guide (see Chapter 3 on *Effective Emailing*).

- **Writing to persuade** requires us to present an *opinion* powerfully; however, we must also integrate facts and evidence as we invite the reader to adopt our position. We must also acknowledge competing opinions to show that we are balanced and fair. Examine the style and content of successful advertisements or campaign proposals. We often want readers to adopt our business ideas, to integrate our professional recommendations, or to react with a particular course of action. As with writing to inform, the key to writing to persuade is also to provide audiences with the most compelling information to make the right decision. *Your* right decision.

  Key tips when writing to persuade:

  - Empathize before you write and acknowledge any opposing views.

  - Consider sending the document to multiple team members, not just "the other side."

  - Strive to maintain brevity while respecting the reader's informational needs.

  - Use the four reader styles (see Chapter 3 on *Effective Emailing*) to tailor the style of argument to your reader.

  - Conclude with hope as a differing viewpoint can be seen as a problem; this approach will turn it into a solution.

Let's contrast how to take one draft memo and turn it into an *informative* piece of writing and a *persuasive* piece of writing.

Draft Memo: What Not to Do

I'm still not sure which commission rate is better, but the one we talked about at the last few meetings in November might be fine for Hubbs Industries—although we could have negotiated other terms with that rate. We can send other marketing materials to them too, but maybe before the signing meeting? There have been a lot of opinions, and I've jotted them down in this memo for us to think about.

Now, contrast the same information with the following:

Memo: What to Do—Writing to Inform

Last Monday, we met with Hubbs Industries about revisiting the negotiation contract, and we will now add the commission increase of 12 percent. The final signing meeting is next Tuesday. For preparation, I've attached a list of the marketing materials they requested. I've also included the meeting minutes from all previous meetings up to this point for final review of contract terms.

In writing to inform, organizing information in a clear chronological and logical order can make all the difference when distinguishing *information* from a garbled stream-of-consciousness report. Conclude with direct statements regarding next steps in an informative situation.

Memo: What to Do—Writing to Persuade

Last Monday, we spoke with Hubbs Industries about revisiting the negotiation contract. Our upcoming signing meeting would be an optimal time to discuss continued financial support for the training programs now that the commission increase of 12 percent has been finalized. Based on the attached budget, there will likely be room to include funding in the coming year. At our meeting Tuesday, we can point to our third-quarter marketing data and highlight the success of our four previous campaigns where we connected training to objectives. A well-trained team is critical to unlocking leading-edge success.

As above, in persuasive writing, we have to combine recommendations and solutions with facts. Always conclude a persuasive piece with a recommendation of what the reader needs to do with the information.

Finally, always consider enhancing both writing types with elements of *writing to entertain,* such as humor (when appropriate!), action language, and sensory details so readers can engage mentally with the summary, recommendation, or solution. Now, we are going to delve into another exciting aspect and consideration on the writing journey—how the kaleidoscope of cultural colors enriches the rhetorical process.

6.4 Thought Patterns Inside and Out: The Kaleidoscope of Rhetorical Styles

> *The greatest possible mint of style is to make the words absolutely disappear into the thought.*
> **—Nathaniel Hawthorne**

So, how does language influence thought? Consider the rhythm of life that we see played out in the change of seasons. The eastward rotation of the earth gives us our stunning sunrises and sunsets from east to west that dictate the patterns of our lives across all cultures. But what if the earth suddenly started rotating in a westward direction?

All of us would be affected. The world would change, eventually transforming habitable landscapes and climate patterns. Apart from the incentive of taking shorter westbound flights—every culture would need to adapt to different patterns of living. We may even develop different words for things, different systems of thought and points of reference, and different ways of representing our reality.

The question of whether language affects perception is richer and deeper than a yes-or-no question. While there are aspects of perception that are humanly universal, language does affect perception. Each language offers unique ways to represent logic, or rhetoric, and expands new opportunities in our human minds. The more rhetorical patterns we "speak," the more doors in our perception are opened.

As global communicators, we must be aware of the intercultural "thought patterns" exhibited across different languages, so that we can better represent reality to diverse audiences. The good news as writers is that this doesn't mean that we have to learn every language of the world, although the more languages we speak, the richer our systems of representation become. All we have to be aware of is the various "thought patterns" that exist in writing; namely, the diverse ways languages and rhetorical systems around the world organize information and manifest it on the page.

As the writer, think of it almost as becoming a "pattern connoisseur." Once we identify *how* our global community routinely consumes information, we can then adjust our writing style accordingly to serve the most easily-digestible platter of content possible. While we all may unknowingly be using these rhetorical patterns on a daily basis, some languages may favor one distinct pattern over another.

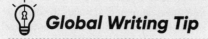

Global Writing Tip

When writing globally, write as others read and read as others write.

As writers, we often leave it up to our stakeholders and consumers to figure out the content. Instead, we have to let go of this practice and become more accustomed to this mantra: *write as others read and read as others write.* Particularly with thought pattern contexts, a growing awareness of global business practices allows all of us to develop quick-to-adapt modes of Global English (see Appendix A on *Global English*) in international business writing. See Figure 6-1. Regardless of cultural background, all of us can adapt to the diverse rhetorical patterns in our writing repertoires that our readers prefer when the situation requires it. Writing is a medium of observable patterns, and we can take the time we need to craft our correspondence and tailor it to diverse contexts and audience preferences.

Explore the following common rhetorical patterns that vary from culture to culture. Keep in mind that cultures and languages are continually evolving through globalization as business cultures continue to integrate complementing features of writing. Let's review a spectrum of the rhetorical patterns in Global English as a means of building a greater awareness around the rhetoric of international professionals writing in this global language of business.

RHETORICAL PATTERN	DESCRIPTION
LINEAR	*Linear rhetoric* begins each paragraph with a main idea statement that is then supported by specific reasons, evidence, and examples. Linear rhetoric tends to be characteristic of English and Anglo-European rhetoric and exposition, where the sequence of ideas flows in a straight line from the opening sentence to the concluding sentence; all paragraph content relates to the central theme and follows a clear thematic progression of ideas.
PARALLEL	*Parallel rhetoric* features paragraphs and sentences built in compounding sequences, using coordinators such as "and" or "but." Rhetoric that is parallel tends to occur in Arab and Persian rhetorical styles. Rather than emphasizing subordinators, such as "if," "because," and "while," for a progression of ideas, this style emphasizes coordinators in order to create a unique repetitive element that builds toward a larger climax of ideas beyond the individual sentence level.
INDIRECT	An *indirect rhetorical approach* examines a topic from a variety of perspectives and viewpoints. The main idea is not analyzed directly and is referenced implicitly through illustrative analogies and metaphors. An indirect rhetorical style may tend to occur in some Asian cultures. In this writing approach, ideas develop toward a main idea at the conclusion and the reader is given an active role in making connections between the writer's observations and the overall theme.
DIGRESSIVE	Writing with features of *digressive rhetoric* may start and end on the same topic; yet, paragraphs are filled with interesting features, engaging detours, and vibrant anecdotes that enliven the content. Rhetoric that is digressive tends to occur in Spanish and French rhetoric, as well as the rhetoric of other major Romance languages. Digressive rhetoric patterns present information dynamically via associated and tangentially-related topics extending from the primary theme.

Through this brief exploration of rhetorical patterns, we can see that *logic* and *rhetoric* are interdependent as much as they are culture-specific. **The above patterns do not mean that everyone from one culture will write or think the same, rather that these are patterns that have become cultural conventions over time.**

Figure 6-1

Invariably, as a *reader,* be aware of how writers from other cultures tend to pattern information in other languages. Look beyond surface ambiguity and be open when reading written materials and correspondence from diverse authors in English. As a *writer,* be mindful of how readers tend to organize information. Try the variety of writing patterns above to guide global audiences toward important information. When writing, we want to lead audiences on a journey through our ideas by providing recognizable frameworks.

Every cultural rhetorical pattern brings rich strengths to the writing *and* reading processes. Cultures with **indirect** style patterns frequently find creating and interpreting powerful metaphors quite easy, whereas cultures with **digressive** patterns often are captivating storytellers and drawn to narratives. Those with **parallel** patterns are usually well-versed at compounding thoughts, while cultures with **direct** style patterns are accomplished at coherence. As we write according to the style pattern of the situation, also consider integrating the rhetorical preferences of your readers to impact the greatest number of minds.

> ## 💡 *Global Writing Tip*
>
> **Integrate the rhetorical preferences of your readers and impact the greatest number of minds.**

Activity: Perspective "Flip-Flop"

When we take flights to conferences or business meetings, we often write a review online afterward. First, read the customer reviews and identify the rhetorical pattern of the original customer review. Then try to rewrite the same review using the rhetorical pattern indicated.

1. We are reconsidering our loyalty to this airline. We realized upon landing that the airline lost our three checked pieces of luggage when flying back home to Johannesburg, South Africa. This setback cost us dearly as the airline had earlier confirmed that our luggage had been stowed in the cargo space. The airline sent an apology with a voucher, however, we would have preferred reimbursement for items we purchased to survive in the interim. We are likely to avoid this airline in the near future. *(Rewrite this review using the* indirect *rhetorical pattern.)*

2. Everyone knows that first-class tickets are not cheap, however during a twelve-hour flight, we eventually gave into paying for the supreme service and comfort. By the way, the food was fantastic! We received really good attention from the crew. I would recommend the new upgrade as it was economical and luxurious. While there are more upgrades underway, we all deserve a little treat now and then. On another international flight last year, I remember thinking how nice it would have been to have more space. In terms of maximizing your money, we would only recommend this upgrade for transatlantic trips. *(Rewrite this review using the* linear *rhetorical pattern.)*

Answers: (1) *Linear,* (2) *Digressive*

6.5 More than Words: Decoding with Schemata

> *Reading maketh a full man, conference a ready man, and writing an exact man.* **—Sir Francis Bacon**

How do we create an architecture with language that rises off the page, immersing our readers in the world of our ideas? Just as architecture cannot exist without human habitants, the environment of our words needs to be multidimensional to appeal to our readers. Imagine entering a luxurious building lobby with arching ceilings culminating in a skywindow to the stars, with shimmering water streaming down a fountain sculpture at its center, vivid art pieces emblazoned on the walls, smooth marble touch surfaces, and a soft scent of lilacs wafting in the air. Architecture can move us when it is multisensory, and in a similar way, our writing can do the same with our readers.

When we experience a physical space, we experience it through our five senses, and it is the same with the architecture of the written word. Effective global writing requires this sensory dimension.

So, when are words *more* than words? We all can read the same content, but why is it that we react in different ways to the same information? Is there a formula or pattern that we should follow? Better yet, how do we create a "good story" that will attract a global audience?

You're in luck—architecture provides an answer! These questions are sought to be answered in the professional work of poets, businesspeople, music artists . . . the list goes on. But one thing remains constant—a certain audience analysis is essential to the creation of any engrossing work, whether we are writing a love letter, crafting a professional email, or addressing a roaring crowd from a stage (see Chapter 1 on *Presentation Skills*). The key is to create *interactivity* with your global audience on the written page.

Audiences regularly experience a phenomenon called *active audience theory,* where individuals interact in an unconscious manner with written content and compare the information and overall messages with that of their own social contexts and cultural norms. Similarly, architects prioritize the interaction between an environment and human habitants in multisensory design. Our goal as writers is to get readers engaged and prompt them to process and store information so that it can be integrated within their frame of mind.

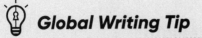

Global Writing Tip

To properly process and store information, readers must inter-act with the content.

The way that we create an exhilarating and affective written experience is by conveying information via activation of the reader's *schemata* (see Chapter 1 on *Presentation Skills*). *Schema* is the cognitive framework that helps people understand and interpret information.

To trigger the *schemata* of audiences that enables them to interact more with a text, appeal to the five senses (i.e., sight, sound, smell, touch, and taste). In writing, this is any technique that connects written content to the sensory world. These senses can be employed through specific settings, examples, or formats to help frame information to the *reader's needs* and allow audiences to logically connect the information to their own experiences—specifically their own past frames of reference.

So, how do we create "interactivity" with our writing? We encourage the reader to move from *observer* to *participant*. We inspire readers to focus not just on *what* we are saying, but also on *how* and *why* we are saying it. The goal is to build context around a topic that allows intercultural readers to access language and connect new information and vocabulary with prior experiences and knowledge.

Techniques for activating *schemata* include enhancing writing with reflective questions, embedded media (e.g., images, video, sound files), compelling statistics, impactful quotes and anecdotes, bouts of action language, strong sensory appeals, or a dose of active voice. The more context we build for global readers, the more we materialize a complete picture in our readers' minds. The technique of activating schemata helps us to see the big picture as illustrated in Figure 6-2. Patterns help us see the big picture interculturally.

Language that *appeals to the senses* can be one of the most effective ways to activate the schemata of your audience. For example, some of our colleagues once competed in a local contest for writing marketing copy for a new muffin among other food connoisseurs where the winner would receive a year's worth of muffins. Yum! Most ads were straightforward and stated something along the lines of "Our new Strawberry Fields Muffin is made from fresh strawberries, a deliciousness all in its natural taste." However, the winning ad went something like this: "In our new Strawberry Fields Muffin, rivers of strawberry run through powdered-sugar-dusted mountains atop a golden honey-infused muffin crust valley." Our mouths were watering just thinking about it!

PATTERNS HELP US SEE THE BIG PICTURE

Activate the reader's schemata –
build context from sketch to full image.

Figure 6-2

As we can imagine, the persuasive nature of activating schemata in writing enables our audience to process information more deeply and memorably—something we strive for whether writing marketing copy for a new restaurant, real estate listings on the market, or the amenities customers receive during a hotel stay. Activating schemata is the source of creating interactivity in writing with global audiences.

Furthermore, the overarching method for activating *schemata* and creating interactivity with the audience is tapping into the cognitive power of story. We build everyday correspondence and documents around narration in the workplace (see Chapter 1 on *Presentation Skills*).

The best way to tailor material of any kind is by identifying underlying narratives and targeting the psychological satisfaction of storytelling for integrating information. When we turn the boardroom into a metaphorical campfire, the minds of our audiences more easily process facts and figures. By storytelling, we deliver information in a more tangible and compelling format. Any information can be made into a captivating narrative with the right storytelling tools and illustrative techniques.

6.6 Tone of Voice: The Other Blueprint in Writing

> *I've learned that people will forget what you said, people will forget what you did, but people will never forget how you made them feel.*
> *—Maya Angelou*

Similar to how fireflies use patterns of flashing light to communicate, we also use variations of language to get our point across. In a small patch of the Great Smoky Mountains along the East Coast of the United States, during certain seasons it's as if the stars may have come to dwell in a shimmering swarm in the woodlands. In this synchronized back-and-forth light show of fireflies, the largest in the Western Hemisphere, communication occurs as flash patterns where the degree of brightness dictates the courting practice in a language unto its own. The modulation of light matters in the communication just as much as the light itself.

Similarly, *tone* is what unlocks true human communication. Words may be the basis of expression, but tone adds perspective to the situation. As we explored in Chapter 4 on *Nonverbal Skills,* tone offers more insight than words ever could, even more so in intercultural situations.

In both informative and persuasive writing, tone is shaped by the words we choose. As *informative* writers, our goal is to present a sequence of facts or events so the reader can draw *their own* conclusions. However, as *persuasive* writers, our goal is to convince the reader to arrive at *our* conclusions.

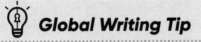

Global Writing Tip

The secret to effective tone in writing is not just attitude, but the right word choice.

In both types of writing, *word choice* shapes the tone of the work. Word choice is our firefly flash pattern. Consider how we use *reporting verbs* in business writing. Rather than use the word "said," *reporting verbs* introduce the research, opinions, or claims of others in business correspondence. Reflect on the following reporting verbs and how they frame information.

TONE OF REPORTING VERBS		
Neutral	**Agreement**	**Disagreement**
Said	Demonstrated	Claimed
Stated	Proved	Argued

If we write "A Harvard research study *claimed* . . ." versus "A Harvard research study *proved* . . . ," we completely change the tone of the information presented. In a piece of business writing, reporting verbs can make a tremendous difference in how we frame evidence and information. Single words can shape the tone of an entire piece.

Explore the "The 4-Tone Analyzer" in Figure 6-3, which contains the four useful categories for analyzing tone: *serious* versus *funny, formal* versus *informal, respectful* versus *flippant,* and *neutral* versus *enthusiastic.* These tones reflect our overall attitude as a writer toward the subject matter created by the words we use. This model also accommodates larger types of global writing, as Eastern and Western cultures often have varying views of what constitutes preferred tones of "respect and politeness" (see Appendix B on *Cultural Contexts*).

Use the *4-Tone Analyzer* to determine how a message can be shifted between tones in writing. These primary tone categories can help position content across audiences, industries, and cultures.

Finally, regardless of our writing purpose, globally, positive language can do wonders for our relationships as well as our professional writing, whereas a negative tone can implant negative scenarios into our readers' minds. Our tone shapes not only our writing and how readers respond to our content, but also how they integrate the content into their own decision-making.

Our advice? Make a conscious effort to focus on employing words with a positive connotation that open a space for more constructive dialogues, joint problem-solving, and stronger relationships with global readers.

💡 Global Writing Tip

Communication has the same goal no matter the channel—to build a relationship.

When we reframe an issue in a positive manner, we welcome others' opinions and move toward solving an issue together. We must remember that we are building a relationship in writing as if having a dialogue—our word choice can make all the difference in motivating our audiences from disagreement to agreement in intercultural business exchanges.

The 4-Tone Analyzer

Explore the four categories for creating tone in global business communications. Tone is created by word choice and reflects the writer's attitude toward the subject. *Which tone dimensions would be appropriate to which industries, messages, and interactions?*

TONE CATEGORY 1	DESCRIPTION:	EXAMPLE: NEWSLETTER SIGN-UP CONFIRMATION
SERIOUS	• Direct/literal tone • Formal/accurate • Plain language • Passive voice	**Automated Email Reply:** *"Your response has been recorded. Further updates will be provided to you in future correspondence."*
Funny	• Playful tone • Slang/irony • Personal pronouns • Active voice	**Automated Email Reply:** *"Sorry, we're out to lunch – you'll have to try again soon. Gotcha! Stay tuned for news and good times."*

TONE CATEGORY 2	DESCRIPTION:	EXAMPLE: NEWSLETTER SIGN-UP CONFIRMATION
FORMAL	• Straightforward tone • Precise information • Courteous/ mannered • Neutral & clear	**Automated Email Reply:** *"Thank you for your registration information. You will receive a message of confirmation shortly."*
INFORMAL	• Casual/ friendly tone • Conversational • Relaxed • Contractions • Personalized	**Automated Email Reply:** *"We're glad you joined the family. Let's keep in touch."*

Figure 6-3a

Take a look at the tone considerations in the *4-Tone Analyzer*. Then, when choosing your words, think about what tone will maximize your content among intercultural readers:

- Determine how you want readers to *think, feel,* or *act* as a result of reading the material.

TONE CATEGORY 3	DESCRIPTION:	EXAMPLE: NEWSLETTER SIGN-UP CONFIRMATION
 *Respectful*	• Proper tone • Sophisticated language • Accentuates service • Polished & refined	**Automated Email Reply:** *"It is our pleasure to receive your request. We look forward to the opportunity to serve you."*
 FLIPPANT	• Irreverent tone • Teasing use of "you" pronoun • Endearing • Cheeky & cavalier • Active voice	**Automated Email Reply:** *"We may include you on our list. Do you expect us to send you an email too? :) Just give us a moment."*

TONE CATEGORY 4	DESCRIPTION:	EXAMPLE: NEWSLETTER SIGN-UP CONFIRMATION
 NEUTRAL	• Objective tone • Factual/concrete • Succinct language • Practical/emotionless	**Automated Email Reply:** *"Thank you for registering. Your response has been recorded."*
 ENTHUSIASTIC	• Expressive tone • Slang/intensifiers • Carefree/outgoing • Colloquial/contractions • Energetic/exclamations	**Automated Email Reply:** *"Hey, it's you! We're so overjoyed to welcome you aboard. We look forward to connecting soon!"*

Figure 6-3b

- Identify whether the *goal* of the document is to inform (to confirm or record information) or persuade (to recommend a course of action or solution).

- Target readers' *expectations* and preferences in terms of clarity, language, and evidence.

- Anticipate readers' *predispositions,* such as prior reactions to the topic and prior level of understanding toward the materials or ideas.

- Highlight the important information that readers need in order to make decisions with particular word choices.

- Target your readers' communication style (see Chapter 3 on *Effective Emailing*).

In writing, we have the ability to make someone feel something with the power of language. Tone is more than the words we use—tone transmits how we feel about a subject. Passion ignites our words and in turn ignites our readers' hearts and minds.

6.7 The "Building Blocks" of Interconnected Thought: Framing at the Paragraph Level

> *Architecture is the learned game, correct and magnificent, of forms assembled in the light.*
> *—Le Corbusier*

Paragraphs are pivotal in business writing. These sections of text are essential—why? Because they organize ideas. Paragraphs are like star clusters that form a large constellation in the sky. The paragraph itself is a grouping of ideas. The "constellation" that connects each "cluster of ideas" is our main message.

To produce a definitive piece of writing, powerful ideas alone are not enough to reach our audience. Our ideas have to be organized for the reader in a logical and impactful way. Like star clusters in a constellation, each paragraph guides our readers through the constellation of our ideas, step-by-step.

So, why *shift* between paragraphs? We shift between paragraphs as we shift between our document's major ideas. Each paragraph contains a central idea, which is called the *controlling idea,* and is supported by details and examples. In English rhetoric, all sentences in a paragraph should contribute to the topic, so that every paragraph is self-contained. The primary difference when writing for global audiences is not just building coherence within paragraph sentences, but also building the best organizational scheme for our paragraphs.

As seen in Figure 6-4, "Choosing Paragraph Patterns," paragraphs in global writing can be arranged in two ways, via *organizational* schemes or via *content* schemes.

First, the following paragraph *organization* schemes provide a framework for creating effective sequences of information for global readers:

At a Glance:
Paragraph Organizational Schemes

- **General-to-specific:** Begin with a general introduction of the topic and proceed to narrow the focus; this scheme is *deductive* and is a characteristic of high-context cultural communication styles.

- **Specific-to-general:** Start with a specific aspect of the topic that broadens into a larger statement; this scheme is *inductive* and is a characteristic of low-context cultural communication styles.

- **Least-to-most important:** Build ideas with increasing force toward the most important point in the paragraph's concluding sentence; this scheme is climactic.

- **Familiar-to-unfamiliar:** Introduce familiar topics first to prepare global readers for new comparative and contrasting topics; this scheme prioritizes what is globally relatable.

- **Spatial or temporal:** Describe a process or sequence from beginning to end.

- **Simple-to-complex:** Highlight straightforward topics before delving into more intricate subject matter.

- **Certain-to-uncertain:** Establish facts and proven concepts before introducing readers to more theoretical information.

Additionally, we can organize paragraphs to guide our global readers based on the purpose of our *content*, such as in the following *content* schemes: *narrative, definition, cause and effect, classification, compare/contrast, persuasive, descriptive, process/chronological,* and *illustrative.* See Figure 6-4 for strategies stemming from these paragraph content schemes that can be used to effectively guide global readers across a variety of content areas and objectives.

As a communication latticework, paragraphs convey a lot about our purpose, but also about our understanding of other cultures. Organizational and content patterns offer numerous possibilities for targeting the styles of our global readers and exploring various combinations of paragraphs in our writing, which can enable us to frame messages effectively for any content, context, and audience. When we learn to form specific patterns using these paragraph "building blocks," we discover *new* patterns that help readers follow the flow of our ideas from one cluster to the next.

Choosing Paragraph Patterns

Use paragraph patterns to guide global readers.

Paragraph Organizational / Cultural Schemes

- **General-to-Specific** – *Deductive*
- **Specific-to-General** – *Inductive*
- **Least-to-Most Important** – *Climactic*
- **Familiar-to-Unfamiliar** – *Globally Relatable*

- **Simple-to-Complex**
- **Certain-to-Uncertain**
- **Spatial or Temporal**

Paragraph Content Schemes

Narrative
Tell a story. Go chronologically, from start to finish.

Definition
Fully define a key term with a detailed definition and at least one example.

Cause & Effect
Explain how one event, the cause, leads to another event, the effect.

Classification
Categorize a large group of items into smaller subcategories. Then, give specific details.

Figure 6-4a

Activity: Power Paragraphs

Choose a recently-published paper or article in your field and select a single in-depth paragraph (seven to eight sentences in length).

1. Determine the type of paragraph pattern used to organize the information.

2. Rewrite the paragraph conveying the same content using *two* different paragraph organizational schemes (*general-to-specific, specific-to-general, familiar-to-unfamiliar, least-to-most important, spatial or temporal, simple-to-complex, and certain-to-uncertain*). Which version (including the original) is most effective? Why?

Compare & Contrast
Describe the similarities and differences between two topics.

Compare and contrast in separate paragraphs or in one paragraph.

Persuasive
Convince the reader of a position with various persuasive patterns; include facts, expert opinions, examples, and rhetorical techniques.

Descriptive
Provide specific details about a situation, event, or object.

Organize content spatially, in order of appearance, by topic.

Process/Chronological
Explain a step-by-step process.

Give specific details in a sequence – first, second, third.

Illustrative
Give examples and explain how those examples prove your point.

Figure 6-4b

6.8 A Professional Frame of Reference: Strategic Messaging

> *There is no such thing as unframed information, and most successful communicators are adept at framing.*
> **—Matthew Nisbet**

Look into the night sky. How would you frame the vastness of the universe to someone else? What might you anchor as a frame of reference? Some may frame the size of the universe in a metaphoric comparison—such as there being as many stars as there are grains of sand on Earth (which includes the grains of sand that make up the ocean floor!). Others may frame the size of the universe using scientific research, such as that the universe could (and that is a big *could!*) be at minimum 250 times the size of the observable universe (46.5 billion light-years).

No matter how we try to frame our explanation, there is no single way to convey the scale of the universe, just as there is no single way to position a message in writing. What matters is choosing the frame that we feel is the most impactful for our message and global audience. Framing is how we strategically lead readers toward an intended outcome, with the goal of tailoring content for a more persuasive result. Enter the mind of professionals in public relations and marketing who frame messages every day in order to engage the public.

To frame messages in writing, we need to determine what (or what not) to say about a topic and how to communicate the information for impact. We need to make the topic as interesting as possible to command an audience's attention away from surrounding distractions. First, identify a target audience based on key indicators (e.g., culture, location, demographics, gender, etc.)—and narrow it within the world's population! Then, focus on the best way to tailor the topic to their specific preferences.

💡 Global Writing Tip

Use message framing as a persuasive method to motivate target audiences.

The "framing effect" was first proposed by cognitive psychologists Amos Tversky and Daniel Kahneman in their innovative research on judgement and decision-making. This cognitive bias describes how we individually select particular combinations of words, phrases, and contexts to rationalize the *value* of a topic within our associated point of view.

Beyond the accuracy of judgement calls, this principle goes on to describe other characteristics and behavioral qualities of the decision-making process with "prospect theory," discussing how we rationalize choices in favor of a topic that is framed as a *gain* or *loss*. And yes—we too are continually influenced by specific phrasing and wording of content that triggers positive and negative emotional outcomes in decision-making, commonly recognized as "gut feelings."

As we can see, many frames exist from which to choose how to present an appropriate message that reaches cultures, customers, or clients. If we are writing to build a brand, we must make sure our frames consistently demonstrate the *value (gain/loss)* of our core message. At the same time, use your "gut feeling" to test the effectiveness of a message frame. Don't just contemplate whether the message is *clear*, but also consider how the communication makes you *feel*. We can use our emotional reactions as feedback that can help refine our written correspondence accordingly.

At a Glance:
How to Frame Messages for Intercultural Readers

- **Tap into values:** Emphasize core values more than facts to motivate decision-making toward an intended behavior.

- **Convey gains/losses:** Highlight the benefits or risks that would result from engaging (or not engaging) in a particular course of action.

- **Create immediacy:** Create urgency and timeliness with words such as *best* and *final*.

- **Use simplicity:** Use Global English, known as plain language, for clarity, comprehensibility, and conciseness.

- **Create metaphors:** Use figurative language to connect intangible topics to the senses.

- **Use visuals:** Incorporate visuals to create a more powerful and memorable impact.

Our frames help us think and perceive. Deborah Tannen, a professor of linguistics at Georgetown University, stated in the journal *Applied Linguistics* that, in terms of frames, we do not approach the world with blank slates, but rather we are "experienced and sophisticated veterans of perception who have stored [our] prior experiences as an organized mass." In other words, we use frames as tools for future interaction. In every culture, we collect frames to make sense of our world. You too can use frames to create windows in your readers' minds.

Why did you buy that tie, latte, or jewelry? Framing is all around us, most notably in the media that we consume. Nowadays, the rise of smart devices and the push toward an "algorithmic economy" has transformed our daily media experiences into an endless list of recommended news, products, and services. It is essential to tap into existing frames when crafting messaging.

Every daily form of communication is likely to have been framed in such a way as to amplify a specific message. Think back through the conversations that you have had, the emails you have read, the news you have skimmed, the music or podcast you have heard—framing is all around us. Use the above principles to develop more awareness of the ways that framing affects our perception of topics, including cultural idiosyncrasies, and apply that awareness in your writing to communicate with a more persuasive appeal across the global landscape.

6.9 Cultural Design Thinking: Rhetorical Windows

The world is waiting for your words. —**Arvee Robinson**

Imagine how you would frame the sight of a great comet in a piece of writing, the kind of comet that is supposed to burn the brightest and only tends to pass by Earth once every twenty to thirty years. During special moments like these, we may begin to frame the experience in terms of where we were, who we were with, why we were there, and why the moment was important to us.

We are actively constructing our lives message by message—or is it *frame by frame?* Both consciously and subconsciously, we process information from what we read and write, regardless of culture, then store these frames in a library of long-term memory in our mind, where they are accessed on a moment's notice to help guide impending choices. Our frames help us understand and react to the world. They guide our preferences and future actions.

When we write, our messages matter, but also our frames matter—*what* we say is as important as *how* we frame it. To create a good cultural frame for our messages, we must tap into the power of schema and use key rhetorical tools. While sculpting our messages, we must also *frame* messages in the most accessible and impactful way for our global audiences. The more we integrate cultural profiles into our audience profiles in professional writing, as outlined in the beginning of this chapter, the more our frames expand to include intercultural audiences and build global engagement within our messages.

Let's look at three integral rhetorical tools that we can use for effective intercultural framing.

6.9a Rhetorical Window 1: Values-Framing

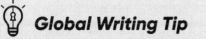

> ### Global Writing Tip
>
> Identify common interests that purposefully join readers in a shared community.

When engaging in business communication within the global community, we can increase our chances of receiving a favorable response by structuring content around shared values, positions, and opinions. We can form a *compatible identity* with others through writing—an identity beyond specific cultural identities and borders. For example, a possible unifying interest between a rice farmer in Vietnam and a cacao farmer in Ecuador is likely to be mitigating the impact of climate change—a shared value and interest. "Values-framing," a term attributed to the work of leading social psychologist Dr. Milton Rokeach, can help build understanding among multicultural audiences by providing a way for "co-cultures" to share a message immediately and deeply.

6.9b Rhetorical Window 2: Cultural Context

> ### Global Writing Tip
>
> Create a shared context with other cultures by targeting prior background or style preferences—avoid overcomplicating or oversimplifying messages.

Every culture has varying degrees of how they prefer topics to be presented. Some cultures favor more information and others prefer less. However, the responsibility doesn't reside only with the writer in English—the reader has certain responsibilities too. The culture, and how much of a shared context already exists with the reader, dictates how much information to provide. Consider the preferences between Western and Eastern cultures (see Appendix B on *Cultural Contexts*).

Typically, Western cultures tend toward a *writer-responsible* rhetoric where the writer is responsible for explicitly conveying information in written formats so that the reader can readily absorb the information. Alternatively, Eastern societies tend to embrace more *reader-responsible* rhetoric where a piece of writing is written with the implicit understanding that there is a shared context of preexisting background knowledge that the reader will bring to the table. Keep in mind that all cultures may alternate between these two style patterns depending on the situation at hand.

Additionally, when framing information across cultures, remember to maintain a general awareness of the direct and indirect preferred styles of writing. Know when to be explicit with your message and when to continually rephrase your core content throughout your text (see Chapter 1 on *Presentation Skills*). Keeping these preferences in mind will help you craft your messages effectively and will help your readers retain key information.

6.9c Rhetorical Window 3: Persuasive Appeals and Devices

💡 Global Writing Tip

Use persuasive appeals to evoke emotion, convey logical meaning, and enhance credibility.

Our minds have not changed much since the days of ancient Greece over five thousand years ago, when Aristotle (384 BC to 322 BC) arrived at the three rhetorical appeals for persuasion—all of which still hold true today. As mentioned in Chapter 1 on *Presentation Skills,* the three appeals in the art of persuasion are **pathos, logos,** and **ethos** (i.e., appeal to emotions, appeal to logic, and appeal to credibility, respectively).

These three appeals are extremely-influential ways of framing information, particularly when you combine two or more appeals in the same piece of writing. When the meteorologist on TV predicts weather forecasts using calculations, that's *logos*. That holiday card with poetic language? You guessed it, *pathos*. The prescription from the doctor—*ethos*. These three *rhetorical dimensions* appear in our everyday lives, framing moments in extremely-influential ways, particularly when combining two or more appeals in the same communication situation.

Consider a funding proposal scenario where a distinguished veterinarian provides a brief biography as a professor of veterinary science and developer of a successful pet vaccine (*ethos*), then discusses charts and graphs for the development of a new veterinary clinic (*logos*), where half of the proceeds will support animal charities (*pathos*).

Furthermore, rhetorical patterns help us to organize information more compellingly for our readers. The use of **rhetorical devices,** such as *parallelism* and *metaphor,* make content memorable across cultures. Firstly, the repetitive qualities of rhetorical patterns like parallelism make the information easier for readers to remember and *anticipate,* such as "Our sales will grow if we *expand* the scope of our business, *extend* our benefits, and *increase* our trade . . ." The three clauses are grammatically similar and parallel in construction.

Equally, metaphor, as part of figurative speech, is effective at connecting an intangible subject to the senses and works across cultures. For example, a phrase such as "his company is a sinking ship" includes an abstract concept of "company" that is made tangible to the reader when connected to "sinking ship"—which illustrates a not-so-subtle detail of the company's future. Always look for ways to connect with global cultures through a combination of rhetorical techniques and appeals in order to frame information more inclusively and powerfully.

6.10 The Greater Perspective: A Culture of Interdependence

> Since "we created our economic and political systems through our perceptions," in turn "we can change them by changing our perceptions." —*John Perkins*

When we write, we can alter the perception of reality. We can choose to write about a glass that is half full or half empty. We can conquer time like the Akkadian princess, Enheduanna, who was the first author known to have signed her name to her work. She reminds us that with writing we can become immortal, conquering death, reaching with words across centuries to whisper inside the minds of the living.

In this globalized and digital age of technology, writing also gives us the power to conquer space. With the right patterns of communication, we send ideas from one civilization to another, from one culture to another, and from one worldview to another—and onward.

How does writing allow us to unlock new perspectives? As writers, the more we practice framing and reframing the world, the more we become consciously aware of and deeply connected with the perspectives of others. Writing is a conduit for building relationships. We arrive at shared perspectives between ourselves and our audiences. We are building relationships in writing as if having a dialogue—remember, communication has the same goal no matter the channel—to build relationships. In the mosaic of content, we can also build new ways to think about the world, together.

Remember there isn't just one way to frame content. Business solutions call for what is termed *design thinking*—the idea of doing "framing experiments." This type of writing enables us not just to discover ways of reaching more audiences, but also to discover new trends. Do framing experiments as frequently and often as you can. When we think of framing as equivalent to critical thinking, we realize that if we continually *re*frame problems, solutions become obvious.

When we start to think of these various writing, framing, and rhetorical *patterns* and how each affects our audiences' perspectives toward particular topics, we reveal practical and new ways of creating ideas and capturing that glow of innovation on the horizon. The result is deeply-shared messaging that becomes the motivation to co-create with the ideas of our audiences. If we can connect each other's patterns of thinking, we can truly connect our ideas across cultures.

Conclusion:
Our Global Mantle

> *Now I know why I'm here. Not for a closer look at the moon, but to look back at our home, the Earth.*
> **—Alfred Worden**

The most influential photograph ever taken was not taken on the earth at all, but from a viewpoint far above—it is the iconic *Earthrise* photo, where the earth is shown rising in the distance beyond the barren lunar surface, captured by the first human crew turning around while their spacecraft navigated the moon in lunar orbit. Imagine the enormity of the earth at that moment as a small, delicate blue ball, a single fragile home to one humanity. A home that we are caretakers of together.

And just for a moment, imagine turning in desolate space at this monumental instant, seeing this blue jewel floating softly before your faceplate. Witness in your "mind's eye" distances vanish and divisions dissolve. A vision of blue and green, with humanity, joined together within this wondrous, but fragile, sphere. A place we've called home for thousands of years. Picture everything we have been, are, and might become right at your fingertips in one singular vision. As the photographer and astronaut of the Apollo 8 mission, William Anders, said about that moment of turning around to look back, "We set out to explore the moon, but instead discovered the earth."

Summoning this vision is important—both as a global communicator and as a world changer. *Earthrise* was humanity's first glimpse of the fragility, beauty, and loneliness of our world. The image went as close to viral as an image could at that time, flooded by international media across the planet. The image was so powerful it helped launch the environmental movement. Most importantly, the photograph brought to eyes and minds on Earth the *overview effect,* passing the illuminating torch of that experience from the hands of astronauts to all of civilization. The photograph offers a timeless gift of perspective. It reminds us that divisions and distances become meaningless in a single worldview—a perspective that transcends societies and comprehends a single geography of cultures, where we exist as living, breathing, miraculous counterparts to one another.

As global communicators—we too must bring ourselves to a similar and singular state of awareness, by viewing Earth, not from a cosmic perspective, but from a global viewpoint that sees and is guided by the interconnectedness of the world within a global mindset. This transformative power already exists within the reach of our own consciousness.

The larger purpose of this book is to link *perception* to specific *behavioral skills*—the skills of global communicators—who not only serve our current global community in the connection between mindset and action, but future generations to come. Below are some final principles:

- **Ignite inside what you wish to spark in the world—build self-awareness as you build global empathy.** Look inward—knowing yourself is the beginning of intercultural awareness. Indeed, the first step to becoming a compassionate global communicator is a deep and intuitive understanding of ourselves as cultural beings.

- **Be a torchbearer that recognizes both the culture and the individual within that culture.** Patterns are helpful guides for our "reading" of cultures when we allow flexibility for individual diversity. Remember cultures materialize differently in different situations, especially when individuals are in mixed intercultural scenarios. All people are individuals and must be respected before integrating awareness of cultural backgrounds.

- **As we recognize the constellations above, learn to integrate communication approaches across the globe.** The goal of global communication is not a place, but a new way of understanding the world. Expanding perceptions, combining approaches, and interweaving cultural communication patterns is what leads us to a global outlook. Every society contains unique patterns of thinking, values, and customs that also intersect at shared points of communication.

- **Be a lighthouse that reflects the communication styles of others— develop an adaptability that looks beyond the surface of culture.** Cultivate open-mindedness and look beyond the surfaces of interactions. Find a shared humanity in others. Being able to adjust our predispositions and being attentive to the subtle intentions of others is the key to bridging understanding. Seeing communication as a system of patterns helps us to nurture a deeper intercultural understanding. Adapting to others rather than believing that others must adapt to us is at the center of interpersonal effectiveness.

- **Breathe and fuse mindfulness with action—develop an attitude of intercultural responsiveness.** We must ground ourselves in every communication moment, with the ability to respond to new situations, and distinguish *being responsive* from simply *being reactive.* Remember that one cultural approach is preferred to another only due to its relevance to the situation at hand—in the larger context of the globe, every pattern and approach has equal value and relevance.

- **In the garden of our earth, cultivate actionable global compassion.** Compassion may very well be our most important human quality. Modeling compassion paves the way for nurturing intercultural patterns of compassion in others. *The true influencers in the world are not successful people but compassionate people.* Awareness is only part of the equation. We must work together to apply our imagination as a rational tool to implement global compassion in a practical, tangible, and actionable way.

This book is meant to be a profound point of departure, a model for future expansion and global compassion, starting with the patterns that already exist between us. However, pattern recognition doesn't just deal with observing and detecting the world, but with *discovering* it as well. We find fresh meaning when we extract information from observed behavior in diverse societies, integrating it with knowledge frameworks and formulating new concepts and knowledge that benefit all of us.

As global communicators, working with patterns is exciting. It's how we learn. Learning is the reconfiguring of previous patterns to create the new. Understanding of our humanity comes from understanding the patterns between our global societies. Each time we interconnect a previous pattern, a new world emerges—a shared world. We also learn that each of our individual tasks and actions matters greatly, for our future as a global community is already being created from the patterns of thought and action each of us in our world enacts every single day.

Astronauts who have given accounts of viewing Earth from orbit have shared core aspects regarding their experience of the *overview effect.* Researchers on behalf of the American Psychological Association examined various astronaut accounts of the effect and reported in the journal the *Psychology of Consciousness* that all the accounts shared "(a) an appreciation and perception of beauty, (b) an unexpected (even overwhelming) emotion, and (c) an increased sense of connection to other people and earth as a whole." Astronaut Edgar Mitchell described the *overview effect* as an "explosion of awareness," an "overwhelming sense of oneness and connectedness . . . accompanied by an ecstasy . . . an epiphany." Similarly, other countries have reported the same findings with astronauts. We too can contemplate the earth from this perspective within our mind, fully feel the emotion, see ourselves and the world differently, and return to ourselves on Earth with a renewed sense of purpose.

We must remember to view the world by fusing two points of perspective, an "as above" view and a "from below" view, similar to what has been called the top-down Platonic view and the bottom-up Aristotelian view. Both approaches, while seemingly independent, are essential to integrate in global communication. We start on the ground, observing patterns of communication across the physical plane of the planet, via modes of email, virtual teams, written international correspondence, intercultural and multinational negotiation, and nations united in policy goals. Then, we also allow new concepts to come into view from an ideal world vision, looking up and down our planet as much as we look across it—and somewhere between the cultural stories and perspectives is a global perspective we can see and feel, a wondrous humanity we all share.

If you are in New York City, stroll through Grand Central Terminal on 42nd Street. Look up at the interior of the domed ceiling in the Main Concourse, and as you tilt your head upward, you will see French artist Paul César Helleu's interpretation of a celestial skyscape on the ceiling, stretching across the entire grand room of the terminal. This panorama of constellations is always awe-inspiring, but when you look a little closer you will arrive at an impactful realization—the constellations are actually inverted and appear in reverse.

Although left open to interpretation by the artist, many believe the constellations were painted not from the perspective as we see the heavens from Earth, but rather to depict a divine perspective. The vantage point of God.

This unique perspective from above the constellations reminds us of a humbling and important service to others. Whether viewing the *Earthrise* photo or looking up at the celestial skyscape at New York City's Grand Central Terminal, each time we shift our mind to a different and greater vantage point, we unlock new perspectives, and we also deepen our approach to our compassion and interactions in the world.

The more we practice expanding our perspective to integrate the cultures of the world and the human family upon it, the more we become consciously aware of and deeply connected with others. For when we shift our "mind's eye," we shift perspective and uncover joint goals as we transform this global canvas—rediscovering ourselves as we voyage together on the path toward our global future.

Acknowledgments

From Raúl and Rod

We send an infinite thank you to our Daddi and Mami. In our home, the breathtaking *Earthrise* photograph rises on the wallpaper of our study, a room where the four of us have shared many precious moments, staring into this photograph of a jeweled Earth floating in space, taking in an astronaut's perspective with the shared wonder of God and the universe. This image fills two adjacent walls from floor to ceiling—the other two walls hold tall bookshelves packed with books. The carpet is white like the moon—and if you lay on the carpet to write, draw, or read a good book, as we've done, you can imagine that you're on the moon, looking out at the earth in space. We know our dear parents and the environment they created shaped our development in profound ways.

Daddi, in that study, you taught us to sculpt our artistic creations from boyhood to manhood, showing us how to dream beyond the constellations with a humility born from grace. Your willpower teaches us that every mountain is an opportunity to touch the sky. As your wisdom reveals, creative vision is not only seeing with our eyes but with our hearts. Daddi, we live by your example, your living legacy is in the strength of our passions, in the pulse of every decision for a better world, in the illumination before each footstep, and in the contours of the men we choose to be in word, integrity, and deed. You are our architect of Dreams.

Mami, in that study you would read color-filled stories to us as we rested our two little heads on your lap. Your voice—the most beautiful sound in the world for us since our conception. Giving us hugs, chocolate chip cookies, and encouraging kisses as we created in that study and grew into young men—always instilling in us God's teachings. Mami, your wondrous heart taught us to cradle the world in our own; the miracle of you is proof that angels do exist on Earth. You are the healer, the anchor, and the nurturer, with a golden look between our eyes revealing that your love makes all things possible. You nourish us with your beloved roots and with the embrace of your branches. The song of your heart helps dreams grow into truth.

The four of us were in that study when we received the news of this book. We cherish that moment. We held each other in joy at the beginning of this part of the path, peering into the starry *Earthrise* sky dawning before us, enveloped in the blessing of family. Daddi and Mami, your love is the light on our life path, guiding us into the realization of every dream and the hope of creating a better future. We love you 4-ever.

Furthermore, a double heartfelt thank you to our kindred spirit, Dan Bullock, for the late night dinner epiphanies, the golden sentiments from the reflection of our connected souls, the glow in our treasured memories, and the exhilarating collaboration of a "three ironmen brotherhood," united in dream and mission—we are deeply enriched with every shared conversation, inspiration, and creation together, always.

From Dan

To my mom and dad for their wellspring of love and encouragement, for being a guiding undercurrent in my own life, and for having built a home that was always full of inspiration and creativity as a child, possibility and wonder as a teenager, and courage and drive as an adult. To my sister Amy for keeping me disciplined and my brother Matt for his straightforward advice.

Thank you also to my Uncle Kenn and Aunt Sue for their willful giving of thoughts and perspectives, and to my extended family for all of their support. Also, to my grandparents who always saw happiness as the true measurement of success.

Also, to a brotherhood that I have forged in writing this book with Raúl Sánchez and Rod Sánchez and our continued collaboration in both words and sketches—this book is and will always be a collective part of us as we continue to go the distance.

From the Team

Thank you to our literary agent Rita Rosenkranz for her steadfast faith, which was a wondrous torch guiding us along this path. We are blessed with our partnership and look forward to the shared dreams and successes to come.

Thank you to Career Press—especially to publisher Michael Pye for his kind consideration, support, and partnership in opening the path for this book—and to creative director Kathryn Sky-Peck for her thoughtful creative direction and gracious collaboration on the book's cover design, as well as Bonni Hamilton, Eryn Eaton, Jane Hagaman, Maureen Forys, and Susan Berge, and the entire Red Wheel/Weiser team who have been integral to helping bring this book into a reality for global communicators everywhere.

Thank you to those global communicators who help others become better people and the world become a better place. To all of you who shared your inspiration and gifts in our classes, workshops, seminars, and trainings—we salute you and the future that you continue to grow for all of us.

Above all, we give profound gratitude to God for the gift that He breathes into our hearts in order to serve. Let each of us be *Your Other Self,* so that we can humbly communicate solidarity, expand unity in the world, and bring your grace, global perspective, and love to this earth.

APPENDICES

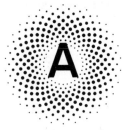

Global English and Brevity

Global English refers to a particular English usage that a communicator has optimized for a global audience. So what exactly is Global English? Essentially, Global English is a purposeful type of English usage adopted by the global business world that is focused on clear and plain language (with a limited amount of idioms and cultural references). As English has become the primary means of communication between businesses in diverse countries, the world is moving toward a new international business English that is practical and useful to corporations globally.

While it's important in business to build rapport, we must consider the degree to which using idioms, slang, and references to events or attitudes specific to American life may hinder clear and effective communication. Instead, in international correspondence, see if you can develop a Global English standard. For example, Americans love culturally-centered references to sports—particularly baseball. However, phrases such as "you're up," "bring your A game," or "out of left field" are not exactly clear to global audiences. Additionally, *business-isms,* such as "get our ducks in a row" and "on the same page" are equally opaque globally. The phrase "throw under the bus" even sounds a bit dangerous!

To achieve Global English, largely focus on general business or commercial terms, rather than specialist vocabulary. Furthermore, if you plan to use jargon or technical terminology, check whether the words you choose are readily found in most standard English language dictionaries. Also, take care when using humor and irony, as these forms of expression are easily misunderstood outside their cultural context.

Another confusing business-ism is the phrase "It is what it is." We've seen many global professionals regard the speaker of this phrase with bewildered sympathy, like *of course,* it is what it is! Also, sarcasm can be very confusing globally. Saying "That's just what we need," particularly when we mean the exact opposite and when the situation clearly is not a good one, can be quite confusing and even offensive.

NON-GLOBAL ENGLISH		
Non-Global English	**Definition**	**Examples of what to avoid**
Idioms	Phrases (groups of words) that have a cultural meaning separate from the literal meaning of their individual words	"Cut and dry" "Off the top of my head" "Come up for air" "Up in the air" "No strings attached" "Go the extra mile"
Cultural references	Culturally-centered expressions or references related to sports/music/TV/advertising/food/geography/film	"Level the playing field" "Bring our A game" "Out of left field" "Keep on rocking" "Think different" "May the force be with you"
Initialisms	The separate pronunciation of every letter in the abbreviation of a longer name or phrase	FBI—Federal Bureau of Investigation ATM—automatic teller machine IBM—International Business Machines
Acronyms	Names or words that are formed when the initial letters abbreviating a longer name or phrase are pronounced as one word	NATO—North Atlantic Treaty Organization YOLO—you only live once EOD—end of day
Business-isms	Corporate jargon (corporate speak)	"Take to the next level" "Lots of moving parts" "Put out some feelers" "Ahead of the curve" "Hit the ground running" "Leverage" (as a verb)
Phrasal verbs	Idiomatic phrases that indicate actions, usually a two-to-three-word phrase that functions as a verb (e.g., verb + preposition, verb + adverb) and creates a different meaning than that of the base verb	"Draw up" "Get ahead" "Zero in on" "Turn on/off/around" "Break it down"
Sarcasm	Saying the opposite of what you mean	"Beautiful day, isn't it?" "Well, that's just what I need." "What a surprise."

We must ensure that when conducting business around the world, we use Global English to optimize the content of our messages to arrive at a clear and effective global communication process.

Cultural Contexts

For us as global communicators, an understanding of communication styles is essential to navigating the cultural dimensions of international business. Pivotal research advanced by renowned anthropologist and scholar Edward T. Hall, social psychologist Geert Hofstede, and renowned linguist Richard Lewis has laid much of the theoretical framework for intercultural communication approaches during the latter part of the twentieth century. Their notable models, adapted for this book alongside other cultural theories, provide a useful intersection of communication patterns for understanding how the norms and values of diverse cultures operate and interact within the intercultural space.

One of the most useful frames of reference for intercultural understanding is Edward T. Hall's concept of **high-context** and **low-context cultures,** which refers to two broad cultural patterns of communication preferences among world societies. Essentially, *high-context cultures* tend to be *implicit* with messaging and the expression of intentions, while *low-context cultures* tend to be *explicit* with messaging and the expression of intentions. This two-pattern concept is useful for understanding the varying communication preferences of people from diverse cultures in terms of professional and personal relationships:

- *High-context cultures* tend to include countries in East Asia, Southeast Asia, the Middle East, parts of Eastern Europe, most of Latin America, the Mediterranean, the Iberian Peninsula, and the majority of sub-Saharan Africa.

- *Low-context cultures* tend to include those in the United States, parts of Canada, Northwestern and North-Central Europe, Scandinavia, and Australia/New Zealand.

(See the region key at the end of this section.)

Keep in mind that in every culture, individuals may vary across high- and low-contextual dimensions. Mindfulness is the key to fusing theory with effective intercultural practice.

The following table is a helpful pattern guide for improving business interactions and relationships with both high-context and low-context cultures in our globalized era.

HIGH-CONTEXT CULTURES	LOW-CONTEXT CULTURES
Direct with communication	Indirect with communication
Extensive and elaborate dialogues	Short and focused dialogues
Implicit in shared views	Explicit in shared views
Value relationships/meaningful interactions	Value time/schedules
Cherish intuition and mindfulness	Prize logic and rationale
Collectivist approach to decision-making	Individualistic approach to decision-making
Favor community and impartiality	Favor privacy and remoteness

Subsequently, one of the later seminal models of national cultural values in relation to international business was developed by Geert Hofstede. His research suggested that cultural dimensions could be used to describe the effects of a culture on the values of its members and, consequently, the relationship of these values to behavior. Hofstede's work led to a core set of five **cultural dimensions,** which provide a framework of national culture values. The following repurposed model adapts this framework of cultural values to our approach for developing a global mindset and enhanced skillset as a global communicator:

- **Collectivist mindset/individualistic mindset:** This dimension describes the degree to which a society's worldview and structures are built around individual fulfillment or group interests. A global communicator navigates independent modes of thinking, which tend to occur in Western cultures, as well as cooperative modes of thinking, which tend to occur in Eastern cultures.

- **Lateral power/hierarchical power:** This dimension describes worldviews regarding the degree to which power should be distributed in social structures. A global communicator is mindful of worldviews that operate with a lateral view of authority spread evenly across parties or that concentrate authority at the highest level of leadership, ultimately respecting the power dynamics that influence decision-making in each culture.

- **Adaptability to change/preference for structure:** This dimension describes the degree to which worldviews find comfort in ambiguous situations versus in situations with clear parameters. A global communicator is sensitive to the comfort level of global partners in light of perceived risk—adjusting communication styles to be either flexible or structured in interaction scenarios.

- **Relationship perspective/achievement perspective:** This dimension describes the degree to which worldviews are driven by quality of life and relationships versus by goal-attainment and tangible successes. A global communicator adapts to shifting levels of value-creating and value-claiming within modes of communication.

- **Short-term results/long-term investments:** This dimension describes the degree to which worldviews depend on tradition and familiar parameters versus reliance on a future vision in the presence of changing circumstances. When interacting with global partners, a global communicator navigates preferences for stability and immediate returns within short-term worldviews or preferences for long-range planning and investments within long-term worldviews.

See Figure 5-4 in Chapter 5 on *Negotiation Skills* for the five decision-making influences in global negotiations.

Keep in mind that while research has shown that it is useful to be aware that countries share larger values such as collectivism or individualism because this information may inform intercultural decision-making scenarios, such as negotiation, it is also important to keep in mind that countries do not always conform to a single prototypical behavior and individual preferences vary across cultures. A developmental view is important for a global mindset that creates successful communication outcomes in today's international business world.

Afterward, Richard Lewis furthered intercultural literacy by creating a model that accommodated individual behavioral preferences alongside cultural norms. His research included a sweeping analysis of executives across multiple countries based on the behavior of individuals in a culture and the cultural roots of national behavior. Focusing on attributes and commonalities prevalent among countries, the **Lewis Model** provides three general dimensions of both individual and cultural behavior that are useful for navigating the communication patterns and conventions of international business. Ultimately, this model triangulates three distinct typologies of cultural interaction styles that Lewis termed Linear-Active, Multi-Active, and Reactive.

The following framework adapts these individual and cultural dimensions to our approach for the development of a global mindset—a global communicator integrates *all* three of the following styles:

- **Linear-Expressive:** As this communication style tends to be task-oriented, direct, and logical, global communicators approach interactions with the awareness that for some global partners, the preferred goal of communication is *information;* therefore, in a mixed audience space, global communicators integrate appeals to logic by including statistics, facts, and relevant research.

  Regions: Often preferred by most English-speaking parts of the world, including the United States, parts of Northwestern and North-Central Europe, Scandinavia, and Australia/New Zealand.

- **Multi-Expressive:** As this communication style tends to be people-oriented, expressive, and instinctive, global communicators approach interactions with the awareness that for some global partners, the preferred goal of communication is *personal connection* and *opinion;* therefore, in a mixed audience space, global communicators integrate appeals to emotion by including a focus on empathy, personal and anecdotal details, and inspirational and creative solutions.

  Regions: Often preferred by most countries in Latin America, the Middle East and North Africa, areas of Eastern Europe and the Iberian Peninsula, the Mediterranean region, and sub-Saharan Africa.

- **Amicable-Expressive:** As this communication style tends to be respect-oriented and indirect, global communicators approach interactions with the awareness that for some global partners, the preferred goal of communication is *harmony;* therefore, in a mixed audience space, global communicators integrate appeals to credibility by including information about character, reputation, and expertise, while also cultivating respect and relationships in the process.

  Regions: Often preferred by most Asian countries, except the subcontinent of India, which is both Multi-Expressive and Amicable-Expressive.

Keep in mind that these cultural context style preferences can vary by individual, occupation, and culture.

Overall, when we cultivate an enriched cultural sensitivity and expanded awareness, bridges are built and connections are made, both within and beyond the workplace. By recognizing and uniting the cultural patterns of global societies, we will not only forge more successful intercultural interactions, but also acquire a deeper appreciation for the richness of world cultures, within the mindset and actions of a *global communicator.*

As a geographic resource, the following regional classification comprises some, but not all, of the countries in each designated region adapted from the United Nations Children's Fund (UNICEF) Regional Classification and the United Nations Statistics Division.

GLOBAL REGION GUIDE	
Asia	**Northeast Asia:** China, Japan, Mongolia, North Korea, South Korea
	Southeast Asia: Cambodia, Indonesia, Malaysia, The Philippines, Singapore, Thailand, Vietnam
	Central Asia: Georgia, Armenia, Kazakhstan, Uzbekistan, Turkmenistan
	South-Central Asia: Afghanistan, India, Iran, Nepal, Pakistan, Sri Lanka
Middle East	Iraq, Israel, Jordan, Morocco, Saudi Arabia, Tunisia, United Arab Emirates, Yemen
Europe	**Western Europe:** France, Portugal, Spain, Switzerland
	Northwestern and North-Central Europe: Belgium, Germany, Ireland, Netherlands, Switzerland, United Kingdom
	Eastern Europe: Hungary, Poland, Romania, Russia, Ukraine
	Scandinavia: Denmark, Estonia, Finland, Iceland, Norway, Sweden
	Mediterranean: Greece, Italy, Turkey
Africa	**North Africa:** Algeria, Egypt, Libya, Morocco, Sudan, Tunisia
	Sub-Saharan Africa
	Western Africa: Burkina Faso, Côte d'Ivoire, Mali, Niger, Senegal, Togo
	Eastern Africa: Ethiopia, Kenya, Madagascar, Mozambique, Rwanda, Somalia, South Sudan, Uganda, Zimbabwe
	Central Africa: Democratic Republic of the Congo (DRC), Cameroon
	Southern Africa: Botswana, Namibia, South Africa

GLOBAL REGION GUIDE	
Latin America	**Central America:** El Salvador, Guatemala, Honduras, Mexico, Nicaragua, Panama
	South America: Argentina, Brazil, Chile, Colombia, Ecuador, Peru
	The Caribbean: Cuba, Dominican Republic, Haiti
North America	The United States, Canada
Oceania	Australia, New Zealand, Fiji, Papua New Guinea

Cognitive Flexibility:
The Global Communicator in a
Time of Change

W e live in a time of constant change that requires versatile, values-driven, and mindful global communicators. For this reason, it's no surprise that **the World Economic Forum lists *cognitive flexibility* as a top ten skill that all professionals need for jobs of the future.** Alain Dehaze, CEO of global workforce leader Adecco Group, stated, "as the world we live in is so unpredictable, the ability to learn and adapt to change is imperative." Successful communicators not only must engage in effective practices, but must reinvent and change themselves in the process. No matter how effective we were yesterday, we will find that today and tomorrow are likely to make new demands on us as global communicators. We must continually reinvent and adapt to meet the impending changes of the twenty-first century and beyond.

For that reason, **cognitive flexibility** is important interculturally because it links global awareness to action. Many of us in the twenty-first century encounter dozens of cultural contexts every day—often in a single day, at work, socially, or online. Research shows that cognitive flexibility is a vital executive function that unlocks the skills of cultural competence—a *global mindset*. In our globally-connected world, we need not only specific linguistic skills for messaging, but also a new *adaptability* to changing circumstances and to new contexts—a global mindset leading to global communication skills. New ways of thinking about culture create new avenues to empathy and global understanding.

Furthermore, cognitive flexibility is also important in terms of the need for adaptability in high-stakes times of international change, such as natural disasters, financial crises, coups, pandemics, or large-scale electrical outages. Beyond having plans in place, we must also cultivate the ability to continually sense and respond to the changing contexts of our intercultural colleagues, stakeholders, and partners. Instead of creating new rules for shifting online and in-person scenarios, we must create new ways of *problem-solving.*

What if our negotiation suddenly has to go virtual? What if our team abroad is caught in a crisis? We have to be both informed and versatile in order to operate in multiple cultural contexts and meet the changes driving a variety of communication scenarios and mediums. For this reason, *remote adaptability* has also become an invaluable skill of the future. Additionally, *empathy,* the ability to share and understand human emotion, is at the core of this versatility—an empathy that comes from continual learning and practice.

Overall, we must think creatively beyond prescribed plans and cultivate adaptability within a global mindset. There's no "playbook" for communicators in the face of a twenty-first-century crisis; however, cognitive flexibility is the key to effectively navigating shifts in our business partnerships, economic markets, governmental structures, and social fabric. The successful global communicator in times of change leverages their capabilities to unify the global community—turning competitors into partners and strengthening the fabric of our human society. Every moment of change, whether of progress or crisis, is an opportunity—a chance for us to grow, create, and build a better world together. When we are responsive and creative in the face of change, we find understanding and innovation within the ever-evolving global business landscape and, ultimately, a sustained future of connection and progress.

Bibliography

"8 Classic Storytelling Techniques for Engaging Presentations: Storytelling Methods." Sparkol, March 30, 2018. *www.sparkol.com.*

"About TfCS." *Tools for Clear Speech.* Baruch College (blog), accessed December 1, 2019. *tfcs.baruch.cuny.edu.*

"Negotiating across Cultures." *Harvard Business Review* video, 2:34, posted February 25, 2016. *https://hbr.org.*

Barthes, Roland and Lionel Duisit. "An Introduction to the Structural Analysis of Narrative." *On Narrative and Narratives* 6, no. 2 (1975): 237–272.

Bower, Gordon H. and Michal C. Clark. "Narrative Stories as Mediators for Serial Learning." *Psychonomic Science* 14, no. 4 (1969): 181–182. *https://doi.org/10.3758/BF03332778.*

Bremer, Nadieh. "Figures in the Sky." *DataSketch,* accessed November 1, 2019. *www.datasketch.es.*

Brooks, Peter. *Reading for the Plot.* New York: Random House, 1985.

Brown, Brené. *Daring Greatly: How the Courage to Be Vulnerable Transforms the Way We Live, Love, Parent, and Lead.* New York: Avery, 2015.

Burian, Richard M. and Robert C. Richardson. "Form and Order in Evolutionary Biology: Stuart Kauffman's Transformation of Theoretical Biology." *University of Chicago Press* 1990, no. 2 (1990): 267–287.

Burkus, David. *Friend of a Friend: Understanding the Hidden Networks That Can Transform Your Life and Your Career.* New York: Houghton Mifflin Harcourt, 2018.

Burt, Ronald S. *Structural Holes: The Social Structure of Competition.* New York: Harvard University Press, 1995.

Cain, Susan. *Quiet: The Power of Introverts in a World That Can't Stop Talking.* New York: Broadway Books, 2013.

Campbell, Gordon. *A Short History of Gardens.* Oxford: Oxford University Press, 2017.

Campbell, Joseph. *The Hero with a Thousand Faces.* Novato, CA: New World Library, 2008.

Coleman, Ken. *The Proximity Principle: The Proven Strategy That Will Lead to the Career You Love.* Mahwah, NJ: Ramsey Press, 2019.

Covey, Stephen R. *The 7 Habits of Highly Effective People: Powerful Lessons in Personal Change.* New York: Simon & Schuster, 2013.

Cron, Lisa. *Wired for Story: The Writer's Guide to Using Brain Science to Hook Readers from the Very First Sentence.* New York: Ten Speed Press, 2012.

Duarte, Nancy. *Resonate: Present Visual Stories That Transform Audiences.* Hoboken, NJ: John Wiley and Sons, 2010.

Dunckel, Jacqueline and Elizabeth Parnham. *The Business Guide to Effective Speaking: Making Presentations, Using Audio Visuals and Dealing with the Media.* Kogan Page, 1985.

Dyer, Jeff, Hal Gregersen, and Clayton M. Christensen. "What Makes Innovators Different?" In *The Innovator's DNA: Mastering the Five Skills of Disruptive Innovators.* Cambridge, MA: Harvard Business Review Press, 2011.

Efron, David. *Gesture Research, Manuscript 1930–1940.* Manuscript. From National Anthropological Archives, Smithsonian Institution, 1941. *www.si.edu.*

Ekman, P. and W. V. Friesen. "Nonverbal Behavior and Psychopathology." eds. R. J. Friedman and M. M. Katz. In *The Psychology of Depression: Contemporary Theory and Research.* Washington, DC: Winston & Sons, 1974.

———. "Nonverbal Leakage and Clues to Deception." *Psychiatry* 32 (1969): 88–105. *https://doi.org/10.1080/00332747.1969.11023575.*

———. *Unmasking the Face: A Guide to Recognizing Emotions from Facial Expressions.* Englewood Cliffs, NJ: Prentice-Hall, 1975.

Ekman, Paul, E. Richard Sorenson, and Wallace V. Friesen. "Pan-Cultural Elements in Facial Displays of Emotion." *Science* 164 (1969): 86–88. *https://doi.org/10.1126/science.164.3875.86.*

Ferrazzi, Keith and Tahl Raz. *Never Eat Alone: And Other Secrets to Success, One Relationship at a Time.* New York: Currency Doubleday, 2005.

"Firewalking Facts." Tony Robbins Firewalker. November 11, 2017. *https://tonyrobbins firewalk.com.*

Fisher, Roger and William Ury. *Getting to Yes: Negotiating Agreement without Giving In.* New York: Penguin, 1991.

Folse, Keith, April Muchmore-Vokoun, and Elena Bestri Solomon. *Great Writing 4: Great Essays.* 4th ed. National Geographic Learning/Cengage Learning, 2013.

Gerritsen, J. S. Roderick and Guido P. H. Band. "Breath of Life: The Respiratory Vagal Stimulation Model of Contemplative Activity." *Frontiers in Human Neuroscience* 12 (2018): 397. *https://doi.org/10.3389/fnhum.2018.00397.*

God, Yu Tim and Hongzhi Zhang. "Intercultural Challenges, Intracultural Practices: How Chinese and Australian Students Understand and Experience Intercultural Communication at an Australian University." *Higher Education* 78, no. 2 (2019): 305–322. *https://doi.org/10.1007/s10734-018-0344-0.*

Goman, Carol Kinsey. *The Nonverbal Advantage: Secrets and Science of Body Language at Work.* San Francisco, CA: Berrett-Koehler Publishers, 2008.

Granovetter, Mark S. "The Strength of Weak Ties." *American Journal of Sociology* 78, no. 6 (1973): 1360–1380. *https://doi.org/10.1086/225469.*

Grant, Adam. "Rethinking the Extraverted Sales Ideal: The Ambivert Advantage." *APS* 24, no. 6 (2013): 1024–1030. *https://doi.org/10.1177%2F0956797612463706.*

Grimley, Brue. "Eye Accessing Cues: The Scales Fall Away and the Eyes Have It." In *Theory and Practice of NLP Coaching: A Psychological Approach.* Thousand Oaks, CA: Sage, 2013.

Hall, Edward T. "Silent Language in Overseas Business." *Harvard Business Review.* April 30, 1960. *https://hbr.org.*

———. *The Hidden Dimension.* Garden City, NY: Doubleday, 1966.

———. *The Silent Language.* New York: Anchor Books, 1973.

Hammer, M. R. "The Intercultural Development Inventory (IDI): An Approach for Assessing and Building Intercultural Competence." In M. A. Moodian (ed.), *Contemporary Leadership and Intercultural Competence: Understanding and Utilizing Cultural Diversity to Build Successful Organizations.* Thousand Oaks, CA: Sage, 2008.

Harden, Paige. "How to Land a Job by Networking." *The Washington Post,* May 23, 2016. *jobs.washingtonpost.com.*

Hasson, Uri, Asif A. Ghazanfar, Bruno Galantucci, Simon Garrod, and Christian Keysers. "Brain-to-Brain Coupling: A Mechanism for Creating and Sharing a Social World." *Trends in Cognitive Sciences* 16, no. 2 (2012): 114–21. *https://doi.org/10.1016/j.tics.2011.12.007.*

Heard, Stephen B. *The Scientist's Guide to Writing: How to Write More Easily and Effectively throughout Your Scientific Career.* Princeton, NJ: Princeton University Press, 2016.

Hofstede, Geert. "National Cultures in Four Dimensions: A Research-Based Theory of Cultural Differences among Nations." *International Studies of Management & Organization* 13, no. 1–2 (1983): 46–47.

Hofstede, G. J. and M. Minkov. *Cultures and Organizations: Software of the Mind.* Rev. and exp. 3rd ed. New York: McGraw-Hill, 2010.

Ingram, Paul and Michael W. Morris. "Do People Mix at Mixers? Structure Homophily, and 'The Life of the Party.'" Columbia University *Administrative Science Quarterly* 52, no. 5 (2007): 558–585. *https://doi.org/10.2189/asqu.52.4.558.*

Johnson, Steven. "The Genius of the Tinkerer." *The Wall Street Journal,* Dow Jones & Company, September 25, 2010. *www.wsj.com.*

Karrass, Chester L. *The Negotiating Game.* New York: HarperBusiness, 1994.

Kennedy, Gavin. *The New Negotiating Edge: The Behavioral Approach for Results and Relationships.* Boston: Nicholas Brealey, 1998.

———. *The Pocket Negotiator.* 2nd ed. London: The Economist Books, 1993.

Kobayashi, Kenji and Ming Hsu. "Common Neural Code for Reward and Information Value." *Proceedings of the National Academy of Sciences* 116, no. 23 (2019): 13061–13066. *https://doi.org/10.1073/pnas.1820145116.*

Land, M. F. and M. Hayhoe. "In What Ways Do Eye Movements Contribute to Everyday Activities?" *Vision Research* 41, no. 25–26 (2001): 3559–3565. *https:/doi.org/10/1016/S0042-6989(01)00102-X.*

Lewis, Richard D. *When Cultures Collide: Leading across Culture.* 3rd ed. London: Nicholas Brealey, 2010.

Lu, Yuhwa. "Underutilization of Mental Health Services by Asian American Clients: The Impact of Language and Culture in Clinical Assessment and Intervention." *Psychotherapy in Private Practice* 15, no. 2 (1996): 45. *https://doi.org/10.1300 J294v15n02_04.*

Merrill, David. W. and Roger H. Reid. *Personal Styles and Effective Performance.* New York: CRC Press, 1981.

Morrison, Terri and Wayne A. Conaway. *Kiss, Bow, or Shake Hands: The Bestselling Guide to Doing Business in More Than 60 Countries.* Holbrook, MA: Adams Media, 1994.

Obama, Barack. "State of the Union Address." The Obama White House video, 1:01, posted January 12, 2016. *www.youtube.com.*

Oshima, Alice and Ann Hogue. *Writing Academic English.* 3rd. ed. White Plains: Addison-Wesley, 1998.

Paul, Margaret and Erika J. Chopich. *Healing Your Aloneness: Finding Love and Wholeness Through Your Inner Child.* New York: HarperOne, 1990.

Pease, Allan and Barbara Pease. *The Definitive Book of Body Language.* New York: Bantam, 2006.

Philippot, P. and S. Blairy. "Respiratory Feedback in the Generation of Emotion." *Cognition and Emotion* 16, no. 5 (2002), pp. 605–627. *https://doi.org/10.1080 /02699930143000392.*

Pillay, Navi. "Opening Remarks by UN High Commissioner for Human Rights Navi Pillay at the Free & Equal Campaign Press Launch." *United Nations Human Rights Office of the High Commissioner.* July 2013. *www.ohchr.org/.*

Plutchik, Robert. *The Emotions.* Rev. ed. Lanham, MD: University Press of America, 1991.

Richardson, D. C., R. Dale, and M. J. Spivey. "Eye Movements in Language and Cognition: A Brief Introduction." Eds. M. Gonzalez-Marquez, I. Mittleberg, S. Coulson, and M. J. Spivey. In *Methods in Cognitive Linguistics.* Amsterdam: John Benjamins Publishing Company, 2007. *https://doi.org/10.1075/hcp.18.21ric.*

Riggio, Ronald E. *The Charisma Quotient: What It Is, How to Get It, How to Use It.* New York: Dodd Mead, 1988.

Robinett, Judy. *How to Be a Power Connector: The 5+50+100 Rule for Turning Your Business Network into Profits.* New York: McGraw-Hill Education, 2016.

Rogers, Everett M., William B. Hart, and Yoshitaka Miike. "Edward T. Hall and the History of Intercultural Communication: The United States and Japan." *Keio Communication Review* (2002): 24. *www.mediacom.keio.ac.jp.*

Rokeach, M. *Understanding Human Values: Individual and Societal.* New York: Free Press, 1979.

Scott, Bill. *The Skills of Negotiating.* Management Skills Library. Brookfield VT: Gower Publishing Limited, 1983.

Solé Sabater, Maria-Josep, "Stress and Rhythm in English." *Revista Alicantina de Estudios Ingleses* 4 (1991): 145–62. *http://dx.doi.org/10.14198/raei.1991.4.13.*

Sommer, Robert. *Personal Space: The Behavioral Basis of Design.* Upper Saddle River, NJ: Prentice Hall, 1969.

State, Bogdan, Patrick Park, Ingmar Weber, Yelena Mejova, and Michael Macy. "The Mesh of Civilizations and International Email Flows." 2013. *https://arxiv.org.*

Tannen, Deborah. "The Pragmatics of Cross-Cultural Communication." *Applied Linguistics* 53 (1984): 189–195. *https://doi.org/10.1093/applin/5.3.189.*

———."What's in a Frame? Surface Evidence for Underlying Expectations." In Roy Freedle (ed.), *New Directions in Discourse Processing.* Norwood, NJ: AbleX, 1979.

The Radicati Group, Inc. Email Statistics Report, 2019–2023. London, 2019. *www.radicati.com.*

"The Future of Jobs: Employment, Skills and Workforce Strategy for the Fourth Industrial Revolution," *World Economic Forum.* Global Challenge Insight Report, 2016. *www3.weforum.org.*

Tversky, Amos and Daniel Kahneman. "The Framing of Decisions and the Psychology of Choice." *Science* 211, no. 4481 (1981): 453–58. *https://doi.org/10.1126/science.7455683.*

Connor, Ulla. "New Directions in Contrastive Rhetoric." *TESOL Quarterly* 36, no. 4: 493–510. *https://doi.org/10.2307/3588238.*

Uzzi, Brian and Shannon Dunlap. "How to Build Your Network." *Harvard Business Review,* August 1, 2014. *hbr.org.*

Wong, Jean and Hansun Zhang Waring. *Conversation Analysis and Second Language Pedagogy: A Guide for ESL/EFL Teachers.* New York: Routledge, 2010.

Yaden, David B., Jonathan Iwry, Kelley J. Slack, Johannes C. Eiechstaedt, Yukun Zhao, George E. Vaillant, and Andrew B. Newberg. "The Overview Effect: Awe and Self-Transcendent Experience in Space Flight." *Psychology of Consciousness* 3 (2016): 1–11. *https://doi.org/10.1037/cns0000086.*

About the Authors

Raúl Sánchez is an award-winning clinical assistant professor and the corporate program coordinator at New York University's School of Professional Studies. He has designed and delivered corporate trainings for Deloitte and the United Nations, as well as been a writing consultant for Barnes & Noble Press and PBS. Raúl was awarded the NYU School of Professional Studies Teaching Excellence Award and specializes in linguistics and business communication. He contributes to *The Wall Street Journal,* HuffPost, Business.com, openDemocracy, and Thrive Global, where he writes about the intersection of global business communication, leadership, and intercultural communication.

 Connect with Raúl: *raul.sanchez@globallycommunicate.com*

Dan Bullock is a language and communications specialist/trainer at the United Nations Secretariat, training diplomats and global UN staff. He also serves as faculty teaching business communication and public relations within the Division of Programs in Business at New York University's School of Professional Studies. Dan was the director of corporate communications at a leading NYC public relations firm, and his corporate clients have included TD Bank and Pfizer. He contributes to *The Wall Street Journal,* HuffPost, Business.com, and Thrive Global, where he writes about the intersection of global business communication, intercultural communication, and professional development.

 Connect with Dan: *dan.bullock@globallycommunicate.com*

About the Illustrator

Rod Sánchez is an award-winning visual communication designer, artist, and filmmaker. He is a lead user experience/user interface designer at Houghton Mifflin Harcourt and has designed and illustrated book covers for Penguin Random House and Scholastic. Rod has directed and designed campaigns for Disney, Nickelodeon, and Baruch College–CUNY and received design awards from the New England Book Show and the Create Awards. Rod's artwork has been exhibited internationally, displayed on billboards in New York City, and published in HuffPost, *El País,* the *Guardian,* Thrive Global, and *Time Out New York.*

 Connect with Rod: *rod.sanchez@globallycommunicate.com*

List of Illustrations